Scottish Newspapers, Language and Identity

To my parents,
and to my fellow Scots

This is my country,
The land that begat me.
(Alexander Gray, 'Scotland')

Scottish Newspapers, Language and Identity

Fiona M. Douglas

Edinburgh University Press

© Fiona M. Douglas, 2009

Edinburgh University Press Ltd
22 George Square, Edinburgh

www.euppublishing.com

Typeset in Goudy Old Style by
Iolaire Typesetting, Newtonmore, and
printed and bound in Great Britain by
CPI Antony Rowe, Chippenham and Eastbourne

A CIP record for this book is available from the British Library

ISBN 978 0 7486 2437 9 (hardback)

The right of Fiona M. Douglas
to be identified as author of this work
has been asserted in accordance with
the Copyright, Designs and Patents Act 1988.

This publication is supported by

Arts & Humanities
Research Council

Contents

List of Illustrations

List of Tables

Acknowledgements

Thanks are due to numerous people for their help and support during the writing of this book, and space permits me to name only a few. An Arts and Humanities Research Council (AHRC) Research Leave Grant and research leave and support from the School of English, University of Leeds made the writing of it possible. David Woolls' computing expertise developed the database that underpins most of the research, and Jean Anderson and Flora Edmonds (University of Glasgow) gave valuable IT assistance in earlier phases of the project. Sarah Edwards provided the opportunity to write the book, and she and Esmé Watson, both of Edinburgh University Press, gave expert guidance throughout the process. The *Daily Record* kindly gave me access to their library resources during the data collection phase. Anthea Fraser Gupta and Clive Upton (University of Leeds) generously gave of their time to read and comment on drafts of the manuscript, as did John Corbett (University of Glasgow). Christian Kay (previously University of Glasgow) gave valuable guidance on the original 1995 research, and I am grateful to the late John Sinclair for his encouragement to publish it. Alison Johnson (University of Leeds) gave much appreciated help with the proof-checking and some useful comments on the last chapter. The faults which remain are naturally my own. Finally, special thanks go to my husband, Ian McFaull, for his unstinting patience, support and encouragement throughout the writing of this book.

Fiona Douglas

Introduction

1.1 SETTING THE SCENE

In recent years there has been a resurgence of interest in Scottish identity and Scottish language varieties, but to date there has been no in-depth investigation of the link between the two. This book attempts to address that gap by focusing on the language of one of the most common and influential text types in Scotland, as elsewhere: the national newspapers. It studies the link between language and identity in the Scottish press and argues that Scottish newspapers create a special relationship with their readers based on their shared Scottish identity by using elements of Scottish language – specifically *Scots* lexis (see section 1.3.1 for definition). The main focus is therefore linguistic, though reference is made to other areas of research such as sociological and historical viewpoints where appropriate.

Contrary to popular opinion, Scottish language is not restricted to the tartan realms of Burns Suppers and poetry readings; rather it forms a contemporary and significant part of most Scots' Scottish identity and daily experience. It is found in the distinctive accents, in conversations overheard on trains, in words used to discuss the weather, and, crucially for this study, in the language of newspapers. Scottish identity is alive and flourishing and there is a new-found national confidence fuelled, no doubt, by the significant changes in Scotland's political landscape with the re-establishment of the Scottish Parliament after a gap of nearly three centuries. This book straddles the pre- and post-devolution years by analysing the language of the newspapers during 1995 and 2005. What, if any, difference has a decade and devolution made?

1.1.1 Scotland today

The northernmost country of the UK, Scotland covers some 30,414 square miles (78,772 square kilometres). Although half the size of England in terms of land mass, Scotland has approximately one-tenth of the population. Mid-2006 estimates put Scotland's population at 5,116,900 (General Register Office Scotland (GRO(S)). The population is mainly concentrated in the Central Belt with its large urban conurbations centred on Glasgow and Edinburgh. Although more than half the geographic area is comprised of the Highlands, less than 10 per cent of the population actually lives there. Scotland takes its name from a Celtic tribe (the Scoti), thought by many to have migrated to Scotland from Ireland in the late fifth century, settling in Dal Riada (Argyll) and merging with the existing Pictish tribes.

1.1.2 Changes in the political landscape

With the Union of the Parliaments in 1707, Scotland relinquished political control to Westminster for a period of nearly 300 years. The Treaty of Union provided for the continuation of Scotland's own church, education and legal systems, but to all intents and purposes Scotland became a 'stateless nation' (see title to McCrone 1992), albeit one with a strongly developed sense of national identity.

Scotland is now post-devolution. The Scottish Parliament was reinstated on 1 July 1999 and although some powers are still reserved to Westminster, a large number, including agriculture, the arts, economic development, education, the environment, forestry and fishing, health, housing, local government, natural and built heritage, planning, police and fire services, prison, social work, sport, transport and tourism matters (Scottish Parliament), are now decided in Scotland by the Scottish Parliament's 129 MSPs. Significantly, the Scottish Parliament has no tax-raising powers, and so it is still economically bound to the rest of the UK, though in July 2007, the Scottish Nationalist Party (SNP), with some cross-party support launched a bid dubbed 'devolution max' to increase the Parliament's powers, thus re-examining the tax-raising issue. When the first set of data for this book was collected in 1995, all this had yet to come, and at that stage it was extremely doubtful whether devolved power would ever be held in Scotland. There was a long-established Conservative government which was opposed to the introduction of devolved powers for Scotland, and although there had been a referendum on devolution in 1979 under a Labour government, it had failed to get the required majority. Scotland did have some measure of control over its own affairs under the auspices of the Scottish Office (see McCrone 1992: 22), but the overall situation was very much dominated by Westminster. By 2005, when the second set of data was collected, all this had changed. Scotland is now a country with some measure of socio-political autonomy. Its nationhood has been, at least partially, restored.

1.2 SCOTLAND'S LINGUISTIC COMMUNITIES

Ongoing migration to Scotland has significantly complicated what was already a historically complex linguistic situation. (See Chapter 3 for further details.) Precise numbers of speakers of most of the languages used in Scotland are not currently available, but the Education, Culture and Sport Committee's report (McGugan 2003) on minority languages in Scotland identified *Arabic*, *Bengali*, *British Sign Language* (BSL), *Chinese*, *Gaelic*, *Punjabi*, *Scots* and *Urdu* as the country's predominant minority languages, and the Scottish Parliament website offers at least some of its information in each of these languages. *English*, though a distinctively Scottish variety of it (see section 1.3.1 and Chapter 3 for definitions and discussion), is the majority language. *Gaelic* language in Scotland is protected by statute, and statistics on the use of *Gaelic* are collected by the Census data. Scotland's Census (2001) Gaelic Report shows that, 'in 2001, over 92,000 people in Scotland (just under 2 per cent of the population) had some *Gaelic* language ability and that almost half of these people lived in Eilean Siar [Western Isles], Highland or Argyll and Bute.' (GRO(S)); of these, 58,650 were *Gaelic* speakers, a drop of 11 per cent from the 1991 Census. Although there are many more *Scots* speakers than *Gaelic* speakers in Scotland, to date there has been no Census question to ascertain their numbers. Interested parties launched a vigorous but unsuccessful campaign to have such a question included in the 2001 Census. The General Register Office cited difficulties for respondents in knowing how to answer the question 'Do you speak Scots?' as the reason why this question was not included. The *Scots* language question was revisited in a 2006 Census Test, and in January 2008, Linda Fabiani, Minister for Culture, announced that 'subject to satisfactory test results', a *Scots* language question might be included in the 2011 Census as part of the Scottish Government's commitment to 'increasing awareness of the Scots language and its literature' and ensuring it honours its European obligations towards *Scots* (Scottish Government n.d.). As examples like this show, the linguistic situation in Scotland is, in some aspects, under-researched. There are estimated figures from a 1996 trial GRO(S) survey which suggested that there might be 1.5 million *Scots* speakers in Scotland. Other estimates suggest the figure should be higher.

1.3 INTRODUCING THE SUBJECT MATTER

This study is based on analysis of a sizeable corpus of newspaper texts which is in two parts: the earlier part covers newspapers published during 1995, two years before the second devolution referendum and four years prior to the inauguration of the Scottish Parliament. The latter part of the corpus focuses on newspapers published during 2005. (More details on the composition of the corpus are given below in section 1.4.) This two-part corpus allows synchronic and diachronic comparisons to be made. Pre- and post-devolution analysis investigates whether the institution of the Scottish Parliament has had any discernible effect on the newspapers' use of Scottish language. The corpus-based approach adopted by this study offers new insights into the linguistic behaviour of the Scottish press. The research is both qualitative and quantitative in approach and it aims to identify key trends within and between newspapers and across both time periods.

1.3.1 Definition of key terms

'Scottish language', the term used thus far, is a rather ambiguous and vague term which can potentially be applied to a range of linguistic varieties. Firstly, it could be used to refer to the Celtic language, Scottish *Gaelic*. However, this book is not concerned with *Gaelic* or even with the use of *Gaelic* in newspapers, although it is worth mentioning an interesting study on the use of *Gaelic* in Scottish newspapers by Cormack (1995), the results of which have some interesting parallels with some of the observations made in the course of this study. Rather, this book is concerned with those 'native' or 'indigenous' (cf. Gupta 2002: 292). Gupta (2002) questions the 'myth of indigeneity', and quite reasonably points out that the Celts and the Germanic tribes were themselves at one time immigrants to Britain (as were the Scots). Language varieties in Scotland which are ultimately derived from *Old English*, that is those varieties that from a linguistic perspective can be put together under the umbrella term *Scottish-English*, which includes everything from broad *Scots* dialect at one extreme to *Scottish Standard English* at the other. The linguistic situation is complex, and in-depth discussion of these language varieties is reserved for Chapter 3, where they can be dealt with more fully. To counteract any possible confusion arising from the use of 'Scots' to refer to the people vs 'Scots' to refer to the linguistic variety, the latter has been italicised throughout, except in quotations where the original form has been preserved. For the sake of consistency, other language varieties, for example *English*, have been italicised also. *English-English* has been used when wishing to indicate the particular form of *English* used in England.

This book concentrates specifically on the use of *Scots* lexis, that is, words and phrases that have Scottish provenance and are not generally shared with *English*, by the Scottish newspapers (*Lexis* (plural); *lexical item* (singular)). *Scots* lexis can be found, though often in different proportions, across the *Scottish-English* varieties, that is in *Scottish Standard English* as well as in *Scots*. Three additional terms are useful for discussing lexis – *types*, *tokens* and *lexemes*. The total number of *tokens* in a text is the total number of word occurrences. Tokens are usually contrasted with *types* – the number of different words that occur in a text. Thus the number of tokens is usually significantly higher than the number of types, as some words are likely to be repeated. So, for example, the preceding sentence has twenty-two tokens but only nineteen types as *the*, *number* and *of* are repeated. The term *lexeme* is used where it is necessary to indicate that what is meant is a group of possible lexical items rather than individual lexical types. So, for example, the lexeme *gae* (to go) includes within it the lexical types *gang*, *gaein*, *gaun* and so on. Any of those lexical types may have multiple occurrences, that is, tokens, so, for example, there may be thirty-five occurrences (tokens) of the type *gaun*.

1.4 THE NEWSPAPER CORPUS: HARD EVIDENCE

The Scottish national newspapers studied are *The Herald* (a Glasgow-based broadsheet), *The Scotsman* (an Edinburgh-based quality newspaper), and the *Daily Record* (a Glasgow-based tabloid and, for a considerable period, Scotland's best selling daily newspaper). There are well-known differences between tabloids and broadsheets both in terms of content and the language they use. Both newspaper types are included to see whether there are noticeable differences in their use of *Scots* lexis, both in terms of quantity and type. For example, it is possible that one type of newspaper will characteristically yield more *Scots* lexis than the other.

The Times (London), and *The Sun* are also examined as controls. As essentially London-based newspapers (though *The Sun* has a Scottish edition, and *The Times* has some Scotticised content such as the 'Écosse' section) we would expect these newspapers to yield much less, or no *Scots* lexis. Chapters 7 and 8 investigate whether this hypothesis is correct. It should be noted that 1995 data for *The Sun* are partial due to the resources available at the time; however, the 2005 *Sun* data are complete. It was not possible to separate *The Sun* data into Scottish and English editions (the newspaper's website similarly had no separate Scottish section), but care was taken to ensure that stories occurred only once. So throughout the data analysis, this newspaper has been referred to as *The Sun*.

Unfortunately the *Dundee Courier* and the Aberdeen *Press and Journal* are not included in the study. At the time of the 1995 data collection, it was not possible to get computerised archive material from these sources, and thus they had to be excluded. Local newspapers such as the *Airdrie and*

Coatbridge Advertiser or free publications such as the Edinburgh *Herald and Post* are also not included in the survey. It can be argued that these newspapers fulfil quite a different function from that of the more 'national' Scottish newspapers, concerned as they are with almost exclusively local news and events.

The corpus data were essentially based on a full year's Monday to Saturday editions for each newspaper, collected systematically over the two research periods – 1995 and 2005. Sunday editions of the newspapers were not included. It was felt that these are very different editions from those published during the week, containing a far greater proportion of feature articles and specialised 'magazine' sections. For each period a full year's data were used, as it was considered possible that there would be peaks and troughs in the amount of *Scots* lexis used over the year, potential peaks occurring around Burns' Night and Hogmanay etc. (see section 5.1 for analysis of this question).

On this basis a substantial computerised corpus of newspaper texts was assembled. As it was not expected that the proportions of *Scots* lexis in the newspapers would be particularly high, it was necessary to collect as large a corpus as possible, thereby removing many of the problems associated with sampling, and trying to address issues of corpus representativeness. The corpus contained full texts, not text samples (for example the first 500 words of each text) as is often done in corpus work. This strategy was adopted because personal observation had indicated that, in some texts, there was often a much higher concentration of *Scots* lexis at certain points in the text, often relating to stylistic choices (see discussion in section 3.2.2). An approach which sampled from texts would inevitably run the risk of missing the *Scots* lexis entirely, or of misrepresenting the situation. The resulting corpus was composed of 14,714 distinct newspaper articles, amounting to 9,467,670 running words of text (that is tokens). Table 5.1 gives more detail on the corpus composition.

There are several important advantages offered by the corpus approach. Firstly, in terms of scale – a large corpus makes for much more accurate analysis of lexis in terms of trends and patterns. As Sinclair (1991: 18–19) notes, the size of the corpus is a primary concern, as less frequently occurring words may not show up at all unless the corpus is large. Secondly, corpus analysis deals with real data rather than relying merely on the intuitions, however well-informed, of the linguist. Several people (for example McClure 1979; Macafee 1983) have written about their observations of the Scottish press, but although their intuitions may have some merit, they cannot be demonstrated to be accurate unless large-scale methodical analysis of the text-type has been undertaken. Corpus analysis

six-footer); and searches on *uplift* meaning, in *Scots*, the verb 'to collect' or a noun meaning 'collection', generated many examples of *English* 'uplifting' as in 'cheering'.

The test word-list yielded 6,204 discrete newspaper articles for the 1995 corpus and 8,510 articles for the 2005 corpus. This methodology was significantly improved on by using *Wordsmith Tools* to create an exhaustive word-list for the 14,714 newspaper articles, that is, every word used in each of these texts was put into one long list. Then, the test word-list and the exhaustive word-list were compared using *Wordsmith*'s 'compare two word-lists' tool. This tool is usually used to identify stylistic differences between texts, but it was used here solely to compare the word-lists themselves. The tool identifies and lists words which appear more frequently in one list than in the other and also those words which occur in one list but not the other. It was thereby possible to discover additional infrequently occurring vocabulary, much of it likely to be *Scots* lexis. This results list was then checked manually to remove non-*Scots* items. The process yielded a total of 1,519 *Scots* lexemes (that is some 1,079 additional lexemes). It also verified the representativeness of the original test word-list in that, other than *ya* (you) (131 tokens) and *burd* (bird – colloquial term for a woman) (107 tokens), there were no additional *Scots* items found with significant frequencies.

The precise technical mechanisms whereby details about the individual newspaper articles were extracted and entered into the corpus are much too detailed for discussion here. Suffice to say that information on publication, date, byline, newspaper section and so on for the articles retrieved, linked to each lexical occurrence, were stored in the Microsoft Access relational database. The database also contained searchable one-line concordance entries for each lexical occurrence. This was useful for analysis purposes and also avoided problems with *LexisNexis*'s conditions of use in terms of permitted length of time for storage of full-text articles. This database forms the basis of the data analysis in Chapters 5 to 7.

1.5 OVERVIEW OF CHAPTER CONTENT

Chapters 2 to 4 outline the key questions and theoretical issues, whilst Chapters 5 to 8 present analysis of the newspaper data. Chapter 2 discusses what Scottish identity is and asks whether there is a single coherent Scottish identity or alternatively multiple Scottish identities. It also explores the roles played by language and stereotypes of Scottishness in this identity. Chapter 3 is devoted to an explanation of the Scottish linguistic situation: what *Scottish-English* is, the different varieties it encompasses and their key characteristics and status, the existence or otherwise of standard varieties, and a brief historical insight into the causes of the present linguistic situation. Also considered is the relationship between the Scottish people and the language varieties they use, focusing on their self-awareness and attitudes. Chapter 4 examines the nature of the relationship that exists between newspapers and their readers and considers how appropriate language use by the press is negotiated. The subsequent data chapters examine the use of *Scots* lexis by the press. Using *Scots* lexis gives the Scottish newspapers an additional and powerful way of relating to their readership, branding themselves as Scottish and cultivating a shared Scottish cultural identity. So Chapter 5 investigates which *Scots* words and phrases occur in the newspapers, in what quantities and densities, where they are found, and offers some explanations for the patterns noted. Newspapers have been argued to exert powerful linguistic forces within society and are usually perceived as using 'correct' or 'standard' language. How does this affect their use of *Scots* (and what might be perceived as non-standard) language? Chapter 6 examines whether there are any differences between newspapers in the types and quantities of *Scots* lexis used, for example tabloid vs broadsheet (or 'quality' newspaper) differences which might indicate readership social class differences, or Edinburgh vs Glasgow-based newspapers which might show East/West regional differences. It also investigates the role played by formulaic language and stereotypes in the press, and considers the sources of these. Chapter 7 investigates whether there is any evidence of a change in the use of *Scots* lexis by the newspapers in a post-devolution Scotland, in terms of quantity, visibility, positioning or type. If so, what conclusions might be drawn? The study concludes in Chapter 8 by considering the wider implications of devolution, for Scottish identity, for the role of *Scots* language, and for the Scottish press. Finally it discusses the importance of playing the language card, and asks whether there are salutary lessons to be learned by newspapers competing in the Scottish market.

Further Reading

1. Sinclair (1991) outlines important issues which must be addressed when working with computerised corpora, such as size, inclusivity, representativeness and sampling, and gives helpful insights on the usefulness of Key Word in Context (KWIC) concordance displays. Adolphs (2006) is a more recent but equally accessible introduction to the principles of electronic text analysis and corpora.

What is Scottish Identity?

Here's tae us; wha's like us?
Gey few and they're aw deid.

The words of that old Scottish toast can perhaps be seen as arrogant self-congratulation, particularly by those who are not Scots, but it does capture an important ingredient of Scottishness – the sense of being part of a distinctive and exclusive group. This chapter deals with the question of identity, and in particular with notions of Scottish national identity. What are the components of such an identity, and how is it constructed and/or maintained? Is it a static phenomenon, or is it a dynamic, constantly evolving entity, open to modification and reformulation? Many linguists (for example Edwards 1985; Le Page and Tabouret-Keller 1985; Joseph 2004) have argued that there is a link between language and identity, and this chapter investigates the symbolic functions of language and asks what part it might play in an ongoing construction and/or maintenance of Scottishness and Scottish national identity.

2.1 WHAT CONSTITUTES IDENTITY?

Identity is both a complex and a fascinating phenomenon. At a basic level, identity is about who we are, and who and what we identify with. However, identity is also about who we want to be, and how we wish to be seen by others.

Joseph (2004: 3–5) distinguishes between individual (or 'personal') identities and group identities, claiming that 'your "deep" personal identity is made up in part of the various group identities to which you stake a claim'. As he goes on to point out, most of us feel that we are rather more than merely the sum of the parts of our various group identities. At its most basic, group identity is about a sense of belonging and sharing with others in the group. It is a simultaneously inclusive and exclusive phenomenon: inclusive if you belong to the 'ingroup'; exclusive if you happen to be a member of the 'outgroup'. An individual may stake a claim to numerous different group identities, and this multiplicity of group identities is generally unproblematic.

So, just as we can all fulfil a variety of roles within society, so we can also have multiple group identities, such as familial identities, gender identities, social class identities, occupational identities, national identities and regional identities, that we hold simultaneously. There may be occasions when these different group identities and their associated value systems come into conflict with each other, but, on the whole, we can cope quite well with the resulting multifaceted personal identity.

So far consideration has been of identities in the here and now, that is, from a synchronic perspective. But identities can also be considered from a diachronic perspective. Plotted diagrammatically (see Fig. 2.1), from a synchronic perspective, an individual's identification with certain groups within society at a particular time can be considered as a horizontal relationship. The diachronic or vertical perspective links individuals through time to others who have held or will hold similar beliefs or espouse(d) common identities, that is, the historical perspective.

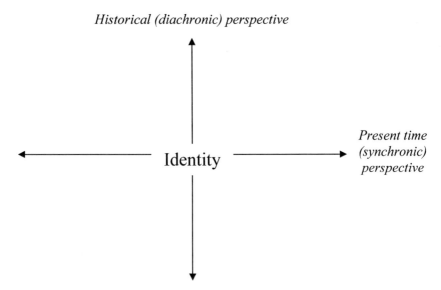

Figure 2.1 Synchronic and diachronic perspectives on identity

To give an illustrative example: I have a synchronic component to my identity as a female Scottish academic that will be influenced by the behaviour and norms associated with the behaviour and expectations of other present-day women, Scots and academics. To some extent, however, there is also an historical or diachronic component to my interaction with these group identities, in that I have some awareness of traditional female roles and the changes brought about by the suffrage and feminist movements, and thus I might choose to situate myself in relation to these; I also have some knowledge of Scottish history and an awareness of family links going back through time to communities in the Scottish Highlands, Lowlands and Ireland; and finally, I might hold strong views on the changing roles and status of the academic over the last twenty years and for the foreseeable future. So there is some sense of continuity and relationship, not just with those around me in the here and now, but also with those who have gone before and those who will come after. In this book, the focus is on Scottish identity, a complex and multifaceted phenomenon which draws on both the vertical and horizontal axes.

2.2 IS IDENTITY FIXED?

William McIlvanney, writing in *The Herald*, argues that 'identity, personal or national, isn't merely something you have like a passport. It is also something you rediscover daily, like a strange country. Its core isn't something like a mountain. It is something molten, like magma' (*The Herald*, 13 March 1999; cited in McCrone 2002). McIlvanney is arguing for identity as a dynamic process rather than as a fixed or static entity. Logic dictates that, if identity is dynamic, then it can be altered and reformulated and, indeed, many sociolinguists have argued that identities, whether they be national or some other identities, are constantly being reformulated. Identity can be altered and reformulated along both the horizontal (synchronic) and vertical (diachronic) axes. Hall's (1996) account also suggests that identities are dynamic, that is that identities are not merely fixed in past time, but that they can also be moulded for future time. He argues (1996: 4) that identities use 'the resources of history, *language* and culture' [my emphasis] as representational icons, and it is to the link between language and identity that attention turns in section 2.3.

Before that, it is worth briefly outlining some of the competing theories surrounding identity as they can also be extended to theories which link language and identity. The key viewpoints can be summarised as reflectivist vs constructivist. The different viewpoints give varying amounts of power, self-determination and choice to the individual vis-à-vis their identity. Whilst this study mainly favours the critical theory standpoint and the idea of identities being constructed, maintained, negotiated and represented, and these are the terms in which the newspapers' interaction with Scottish identity are discussed, it also recognises that the reflectivist approach has some merit.

The reflectivist viewpoint says that because someone has a certain identity – for example as a man, a businessman, a Scotsman – that they will behave in a way that reflects that identity; that is it is more or less inevitable. So they will behave, use language and speak, like a man, a businessman, a Scot, because that is what they are. The reflectivist view is the one that underlies some, but not all, sociolinguistic accounts of language variation.

The constructivist viewpoint takes a critical theory stance and says that individuals do not merely reflect what they are, but play an active part in the representation, negotiation, construction or maintenance of those identities to which they have an allegiance; that is that individuals behave in a way that signals their membership of certain social groups. We 'perform' identities to claim membership of particular social groups (c.f. 'Acts of Identity' in section 2.3). Joseph (2004) speaks about individuals staking a claim to identities, thus implying their active involvement in and uptake of certain identities. Hall's (1996) discussion of the 'representation' of identities allows both for others representing us as having particular identities, and for us as individuals choosing how to represent our own identities. Hall's viewpoint again underlines the role of the individual in how they choose to represent their own identities. They are not restricted to merely being the passive recipients of someone else's idea of what they should be. 'Negotiation' suggests not only internal forces (that is people choosing to enact certain social identities), but also the pressure exerted by external forces on the individual, that is the individual must negotiate their membership of a certain social group with other members who belong to that social group. In order to be a member of the ingroup, as well as electing to join the social grouping, the individual must satisfy the tariffs set for group membership by the existing group members – that is they have to be accepted. So to return to the earlier example, if an individual wants to be accepted as a bona-fide Scottish businessman, he must behave and sound like a Scottish businessman (c.f. discussion of discourse communities and linguistic tariffs in section 2.3).

With 'construction' vs 'maintenance' of identities, there is something of a chicken and egg question. Do identities pre-exist and therefore they are maintained by certain 'acts of identity', or alternatively, does the performance of 'acts of identity' actually construct identity? Of course, these two are not necessarily mutually exclusive. On the constructivist viewpoint, see, for example, Wodak et al.'s (1999) discussion of the discursive construction of national identity, and Schlesinger's (1991) examination of the link between the media and national identity. The constructivist approach has certain advantages. If, say, a child was born in England to English parents, and then moved to Scotland at the age of five, he or she might choose, for various reasons, such as fitting in at school, to construct a

Scottish identity for himself/herself. However, we may want to stop and consider whether saying that identities are entirely constructed phenomena might be taking things too far. Hall (1992) (cited and discussed in McCrone 2001: 152) argues that identity is not a free-for-all but must work within existing cultural representations. So to some extent we can choose what a Scottish identity looks like, but that choice will be formulated and to some extent constrained by the ways in which Scottish identity has been constructed in the past and also by the ways in which others perceive it. It may also carry significant linguistic tariffs, as discussed in the following section.

2.3 LANGUAGE AND IDENTITY

In order to consider the role of language with respect to identity, we need firstly to think about language not merely as a vehicle for communication but also as symbol. Many linguists, for example Jakobson (1960) and Edwards (1985) have emphasised that language does not always function only to facilitate communication. Language can fulfil a variety of functions, and it can be argued that language has a symbolic function for identity. Edwards (1985: 17) makes the distinction between language for communicative purposes and 'language as an emblem of groupness, as a symbol, a rallying point'.

Language can emphasise group identity, in that members of the group share the same language or language variety; but it can also highlight the differences between that group and others around them. As McCrone (1992: 28–9) notes, language can be a 'cultural identifier' (c.f. Gellner 1983), and thus, when used to negotiate identity, can be simultaneously inclusive and exclusive as it erects group membership 'tariffs'. The notions of 'discourse communities', where the knowledge and use of certain linguistic forms determines group membership or exclusion (see Bex 1996) and 'communities of practice', where communicative practice is one of a raft of group norms and behaviours (see Eckert and McConnell-Ginet 1992; cited in Joseph 2004: 65), stress the importance of meeting these linguistic tariffs. Those who are part of the shared linguistic community feel as though they belong to a group with common aims and ideology; those who do not have the necessary linguistic skills are, however, excluded. Their lack of shared linguistic competence precludes them from partaking of full group membership.

Many studies have focused on the perceived link between language and group identity (for example Le Page and Tabouret-Keller's (1985) highly influential concept of 'Acts of Identity'), language and national identity

(Wodak et al. 1999), or language and ethnicity (Edwards 1985; Fishman 1989; Wood 1979)). Bakhtin's theory of dialogism (Bakhtin 1981), which stresses the ongoing interaction between meanings, the constant reformulation of the meaning of utterances or words in the context of what has gone before and what is still to come, views identity 'not as fixed, closed and unchanging, but as formed and reformed through *dialogue*' (Crawford 1994: 57, my emphasis). So language is integral to the reformulation of a dynamic identity. Anderson (1991: 6), again from a constructivist viewpoint, argues that languages help to create a sense of national identity. He concentrates on the historicity of languages, the sense we have that they have always been there and that they are therefore a link between ourselves and our ancestors, between the present and history. A sense of history, of a nation stretching backwards through time, he argues, is of profound importance in the concept of nationhood, and language forms part of that sense of continuity. So Anderson subscribes to the vertical (diachronic) dimension of identity. He also recognises the horizontal (synchronic) dimension, speaking about the role of language in bonding the 'contemporaneous community' together (Anderson 1991: 145).

2.3.1 Language display

Having examined the link between language and identity, it is useful at this point to consider a related concept, that of 'language display', and think about how it can be used to negotiate identity. The concept of language display strongly emphasises the purely symbolic role that language can sometimes have. Eastman and Stein (1993: 187) use the term to refer to a special type of borrowing or code-switching whereby individuals use foreign languages as a way of associating themselves with the attributes of social groups beyond their own. For example, by using the expression *Veni, Vidi, Vici* ('I came, I saw, I conquered'), I might be successfully demonstrating my knowledge of *Latin* and hence associating myself with those individuals who have received a classical education, displaying my knowledge as a historian, or flashing some literary credentials. By insisting on ordering my cappuccino with an attempt at an Italian accent, I might be demonstrating just what a cosmopolitan and well-travelled (or alternatively what a sad and attention-seeking!) individual I am. Language display can thus be used to negotiate an identity. Eastman and Stein argue that the pragmatic force of the utterance in language display is symbolic rather than semantic, that is, what it means is less important than the association of group characteristics that it evokes. Interestingly they also suggest that language display is at its most successful when used in a context where it is unlikely to be challenged (c.f. discussion of language display and proverb displays in section 6.4).

As will be evident from the discussion to follow in Chapter 3, *Scots* and *English* cannot be classed as 'foreign languages' to each other in the sense that *English* vs *French*, *German* or *Latin* are; rather *Scots* and *English* are different linguistic varieties contained within the same overall system. For the purposes of this study, the term 'language display' can be usefully adapted to refer to the symbolic rather than communicative use, not of a foreign language, but of a different heteroglossic (c.f. Bakhtin 1981) linguistic variety – in this case, *Scots*. It will be argued in the data chapters that the symbolic use of *Scots* lexis by the newspapers is itself a type of language display. (Cormack (1995) argues the same point concerning the use of *Gaelic* in newspapers.)

2.4 A DISTINCTIVE SCOTTISH IDENTITY

This section reviews what Scottish identity might be considered to be. This is an important broad sociological question about Scotland and the Scottish people, a full analysis of which extends well beyond the scope of this book. Certainly identity, and Scottish identity in particular, are recurring and popular topics, both in the academic literature with numerous studies such as those by Broun et al. (1998); Ferguson (1998); McCrone et al. (1995); McCrone (2001); Pittock (2001); and Watson (2003); and also in non-academic texts such as Devine and Logue (2002). Devolution seems to have increased interest in an already perennially popular topic. As Bond and Rosie (2006: 141) point out, it has 'increased the salience of national identity as an area of academic research and wider popular concern'.

2.4.1 Defining Scottishness

So – what is Scottishness? Ostensibly it is merely a matter of nationality but even nationality is a rather prickly thistle to grasp. Is it about place? McCrone (2002) suggests this is the critical factor. Does being born in Scotland make you Scottish or is it complicated by issues of parentage, grandparentage or wider ancestry (often a matter for discussion when choosing the national football or rugby teams), or even of ethnicity? What about those Scots who operate with hybrid identities such as Scottish Pakistani, Scottish Muslim or Glasgow Italian (see Saeed et al. 1999)?

Alternatively, is it about history, that is, the vertical dimension discussed previously? Ferguson (1998), as a historian, stresses the construction of identity by history, and investigates Scottish identity's origins and development arguing that Scotland's history, but also its myths and legends, have been important influences on the development of its identity (see also Smout 1994: 108). Ferguson's argument suggests that the need for a sense of historicity is so strong that, on occasions, the historicity may be actively or deliberately constructed or reconstructed. Though some of the myths and legends are somewhat fanciful, that does not appear to prevent them from being used as foci for identity. Ferguson's discussion has echoes of Anderson (1991) in terms of the significance of historicity, but interestingly it also emphasises the fact that things do not need to be true to serve as signifiers of identity.

McCrone et al. (1995), writing from a sociological perspective, approach the question of identity from the related viewpoint of heritage. They argue that Scottish heritage and iconography, whether authentic or not (for example tartan) are very important in legitimising Scottish identity.

> In asking who we are, the totems and icons of heritage are powerful signifiers of our identity. We may find tartanry, Bonnie Prince Charlie, Mary Queen of Scots, Bannockburn and Burns false descriptors of who we are, but they provide a source of ready-made distinguishing characteristics from England, our bigger, southern neighbour. (McCrone et al. 1995: 7)

Once again, the idea of a historic basis (the vertical identity axis) for the nation seems to be integral to Scottish identity, even when 'history' is transformed into 'heritage'. The use of tartan as a cultural icon of Scottishness is an interesting one, many of the tartans having little historical basis, and the kilt being a modern interpretation of the *philabeg* (large tartan plaid cloth) (see Donnachie and Whatley 1992: 150–1). It is important to note that we do not necessarily have to agree with these 'totems' of our nationality in order to make use of or reference to them. It does not ultimately matter whether or not these things to which we cling as making us Scottish are particularly 'authentic', if indeed true authenticity can ever be claimed. What matters is that we subscribe to these cultural totems and icons, invest them with salience, and use them to validate our sense of Scottish identity.

So are there key defining characteristics that 'make' a person Scottish? Kiely et al. (2001: 36), sociologists, identify ten 'identity markers' which people use to claim or attribute identity: 'place of birth, ancestry, *place of residence, length of residence,* upbringing and education, name, accent, physical appearance, *dress* and *commitment to place*' [my emphasis], some of which are treated as 'fixed', and others (in italics) which are seen as 'fluid'. Of course, people differ in the degrees of emphasis they place on any of these 'markers', with some markers, such as accent, tending to outweigh the effect of others.

Or, is Scottishness, as is often claimed, an identity of 'otherness' and particularly of non-Englishness? McCrone at al. (1995: 7), quoted above, talk about the icons Scots use to distinguish themselves from their English neighbours. Can you be born to Scottish parents living in London and still consider yourself a Scot? (C.f. Bond and Rosie (2006) who found that being born in England was a 'significant barrier' to claiming Scottish nationality.) Joseph (2004: 37) discusses the identity paradox of *sameness* and *uniqueness*. Wodak et al. (1999) make a similar distinction by arguing that all national identities are constructed according to the polar binaries of *sameness* (those within the group) and *difference* or *otherness* (those outside the group). Benhabib (1996: 3ff); cited in Wodak et al. (1999), writing on global democracies, comments that 'since every search for identity includes differentiating oneself from what one is not, identity politics is always and necessarily a politics of the creation of difference'. So essentially identity is about ingroups and outgroups (van Dijk 1998).

Reading Devine and Logue's (2002) edited collection of 100 essays on *Being Scottish: Personal Reflections on Scottish Identity Today*, written by contributors from a variety of walks of life, some native Scots, others naturalised Scots, it is noticeable that conceptions of what it means to be Scottish and what Scottish identity is are remarkably coherent; the same themes such as a sense of place, a sense of history, and a sense of nation recur time and time again. Many of the writers also comment that there is no one Scottish identity, but that it is a shifting and dynamic phenomenon. National identity often seems to surface at national football or rugby matches, and it is an ex-Scottish rugby player, Gregor Townsend, writing in Devine and Logue (2002: 264), who notes that

> national identities are difficult concepts to define. No doubt we would all prefer to belong to a nation that we think is unique and different. Thus there is inevitably much subjectivity in how we determine our national identity. Being Scottish must be considered as more than a question of nationality or place of birth. It is an expression of who we think we are, or, in other words, a state of mind.

2.4.2 The imagined Scottish community

On a literal level, Scotland is, of course, the country in the northern part of the British Isles. However, Scotland is not just about the physical place and its inhabitants; Scotland is also a mental construct. In other words,

Scotland is made distinctly Scottish partly by the attitudes and values held by those who live there, and their sense of Scottish identity. To clarify the point further, from the dissolution of the Scottish Parliament in 1707 until devolution in 1999, Scotland was largely governed from Westminster, as an integral, if distinctive, part of Britain. However, although Scotland had none of the traditional attributes which might usually be considered to make it a nation state, such as political autonomy, self-determination, consistent use of its own language and so on, attitude surveys (for example McCrone 1992; McCrone et al. 1995) clearly show that many of its inhabitants still considered it to be a nation of sorts, if not in actuality, at least as far as their mental attitude towards it was concerned. Anderson's highly influential book *Imagined Communities* (1983; later edition 1991) suggests that a nation can be considered as an imagined political community. McCrone (1992), adding to Anderson (1991), underlines the importance of a sense of belonging to this imagined community. The community has to be imagined because it links us affectively, not just to people we know, but also to people we will never meet, living in the past, the present or the future. Anderson (1991: 26) conceptualises the nation 'as a solid community moving steadily down (or up) history'.

So nationhood is not just to do with political principalities, but rather it is based on a more fundamental sense of belonging to a distinctive community which is rooted in history. Furthermore, that nationhood implies a shared sense, not just of synchronic (horizontal), but also of diachronic (vertical) identity. That is not to say that all Scots necessarily share exactly the same ideas as to what Scotland is all about, and what makes them Scottish; but there will be a pool of generalised concepts about Scotland and Scottishness, from which the individual can construct his or her own Scotland. For some those concepts may be mainly historical, for others cultural, for some linguistic and so on. As McCrone (1992: 17) observes, 'Scotland as "country" is, then, a landscape of the mind, a place of the imagination. As such, notions of the essential Scotland are what people want it to be.' A mental consciousness of being Scottish whether based on historic fact or fiction, cultural 'totems' and icons, Scottish heritage, or Scottish language, is still pervasive in Scotland today.

So it seems that Scottishness is not a monolithic unalterable identity, but rather that it is a dynamic process whereby individuals can 'stake a claim' to those facets of Scottishness that appeal to them, and they are therefore directly involved in the construction and maintenance of that identity. As discussed previously in section 2.1, individuals can also align themselves with multiple social groupings. The Scottish national identity is multi-faceted, but it is necessary also to consider how it integrates with other identities. In addition to having a Scottish national consciousness, most people will also have a distinctive 'local' identity; so for someone living in Glasgow, their notion of what it means to be Scottish will be bound up with their experience of being a Glaswegian, with its attendant value systems, local stereotypes and so on. Someone living in Inverness may well have a quite different experience of being Scottish, based on their experience of life in the Highlands, perhaps a more rural Scottishness, a more conservative value system, and a stronger sense of local community. In addition to a national and local identity, most Scots will also have a class identity. This will be dependent on a number of inter-related factors such as their education, financial status, family background and general outlook on life. Scotland still has quite a strong system of class identity, although it has traditionally been believed in Scotland that, if one works hard and gets a good education, it is possible to rise above one's humble origins (that is to be a *lad o' pairts*). Individuals may key into different identities on different occasions, sometimes choosing to highlight their national Scottish identity, and at others choosing to foreground their local, or class, or religious identities. So, national identity may well be mediated by local and/or class identities. This idea will be returned to in section 6.1.2 when considering differences in East/West and tabloid/broadsheet newspapers.

2.4.3 The role of Scottish language

Section 2.3 discussed the link between language and identity. Now consideration turns to the more specific question of the role of Scottish language in constructing and/or maintaining a sense of Scottish identity. Reading the personal accounts in Devine and Logue (2002), one notes the recurring emphasis placed on language as a factor in Scottish identity. Many contributors comment overtly on the status of *Scots* language in their conception of Scottish identity. Many others simply use identifiably *Scots* lexis and idiom, without comment, in their essay contributions. Certainly personal observation, as a Scot currently resident in Yorkshire, suggests that distinctively Scottish features (mainly pronunciation, lexis and idiom) in an individual's linguistic repertoire are what immediately identify them as a Scot to others. Difference (or indeed similarity) can be primarily indicated through language. What marks out the majority of Scots is not the (usually non-existent) tartan garb, the wee dram or can of Irn-Bru lurking in the sporran, the wriggling haggis under the arm, or even the thrawn and dour persona. Rather, what most significantly mark the Scot, in the spoken mode, are the identifiably Scottish accent and the use of Scottish vocabulary and idiom. Some Scots will also use identifiably Scottish grammar (see discussion in section 3.2.1 for distinguishing features of *Scottish-English* varieties).

Accent is probably the most readily recognisable marker of Scottish identity. Bond and Rosie (2006: 153–4) discover that a Scottish accent can be an 'identity resource' which may act as a 'proxy marker' of prolonged Scottish residence and/or birthplace which can authenticate a Scottish identity for individuals who may 'lack (or appear to lack)' other markers of Scottishness. As they note, accent is also usually more readily discernible than place of birth or ancestry claims, both of which would usually require longer acquaintance or elicitation. Kiely et al. (2001: 36) cite accent as one of their ten identity markers and it is interesting to consider whether it is an essential element in the successful negotiation of an individual's Scottish identity (see Bond 2006: 616–17). However, salient as it is, because accent is confined to the spoken mode it is of limited relevance to this study, though arguably some Scottish pronunciations can be reflected in orthography (see discussion in sections 3.2.1 and 3.3 for further details, and section 5.8 for analysis).

In the written mode, the observable markers are those of *Scots* lexis, idiom, orthography (spelling), and, to a lesser extent, grammar. It is, however, easy to overstate the case. Glauser's (1974) examination of the fuzzy nature of the Scottish/English linguistic border indicates that many words that a Scot might think of as essentially Scottish are, in fact, for historical reasons, shared with *northern English* dialects such as the *Yorkshire* dialect. So, for example *aboon* (above, over), *blether* (talk nonsense), *jaloused* (suspected), *lug* (ear), *sneck* (door latch) and *skelped* (given a good hiding, smacked) are shared and others have very closely related meanings: *anent* (*Yorkshire*: next to; *Scots*: concerning, about), *clarty* (*Yorkshire*: muddy; *Scots*: also dirty), and *threap* (*Yorkshire*: argue; *Scots*: argue or nag at). (Definitions are taken from the Yorkshire Dialect website.) Section 3.1 explains in more detail why many such lexical items are shared across the Scottish/English political border. Does it matter that the items people think are distinctively Scottish or Yorkshire may, on occasions, not be so? Not really, and lexis and its isoglosses are notoriously slippery anyway. What matters for the present study is that the items appear in the major *Scots* language diction-aries (*Scottish National Dictionary* (SND), *Dictionary of the Older Scottish Tongue* (DOST), *Dictionary of the Scots Language* (DSL) and they are felt to be Scottish words/phrases by Scots themselves. Returning to the ideas behind Anderson's (1991) imagined communities, a body of people believing these items are essentially distinctive is actually enough. That is, they invest them with a Scottishness that makes them salient.

Linguists disagree on the role that *Scots* language can have as a symbol or focus of Scottish cultural identity. Ager (2003: 62) baldly asserts that 'despite the existence of a major poet (Robert Burns) writing in the language, *Scots* has not acted as a major symbol of Scottish identity', and McCrone (1992: 174) even goes as far as arguing that Scotland lacks linguistic cultural markers. Donaldson (1998: 194–5) takes the opposite view. He is discussing speech, but the general point applies. He argues that *Scots* language defines people as 'insiders' and keeps outsiders out, whereas *English* is used as a 'bridge' with the outside world. McCrone (1992: 28–9) argues that there are additional factors that are involved in the generation of national identity, and that language will not necessarily function as a 'cultural identifier' in the same way for everyone. Edwards (1985: 3) argues that language is only one of the factors that goes into the formation of an individual's sense of identity, other factors being things like age, sex, social class, geography, religion and so on, and these are important provisos.

The situation in Scotland is complicated by *Gaelic* which has competing claims as Scotland's linguistic identifier even though spoken by a small minority of the population. Note that one does not have to understand *Gaelic* to relate to it in this way. Its symbolism as a Scottish language and its 'otherness' allow it to function as a cultural identifier, even for those outside the *Gaelic*-speaking community. Cormack's (1995) work on the symbolic function of *Gaelic* in the newspapers argues that it is a salient symbol of Scottishness even for those who do not understand the language.

Scottish Standard English further complicates the language and Scottish identity situation. This study argues that *Scottish Standard English* can also function as a potent symbol of Scottishness (see discussion in section 3.3). Indeed, in many cases it may be a more potent symbol, especially in the written mode, than *Scots* (or *Gaelic* for that matter) because it lacks the problems of comprehensibility often associated with the other two varieties.

2.4.4 Language, identity and nation states

When considering the link between language and identity, it is important to stress that linguistically determined boundaries may or may not correlate with nation-states (see section 3.7 for discussion of language as a socio-political construct). There is nothing to say that because a group has a distinctive language and/or culture they will automatically have an autonomous nation-state. However, for those cultures which have once had, and for whatever reason have now lost, nation-state status, language can continue to be a strong unifying force. As Cooper (1989: 12) notes, the fact that language continues to be a strong force in a sense of national identity in such communities is evidenced by the attempts which are often made to revive a language, which go hand-in-hand with nationalism or nationalistic ideologies, for example the promotion of *Hebrew* in Palestine and *Nynorsk* in Norway.

The case of *Scots* language and Scottish national identity is a particularly interesting one due to the problematic status both of language and nation. Chapter 3 deals more fully with the problematic status of *Scots*, and the ways in which it is used, but for now it is useful to consider the impact of Scotland's problematic nation status. Edwards (1985: 18) argues that the communicative and symbolic functions of language can be separated, and that it is possible for the symbolic function of a language as a focus of identity to persist, even when the language is no longer used in its communicative function. In other words, the symbolic function of language as a rallying point or emblem of group identity can persist even when the communicative function of that language is reduced or lost.

This study argues that language is a powerful factor in Scottish identity. As has already been hinted, and as will be discussed in more detail in Chapters 3 and 5, problems with the status of *Scots* mean that, for some Scots, broad/dense *Scots* dialect will not be a strong cultural identifier and may not even be understood, that is, it has lost its communicative function. However, that need not fully detract from its symbolic function. Section 6.4 discusses an ongoing exchange of *Scots* proverbs in one of the newspapers, where communicative import seems much less important than visibility and symbolic function.

2.4.5 The role of Scottish stereotypes

Newspapers are well known for keying into stereotypes, as these give the journalist a shorthand method of establishing common ground. Fowler (1991: 17) describes stereotypes as being 'a socially-constructed mental pigeon-hole into which events and individuals can be sorted, thereby making such events and individuals comprehensible'. Stereotypes, as his definition suggests, can be wide-ranging and are extremely pervasive in the language of the press; for example, the well-known stereotypes associated with women, especially in the tabloid newspapers: often blonde, beautiful and defined in relation to men. Stereotypes relate individual mental constructs to socially-shared categories, and help us to make sense of the world (see van Dijk 1998: 83–5). By definition, stereotypes need not be, and indeed are unlikely to be, entirely accurate reflections. They are a selective representation or simplification of a much more complex and varied situation. Although stereotypes may have some basis in truth, they may be exaggerated or simply untrue. As discussed earlier with respect to

Scottish 'totems', this need not detract from their influence or pervasiveness. We do not need to believe that all Scotsmen wear kilts, eat haggis and play the bagpipes in order to make use of that stereotype, or even to promulgate it, when the occasion suits.

For the purposes of this study, there are three Scottish stereotypes that need to be considered. These are Tartanry, the Kailyard and Clydesidism. McCrone (1992: 177ff.) discusses and defines these three key 'mythic structures'. (Note once again the use of 'mythic', suggesting that these stereotypes are not necessarily true.) McCrone describes the Kailyard stereotype, as 'a popular literary style celebrating Scottish rural quaintness' which helped elevate the mythic status of the *lad o' pairts*. He notes that it 'is usually attributed to the critic George Blake, who described its essential elements as domesticity, rusticity, humour, humility, modesty, decency, piety and poverty'. Key features associated with the Kailyard are the importance of the minister and the schoolmaster or *dominie*. This is the Scottish stereotype often portrayed by television, for example in *Dr Finlay's Casebook* and earlier episodes of *Take the High Road* (Corbett 1997: 185). Tartanry was not a literary movement and it includes elements like the kilt, the bagpipes, a noble Highland ancestry, patriotism, Jacobitism, Scotch whisky etc. (Corbett 1997: 186). McCrone (1992: 180–1) describes the famous music hall performer, Harry Lauder as 'the fusion of both tartanry and Kailyard' and argues that Tartanry 'has come to stand for tourist knick-knackery, visits to Wembley, and the Edinburgh Tattoo'. The final Scottish stereotype to consider is Clydesidism (see McArthur 1981; 1982). Some of the key attributes associated with Clydesidism are, borrowing from Corbett (1997: 187), being working-class, male, a skilled worker, a hero, coupled with associations of oppression, violence, alcoholism and socialism. A key representative of this stereotype would be Billy Connolly, himself an ex-shipyard worker, who makes jokes about the working-class ethos, drinking and so on. As society changes, other stereotypes will emerge, and even the more recent stereotype of Clydesidism is nowadays, in many ways, outdated. Works such as *Trainspotting* and others by writers like Irvine Welsh and James Kelman are a modern version of Clydesidism. The TV character Rab C. Nesbitt is another modern adaptation of this stereotype. Clydesidism has often been argued to be more realistic than either Kailyardism or Tartanry, as it was ostensibly based on the real experiences of the working classes; but with the closure of the shipyards, McCrone (1992: 187) queries whether this is really the case and suggests this stereotype too is on its way to being a historical construct.

Many of the elements of these Scottish stereotypes have become clichéd in Scotland, and beyond. Tartanry, although an extremely successful marketing ploy, has often been heavily criticised, part of the criticism being that Scots are content to accept and put forward debased images of themselves for external consumption (for example the misleading representations of Scottish history or culture projected by films such as *Braveheart* and *Brigadoon*), rather than seeking to project the 'real' Scotland (whatever that might be). For a more in-depth discussion of representations of Scotland on film see McArthur (1982: 40–69), where he notes that even the Scottish film industry has failed to shake off Tartanry and the Kailyard in its representations of Scotland. It is interesting to consider in passing whether 'realistic' books and films such as the more recent *Trainspotting* are any more 'real'. It would appear, however, that not all the trappings of Tartanry are universally despised in Scotland. Many people still choose to get married in kilts, and to have a piper play them down the aisle, with a ceilidh afterwards at the reception. In that guise it seems to be perfectly acceptable. Nevertheless, there is a rather wry appreciation that the Scots have come to be viewed as a tartan-bedecked, haggis-eating nation; it is a stereotype which many Scots seem to promulgate themselves, albeit with a sense of humour. For example, there was a billboard advertisement displayed in Edinburgh to announce the opening of the new Ikea furniture store, which depicted the store wrapped up like a box of petticoat tails shortbread, but claiming that the contents of the Ikea box were much more interesting than the usual shortbread.

Stereotypes, just like identities, are not necessarily foisted upon people, and then left unchallenged or unaltered. People can choose to engage with the stereotypes, perhaps challenging them, or modifying them for their own purposes. Thus there is a dynamic relationship between the stereotype and either its referent or those who invoke it. Fowler (1991: 17), arguing from a constructivist approach, cautions that 'they are categories which we project on to the world in order to make sense of it. We construct the world in this way.' Corbett (1997: 188–9) also argues that, as individuals, we are actively involved in the construction and maintenance of these stereotypes; we can choose to 'celebrate' these shared cultural representations, or alternatively we can choose to question, subvert or deny them, but that ultimately we use them as a form of 'shared culture'. Section 6.10 considers whether newspapers are more likely to use some Scottish stereotypes than others, and also whether the use of certain *Scots* lexical items triggers particular Scottish stereotypes.

2.5 Conclusion

This study focuses on the linguistic construction of Scottish identity by the newspapers, but also acknowledges that the newspapers are drawing on ideas about Scotland and what it means to be Scottish which are already prevalent in society. Scottish newspapers can therefore be viewed as involved in both the construction and maintenance of Scottish identity. By using *Scots* lexis, the newspapers are, to some extent, erecting linguistic tariffs which simultaneously include Scottish readers and exclude non-Scottish readers (or those with no knowledge of *Scots* lexis). As will be discussed further in section 4.4.5.2, they are also involved in a process of negotiation with their readers as to what that Scottish identity will be, and the appropriacy of the language used to evoke it. Scottish identity is a multifaceted phenomenon, and therefore readers may tend to choose newspapers which espouse those particular facets of the Scottish identity to which they adhere, and not choose those which emphasise a different side of that identity. This is likely to be most evident in a class-based split between the tabloid and broadsheet readerships, and this is investigated further in the data chapters. The construction of Scottish identity by the newspapers may rely, to some extent, on formulaic elements and key Scottish stereotypes, and so these factors are investigated in Chapter 6.

FURTHER READING

1. Anderson [1983] (1991) is the classic and frequently referred to work on the imagined community. It has been seminal in numerous academic fields of study.
2. Joseph (2004) is a well-written, readable and useful overview of identity, particularly as it relates to language.
3. McCrone (1992) gives a useful overview of Scottish identity and its features. McCrone (2001) updates this earlier work and gives a useful post-devolution perspective. The Institute of Governance Identity Briefings (Bechhofer et al. 2006; Rosie et al. 2006b; 2006c and others available online from the Institute of Governance website) investigating Scottish identity are accessible and brief sociological overviews which usefully combine quantitative and qualitative analysis.
4. McCrone et al. (1995) provide a useful summary of the main Scottish stereotypes, and their impact on Scottish culture.

3

What is Scottish Language?

This chapter gives an overview of the complex linguistic situation in Scotland and links it to discussion of the language of the newspapers. It outlines how the linguistic situation that exists in present-day Scotland arose, and suggests various ways to make sense of the range of Scottish varieties encompassed by the superordinate term *Scottish-English*. A range of questions surrounds the status of *Scottish-English* varieties: whether they are best described as discrete languages in their own right or alternatively as dialects of *English*; the existence or absence of a Scottish standard variety; and status and register constraints. Also under discussion are issues such as how people in Scotland feel about the language they use, focusing particularly on their self-awareness, ambivalent attitudes and the frequently encountered linguistic insecurity. Finally, this chapter considers the relevance and implications of these factors for an analysis of Scottish newspaper texts.

As discussed briefly in Chapter 1, this study is concerned with those language varieties in Scotland I have collectively termed *Scottish-English*. *Scottish-English* is a localised form of *British English*, and, on a global scale, of *World English*. The varieties within *Scottish-English* (including the two key varieties *Scots* and *Scottish Standard English*) are characterised to varying degrees by the inclusion of *Scots* lexis and idiom, Scottish grammatical features (both syntactic and morphological), Scottish pronunciation, and, in the written mode, sometimes by distinctive orthography. Before discussing the present-day characteristics of *Scots* and *Scottish Standard English* and how this relates to their use in the newspaper texts in more detail, it is helpful to examine their origins; firstly the development of the variety I have termed *Scots*; and secondly the subsequent development of *Scottish Standard English*. Many of these historical developments can be usefully illustrated by using the *OED* to trace the etymologies of some of lexical forms found in the newspapers.

3.1 THE HISTORICAL CONTEXT

Two fundamental theories of language change can be used to explain the development of, and also the current situation as regards these *Scottish-English* varieties – the tree and the wave models (Smith 1996: 50). The tree model emphasises descent or linguistic inheritance. So, for example, we can trace the development of the word *gallus* (which means 'self-confident' or alternatively 'good, impressive' and is used in both senses in the newspaper data) from *gallows* (fit for the gallows, daring, wild). *Scots* and *English* are closely related cognate Germanic language varieties, and so sizeable proportions of their lexicons are made up of cognate vocabulary, for example *Scots hame* and *English home* (see section 3.6 for further discussion).

Their shared historical origins in *Old English* also mean that *Scots* and *English* share a body of material (both lexical and grammatical) which is usually referred to as 'common-core' and which the lay person may consider simply to be *English*. This material 'has since the outset been common ground' (Aitken 1979: 85), for example, items such as *name, hole, before* (Aitken 1984a: 520). As can be seen from the examples, these common-core items have the same orthographic form in both *Scots* and *English*. Although such items belong no more to *English* than they do to *Scots*, they are not included in this study, as only items that are markedly *Scots* are immediately discernible from *English* in the written mode, and can therefore be used by the newspapers to mark Scottishness.

Scots developed from the *Anglian* dialects of *Old English* which straddled the present-day political border between England and Scotland, thus explaining why similarities are found even today between *Scots* and the *northern English* regional dialects. So, for example, the newspapers contain words such as *mickle* (sometimes *muckle*) which are still found both in Scotland and in some *northern English* dialects though not in *English* generally. (In the newspapers the word may also be contained within the idiomatic expression *mony a mickle maks a muckle* (many little things make a big thing) an expression that is often said to be corrupted given that *mickle* and *muckle* are actually the same word.) The word can be traced back to *Old English* (*micele*) and its cognate forms in *Middle Dutch, Old Saxon, Old High German, Old Icelandic* and so on (OED) usefully demonstrate *Scots'* and *English's* shared Germanic and ultimately Indo-European roots. Given its origins, *Scots* can certainly be linguistically (although perhaps not ideologically) classified as a type of *English* (see discussion in section 3.7).

The wave model emphasises language contact and interaction. It is very useful when considering languages, such as *Scots* and *English*, which have a long history of development in close geographical proximity. Although having originally developed from different dialects of *Old English*, as Macafee (2007) notes, *Scots* and *English* have not developed in isolation from each other; rather they 'have always formed a geographical continuum of dialects within which linguistic changes diffused and spread'. Until the late fifteenth and early sixteenth centuries, the descendant of *Old English* in Scotland was, like the variety used in Northumbria, termed *Inglis*. It was only then that the Scots began to differentiate their variety by terming it *Scottis* (see McClure (1981) for fuller discussion of the names of these varieties, and section 3.7 for discussion of the significance of names in the present day). So *Scots* and *English* have had a longstanding relationship both in terms of their shared historical origins and ongoing contact. Some *Scots* items occurring in the newspapers such as *glaikit* (foolish), *haar* (East coast mist), and *pawky* (dry sense of humour) are shared with some *northern English* dialects and therefore illustrate this lexical continuum, but the precise etymologies of many such words are unclear.

Scots, like *English*, was influenced by *Old Norse*, *French* and *Latin*, but as McArthur (1998: 146) notes, *Scots* was influenced 'in different ways, to different degrees, and under different conditions'. *Old Norse* influence can be seen in *skite* (slip, slide) (though the etymology is somewhat unclear), an item which is found in the newspaper texts and in some *English* regional dialects. *Old French* and/or *Anglo-Norman* influence can be seen in words like *poke* ('bag' in *Scots* and some regional *English* dialects not restricted to the 'pig in a poke' idiom) and *vennel* ('a narrow passageway'), also found in some *northern English* dialects. Most, though not all, scholars agree that the influence on *Scots* from *Gaelic* has been minimal but the newspapers quite frequently use *Scots* lexical items that indicate *Gaelic* influence, for example *Sassenach* (a somewhat derogatory term for 'an Englishman', from *Gaelic Sasunnach*) and *sonsie* (plump, attractive – applied to women and children, from *Gaelic sonas*). Many of these influences can be explained by historical events which brought these different language varieties into contact.

Until the arrival of Anglian invaders in 547 and the establishment of the kingdom of Bernicia, the language of Scotland was predominantly Celtic, that is, *Gaelic*. The Anglian invaders brought their Germanic dialects, what is now termed *Old English*, with them. The arrival of Viking invaders and settlers from the eighth century substantially complicated matters, and explains the significant influence of *Old Norse* (another closely related Germanic language) that can be seen, both in *English* and in *Scots*, to the present day. The *Norse* influence on *Scots* was extensive, beginning with the arrival of Viking raiders to the northern and western isles of Scotland in the eighth century and continuing with ongoing waves of attacks and later settlement both north and south of the present Scottish/English border. A good indication of settlement patterns is given by placename evidence, for example in *–by* and *–wick* elements. (See Scott (2003) and also Macafee (2007) for discussion of Scottish placename elements.) In Scotland, there was significant settlement in the Orkney and Shetland islands, and present-day *Insular Scots* still shows significant influence from the Norwegian variety *Norn* (the descendant of *Old Norse* spoken in these islands until the eighteenth and nineteenth centuries respectively). There were also areas of Viking settlement in Caithness, Sutherland, Galloway and Argyll. Viking raids and settlement persisted from the late eighth to the twelfth century. South of the border, there were significant Viking settlements in the area known as the Danelaw from the ninth century onwards. So both *Scots* and *English* were heavily influenced by *Old Norse*, and even a cursory investigation of the etymology of many common *English* and *Scots* words will bear this out. *Scots* has many *Norse*-influenced words such as *kirk* which is cognate with *English* 'church'. (*Kirk* occurs frequently in the newspapers and can be considered a 'cultural Scotticism' (see section 3.10).) Some scholars (for example Poussa 1982) suggest that, because the languages of the Anglian and Viking settlers were cognate and to some extent mutually comprehensible, an Anglo-Scandinavian creole situation developed. The displacement of *Gaelic* by the Anglo-Scandinavian variety later known as *Scots* was a very gradual process, and indeed, until the twelfth century, *Scots* was restricted to the areas in the south and southeast of Scotland, the areas to the north being *Gaelic* speaking (see McClure (1994) for further discussion).

The arrival of Norman-French overlords following the Conquest in 1066 had far-reaching linguistic as well as political effects in Scotland, as in England. *Scots* shows influences from this period of *Norman French* and also of a strengthening of the Anglo-Scandinavian variety spoken by the Norman lords' servants and retainers. Further *French* influence on *Scots* came from ongoing contact with France via the Auld Alliance (1295–1560) as well as later influence from *Central French* borrowings in *English*. So there are *Scots* words such as *ashet* 'an oval, flat plate or dish, generally large, on which a joint or other food is served' (*DSL*) – often applied to a type of pie (Fr. *assiette* – also found in some *northern English* dialects) which occurs thirteen times in the newspaper corpus.

Scots, like *English*, experienced ongoing influence from *Latin*. But by 1390, Scottish Acts of Parliament, which hitherto had been recorded in Latin, began to be written in *Scots* (*Inglis*). By the fifteenth and early sixteenth centuries, *Scots* was being used in increasingly formal registers – it was the language of the Scottish court, was often the language used for government and administrative documents, and it had a burgeoning and well-established literary tradition with writers such as Douglas, Henryson and Dunbar. However, during the sixteenth century, *Scots* increasingly became seen as a homely or more domestic language, and not always suited to more lofty purposes. Evidence of this reduction in status of the language can be seen even today (see section 3.7), and the newspaper evidence demonstrates it too (see analysis in Chapter 5). The introduction of printing to Scotland in 1508 had a far-reaching effect as printers 'normalised' *Scots* lexical and grammatical forms to their *English* counterparts. The Scottish Reformation in 1560 and the attendant exposure to *English* through the English version of the Bible changed things still further. There was a recovery in Scottish literature for a few years under the aegis of James VI, but with the relocation of the court south and the Union of the Crowns in 1603 and the Union of the Parliaments just over a century later in 1707, the *Scots* language declined in status, and over a period of time began to be somewhat displaced by *English*, at least in intention if not in actual realisation, by its more upwardly mobile speakers. As Murison (1979: 9) observes: 'Scots . . . lost spiritual status at the Reformation, social status at the Union of the Crowns, and political status with the Parliamentary Union.' During the seventeenth century there was an increase in the amount of contact between the Scots and the English, and the numbers of Scottish gentry marrying into the English gentry rose sharply. There was a corresponding decline in the fortunes of Scottish literature, and this situation continued until what is now termed the Scottish Enlightenment in the eighteenth century, when there was a resurgence of interest in things Scottish. The work of writers such as Burns, Ramsay, Ferguson and later Walter Scott revived the use of *Scots* in literature. However, this revival also reinforced negative attitudes to *Scots*. Lectures on how best to expunge one's language of Scottish 'barbarisms' became extremely popular in the eighteenth century, partially influenced by the Augustan distaste for anything vulgar or barbaric; and increasingly those higher up the social ladder sought to emulate the language of England as they had closer and more frequent contact with those in the south. It was against this background that *Scottish Standard English* originated as a linguistic compromise of the aspiring middle classes between the *Standard English* of London and *Scots* (McClure 1994: 79). *Scottish Standard English* became, and is now in the present day, established as a prestigious variety in its own right.

Scots increasingly came to be viewed as homely and domestic, and not suited to high style writing or serious prose, and this is a situation which largely persists today. *Scots*, unlike *English*, historically failed to achieve a standard variety. Various attempts have been made since to set up a standard variety of *Scots*, but with limited success. In the twentieth century there was an attempted literary revival of *Scots* using a synthetic variety known as *Lallans*, the main proponents being followers of the poet Hugh MacDiarmid. However many writers reject *Lallans* as a false, plastic *Scots* which is not rooted in any discernible time or place. It is a written variety seldom used by ordinary Scots people; in fact, most are unlikely to be aware of its existence. Nowadays the position of *Scots* in Scotland is very much overshadowed by *Scottish Standard English*, which continues to be the prestigious form most often used in formal situations. This has serious implications for the use of *Scots* by the newspapers.

3.2 THE LINGUISTIC CONTINUUM

Present-day *Scottish-English* is perhaps best thought of as containing a whole spectrum of linguistic varieties which may be regionally and/or socially defined. It has been suggested (Aitken 1979; McArthur 1979; and others) that the present linguistic situation in Scotland is best considered as a bi-polar linguistic continuum, with *Scots* at one end being the variety which is most markedly Scottish and *Scottish Standard English* being the least so (see Fig. 3.1). Individuals, taking account of external factors such as context of situation, social class, education and so on, are able to move along the continuum in either direction; thus it is bi-polar.

Scottish-English

Scots ◄──────────────────────────────► *Scottish Standard English*

Figure 3.1 *Scottish-English* linguistic continuum

3.2.1 Varieties along the continuum

To complicate matters further, the term *Scots* does not describe a homo-geneous linguistic situation, and it can be used to cover a whole range of linguistic varieties. It is generally held to include localised Scottish verna-culars known variously as *broad Scots* or *dialect Scots*, for example, rural or more traditional varieties such as the *Ayrshire* dialect or the *Doric* of northeastern Scotland. It can also be used to describe *Lallans*. Although I include modern urban dialects such as *Glaswegian* in the definition of *Scots*, this practice is by no means universal. So for me both of the following excerpts from the newspapers would qualify as *Scots* though clearly of very different types.

Shairly ane o the weirdest contradictions o Scottish culture is that while we're often fond o crawin aboot oor mony claims tae fame, we often hae nae mair confidence than wee coorin timorous tung-tied beasties when it comes tae expressing oorsels in oor ain native Lowland Scots. We pey respectfu homage tae oor great national Bard aince a year, but for the rest o the time luek doon oor snoots at onybody that actually tries tae yaise the very tung that Burns immortalised. In maist Scottish schuils, the annual Burns' Competition has been the only time o year when ony kinna Scots wis tholed. (John Hodgart, language activist, writing a feature article entitled 'Time tae cure oor cultural cringe aboot native tungs' in *The Herald*, 12 September 1995)

When ah first got doon ah arrived at Victoria an' then a walked fae Victoria intae the West End and a met a couple o' pals fae ma home toon. Ah didnae know they wur doon here, ah just seen them by chance. Ah wiz walkin' by Westminster an' ah heard somebdae shoutin' 'Tony!' an' ah turned roon' an' it wiz them shoutin' oan me. Ah've spent most o' ma time wae them since. (Gerard Seenan narrating a young homeless man's story, ostensibly in his own words, in an article with the headline 'London's bright lights don't look so good from a cardboard box' in *The Herald*, 13 June 1995)

The Hodgart extract is written in a dense *Scots* which can be put at the extreme *Scots* end of the continuum. The Seenan article is rather less markedly *Scots*, is written in such a way as to represent spoken urban *Scots*, and uses some forms such as *wiz* that are used to represent a particular pronunciation but would not be found in a *Scots* dictionary. (As you may have noted, the Seenan article also uses apostrophes to indicate so-called 'missing letters' – something few, if any, Scots language activists would condone.) As these examples show, written and spoken *Scots* can be rather different animals and this is something returned to in section 3.3.

Present-day *Scottish Standard English* is a widespread and important variety. In the spoken mode, its key distinguishing feature is pronunciation. However, it also has characteristic vocabulary, idiom and to a lesser extent grammar, all of which can be reflected in the written mode. Examples of *Scottish Standard English* which illustrate grammatical difference from *Standard English-English* would be *The car needs washed* (Scottish Standard English) vs 'The car needs washing' (Standard English-English) or *She has **the** cold, **the** flu* rather than *Standard English-English* 'She has a cold'; 'she has flu'. *Edinburgh was dreich yesterday* would be a lexical example. An example of *Scottish Standard English* (that is the extreme opposite end of the continuum from the Hodgart article) in the newspapers would be something like the following:

> Scots has of late been hitting the headlines. James Kelman and the Booker (how late it was how late it was indeed!). Trainspotting at last released by Irvine Welsh from its associations of coorying in with a notebook, pencil, and flask and happing up with anorak hood. People write about Scots in the papers. They proclaim its 'mither tongue' status and its fitness for all linguistic purposes – or they deny its relevance, or even existence. (Dr Anne King, an academic with expertise in *Scots* language, writing a feature article, again in *The Herald* (7 October 1995), entitled 'A language beyond the pail')

Other than *coorying* (snuggling), *happing* (covering up – OED has distribution as Scottish and some English dialects) and *mither tongue* (mother tongue), the last marked off by the use of inverted commas, this extract is written in unremarkable *Standard Written English*. It is only the inclusion of these occasional *Scots* lexical items that make it *Scottish Standard English*.

Both *Scots* and *Scottish Standard English* have some (though limited, especially in the case of *Scottish Standard English*) recognised morphological features which inevitably impact on the forms of some lexical items, for example –it, –in endings in section 1.4.1), and these are found in the newspaper data. *Scottish-English* varieties have other distinctive features such as a rather different distribution of modal verbs from *English-English*, for example, the use of *can* or *could* rather than *may* for permission is more usual, and some syntactic differences from other varieties of *English*, but these are beyond the scope of this study. Although this study does not investigate elements of Scottish syntax, it does look at closed class or grammatical lexis in section 5.5.2.

Although varieties along the *Scottish-English* continuum have common characteristics, there are certain phonological, orthographic, lexical and even a few grammatical features which are regional. Some orthographic forms show regional differences, for example *canna* (east) vs *cannae* (west), and certain lexical items are associated with particular parts of the country for example *bairn* and *wean* (both meaning 'child', but *wean* being the preferred word in West Central Scotland). Both these items were found in the newspapers and section 6.1.2 assesses whether there is any evidence of a regional split (see Table 6.4). *Scottish-English* varieties can also be socially defined, and indeed, defining. Linguistic choices in matters of grammar, lexis, phonology and idiom can be socially marked, with certain lexical features being treated as linguistic shibboleths, particularly by the middle classes, for example *yous(e)* (you (plural version of the 2nd person pronoun)), an item that occurred sixty-five times in the corpus and was found in all the Scottish newspapers.

3.2.2 *Polarisation, code-switching and style-drifting*

A linguistic continuum suggests that individuals can vary their style across the whole breadth of the range according to circumstance, but in practice their linguistic choices are more likely to be skewed towards one end of the continuum. Not all speakers have equal access to both the *Scots* and *Scottish Standard English* systems, and the choices of a particular individual may be restricted by a number of social and contextual factors. Thus it is a polarised linguistic continuum (Aitken 1984b) where people tend to favour one or other pole. Pole choices broadly conform to social class divisions, with middle-class speakers preferring the *Scottish Standard English* pole and working-class speakers tending towards the *Scots* pole. Working-class speakers will usually tend towards the *Scottish Standard English* pole in more formal contexts. There are often register implications associated with moving along the continuum in either direction. It should also be noted that individuals can move across the continuum within the same piece of discourse. So, for example, a speaker or writer may mainly use *Scottish Standard English* but switch to using *Scots* to make a particular point. Aitken observes that

> Some such speakers can switch quite cleanly from one to the other – these people have been called *dialect-switchers*. Others again cannot or do not choose to control their styles in this way, but they do shift styles in a less predictable and more fluctuating way – these people we may call *style-drifters*. (Aitken 1979: 85–6)

Individuals can therefore switch between the different bases in different circumstances (code-switching – often deliberate and stylistically motivated), or can drift between styles (style-drifting). As outlined in section 1.4, this was one of the main reasons for using full texts rather than text samples.

3.3 Written vs Spoken Varieties

The range of linguistic choices along the continuum is often very different in the written and spoken modes. It is a very curious anomaly that those individuals who speak *Scots* are generally unable to write it and/or read it;

those who are most likely to be able to read and perhaps even write it are usually well-educated middle-class non-*Scots*-speaking individuals. The education system, for most people, has largely ignored developing writing skills in *Scots*, and even study of literature written in *Scots* is usually heavily limited. There are currently moves afoot to change the schools' English curriculum and to redress this balance somewhat and the 5–14 Guidelines on English Language and the Curriculum for Excellence (Learning and Teaching Scotland (LTS)) do make some mention of *Scots*. But the fact remains that there are a large number of people in Scotland who know little or nothing of *Scots*, even though some of them may speak it. Thus there is a divorce of styles between the written and spoken modes.

Nowadays *Scots* is primarily a spoken language, so much more *Scots* is spoken than is written. We might therefore expect to find more *Scots* lexis in direct speech contexts than in straightforward narrative contexts within the newspapers, and section 5.7 investigates this hypothesis. In the written mode, because *Scots* historically failed to achieve standardisation, a standardised system for its orthography has never been agreed (Scottish Language Dictionaries 2008), though there have been ongoing attempts. Smith (1996) draws a contrast between the different degrees of standardisation achieved by *English* and *Scots*, and introduces the useful terms *fixity* and *focus*. Fixed varieties (for example *English*) are those that have an agreed standard form; by contrast focused varieties (for example *Scots*) have 'a centripetal norm towards which speakers tend, rather than a fixed collection of prescribed rules from which any deviation at all is forbidden' (Smith 1996: 66). The fixity/focus model is useful when discussing the differences between *English* and *Scots* in terms of the degree of standardisation achieved especially as regards orthographic conventions. Present-day *Standard Written English* is a fixed variety, and only a few spelling variants are allowed, for example between *jail/gaol*, *gipsy/gypsy*, *focused/focussed*. The fact that exceptions can be listed illustrates how exceptional they are in the overall picture. *Scots*, by contrast, is a focused variety, and a brief perusal of any of the large *Scots* dictionaries such as *SND*, *DOST* or *DSL* will show that, although *Scots* has, to some extent, been codified there, it is not prescriptive codification. The major *Scots* dictionaries offer a range of possible spellings for most lexical items, with no one spelling being considered 'correct'. Thus there is variation in orthographic practice with some forms being justified by writers on the grounds of etymology, others being justified on the grounds that they represent pronunciation, and others being a matter of personal preference. However, it would be erroneous to imagine that spelling in *Scots* is a free-for-all. On the contrary, there are agreed tendencies and orthographic patterns can be discerned for example choice of –ie or –y endings on words like *bonnie/bonny* (attractive to look at), or the variation between –ou– and –oo– spellings in words like *fouter/footer* (to potter/fiddle, or someone who does this). Section 5.8 assesses the extent to which the newspapers have normalised the orthographic forms they use and uses this to ascertain whether they are or are not adhering to in-house or other standards.

In the written mode, most Scots will habitually write in *Standard Written English* (or sometimes *Scottish Standard English*, depending on content, context and so on) because that is what the Scottish education system has conditioned them to do. So Scots cannot necessarily be identified as such by their writing. However, they will usually have within their linguistic repertoire items that are distinctively Scottish. *Scottish Standard English* is, of course, like other standard forms (*Standard English-English*, *Standard Irish English*, *Standard American English* and so on), subsumed within the overall category of *World/International Standard English*. So, for example, there are a few occurrences of distinctively Scottish features (for example *thrawn*, *furth*) in the general narrative of this book; therefore I would contend that it is, at least in parts, written in a distinctive form of *Standard Written English* that can be termed *Scottish Standard English*. *Scottish Standard English* unproblematically allows the inclusion of what can be termed *functional Scotticisms*. Functional Scotticisms are items of *Scots* lexis which transcend register boundaries and are acceptable in even very formal contexts from which *Scots* lexis would generally be precluded, and they include items such as the already discussed *furth* (outside), *leet* (list of candidates for a job), *outwith* (outside, beyond), *retiral* (retirement) and *uplift* (collect). They can be found in a range of formal and public discourse types including official output from local authorities, human resources departments and, of course, newspapers, where they occur quite frequently, especially in the broadsheets (see discussion in section 6.1.1).

The inclusion of national or regional forms in a standard variety is, of course, not something that is restricted to Scotland and *Scottish Standard English*. (See, for example, discussion of various *Standard Englishes* in Kachru et al. (2006).) World Englishes are often characterised by particular lexical, idiomatic or even grammatical forms which lend the varieties national or regional 'colour' without detracting from their 'standard' status (see discussion of *Singlish* and *Australian English* forms in newspapers in section 5.5.1). Perhaps the most important thing to note about *Scottish Standard English* is its status as a standard variety (more about status later in section 3.7). In both the spoken and written modes, it is the variety most commonly aimed at by Scots in formal situations, and both McArthur (1979: 50) and McClure (1994: 79) note its prestigious status as a national standard variety of *World* (or *International*) *Standard English*. *Scottish Standard English* is a persistent, prevalent and influential variety in Scotland today, and can serve as a useful focus for Scottish identity. Indeed, because many Scots would find writing (or for some even speaking) in *Scots* very difficult, if not impossible, as argued in section 2.4.3, I contend that it is often a more significant emblem of Scottish identity than dense *Scots*. *Scottish Standard English* is understood and used by the majority of the Scottish populace, as it is the variety most often used in Scottish education. It is in widespread use in Scotland today, enjoys high status and, acts as a potent marker of 'Scottishness'.

All of this means that writing in *Scots*, as opposed to speaking it, is seldom likely to be a subconscious act. Writing in *Scots* is generally a stylistically and/or politically (with a small 'p') motivated action. These factors have important implications for the newspaper texts, especially given the additional language 'checking' afforded by spell-checkers (*English*) and copy editors. We would expect, therefore, that the newspapers would generally be written in *Standard Written English* or *Scottish Standard English*, and we might also predict that the tabloid newspapers, with their allegedly predominantly working-class readership, would be less likely to use extended passages of broad *Scots* than the middle-class broadsheets, as much of their readership might have little familiarity with *Scots* in the written mode. Section 6.1.1 ascertains whether this is indeed the case.

3.4 THIN AND DENSE SCOTS

The concept of a linguistic continuum is useful in the abstract, but it is less helpful when faced with a text and trying to categorise it or position it along the continuum. *Scots* and *Scottish Standard English* are traditionally defined in the academic literature (and a practice followed in this study) by the extent to which they differ from *Standard English*, though McClure (1979: 30) takes pains to point out (vis-à-vis *Scots*) that this descriptive convention should not be taken as implying 'in any real sense a deviation from a standard represented by English'. Others, such as Gupta (2006), have continually argued against the 'deviance model' of language description more broadly. Certainly much of the academic literature describing linguistic varieties does so in terms of their distinctiveness or perceived differences from other varieties, differences and distinctiveness which, in the wider context of British or even World Englishes, may well turn out to be shared with other varieties.

However, with these caveats, quantitatively and qualitatively, how Scottish does a text have to be to qualify as *Scots* rather than *Scottish*

Standard English? McClure (1979) has developed a model which seeks to address this problem of analysing individual texts. His model is based on two pairs of concepts: firstly that of 'thin' and 'dense' *Scots*, that is a quantitative analysis; and secondly 'literary' and 'colloquial', a qualitative analysis. McClure's terms 'thin' and 'dense' *Scots* have their basis in the concept of the linguistic continuum, that is, of being more or less Scottish. He suggests (McClure 1979: 30) that in the written mode it is possible to differentiate between dense and thin *Scots* whereby thin *Scots* contains few *Scots* words and other *Scots* features, and dense *Scots* has significant quantities of *Scots* lexis, contains orthographic forms that betray *Scots* pronunciation or etymology, and has *Scots* grammar and idiom. He goes on to say (McClure 1979: 30) that 'the limiting case, as it were, of 'thin' Scots would be Scottish-English, that is Standard English, the international *lingua franca*, as spoken by educated Scotsmen' (N.B. McClure's use of the term 'Scottish-English' here equates to my use of the term *Scottish Standard English*). McClure also proposes that a qualitative distinction be made between 'colloquial' and 'literary' writing, but this is less helpful for categorising the language of the newspapers.

Some difficulties are encountered when attempting to distinguish and describe interim points on the *Scottish-English* linguistic continuum. This is especially true in the written mode as there can be no assistance gained from an analysis of accent. There will be many cases where it is evident that a certain text is *Scots* and another is *Scottish Standard English*; but as McClure's description suggests, there are grey areas in the middle. Some texts seem to fall mid-way between these two poles. That is to say there can be degrees of linguistic 'Scottishness'. One of the issues addressed by section 5.5 is the density of the language used in the newspapers. Macafee (1983: 31) notes that 'the [linguistic] continuum can be extended further in either direction in writing than in speech – not only are more formal types of St E [Standard English] possible in writing, but also more dense types of Scots'. So it is possible, though based on the foregoing discussion unlikely, that the newspapers could exhibit some very densely *Scots* texts. This study uses essentially quantitative methods to ascertain the densities of the newspaper articles by calculating the proportion of *Scots* to non-*Scots* lexis (see section 5.5.1).

3.5 Open vs Closed Class Scots Lexis

In linguistics generally, a basic distinction is drawn between content (open class) lexis and grammatical (closed class) lexis. Open class lexis consists of nouns, verbs, adjectives and adverbs; closed class lexis is determiners, auxiliary verbs, pronouns, prepositions, conjunctions, interjections and negatives. It is hypothesised that the split between open and closed class *Scots* lexis or, to put it another way, the distinction between content *Scots* lexis (that is the open class words which carry meaning) and non-content *Scots* words (closed class words which organise meaning), is potentially significant for newspaper language. It seems likely that open class *Scots* lexis is more likely to be used for language display than closed class *Scots* lexis. Hence open class *Scots* lexical items are likely to be found in isolation in thinner contexts, often with no examples of *Scots* closed class lexis, other than as found within the confines of particular idiomatic expressions. It is very unlikely that a text would have *Scots* closed class lexical items such as prepositions, conjunctions and determiners but not *Scots* open class lexical items such as nouns, verbs or adjectives. It is posited further that, where texts have *Scots* closed class items, they are likely to lie fairly close to the dense *Scots* end of the spectrum, whereas if they have only open class *Scots* lexical items, then they are more likely to tend towards the thin *Scottish Standard English* end of the continuum. The text examples given in section 3.2.1 illustrate this tendency, and section 5.5.2 quantitatively investigates whether this trend is upheld in the newspaper data.

3.6 Cognate vs Non-Cognate Lexis

As noted in section 3.1, *Scots* and *English* are cognate varieties. Because of this, there is a large group of *Scots* lexical items that are also found in *English*, but are distinguishable as *Scots* in the spoken mode by pronunciation and in the written mode by orthography. So, for example, all the Scottish newspapers use the *Scots* word *hame* which is cognate with *English* home. Of course, they also often use *home*. Similarly, some of them use the word *bile*, cognate with *English* boil, often as part of the colloquial imperative *bile yer heid* (see sections 6.6 and 6.7 for further discussion of this item). The *Scottish-English* varieties also contain lexis which have no cognate forms in *English*. So, for example, *wean* and *bairn* vs *child* as discussed above in section 3.2.1, or *dreich* which is not really synonymous and is certainly not cognate with *dull*. (C.f. Aitken's (1979; 1984a; 1984b) five-column model.)

If encountering a *Scots* word for the first time, someone who is familiar with *English* might well be able to guess at a cognate item if they have internalised either some of the features of Scottish pronunciation (in the spoken mode), or some of the features of *Scots* orthography (in the written mode). Alternatively they may deduce the meaning of this 'new' word purely on the grounds of its similarity with a known *English* one. Due to an often encountered lack of awareness of *Scots* language and its features (see discussion in section 3.9), coupled with the overwhelming hegemonic pressure to write using (*Scottish*) *Standard Written English*, on some occasions cognate items of *Scots* lexis may well be interpreted by both Scots and non-Scots individuals (erroneously it must be added) purely as self-consciously Scotticised versions of *English* words. Therefore they may be seen in some ways as less 'acceptable' than non-cognate (and hence 'bona-fide') *Scots* words such as *bairn*. Cognate *Scots* items may also be misinterpreted as pronunciation spellings, and consequently be rather problematic for language display in a discourse type such as a newspaper, especially in more formal article types. For non-cognate items of *Scots* lexis, there are no such clues, and the individual encountering such an item for the first time may well have to look the word up in a dictionary to ascertain its meaning. So such items are usually more allowable as local exoticisms and more acceptable for language display.

Both types of *Scots* lexis (cognate and non-cognate) are to be found in the newspaper data, though arguably they have rather different significances which might lead to rather different distributions. This in tested in section 5.6 under the question of 'How different does it have to be from English?'. Section 5.6.2 investigates whether there are any differences in the densities of the texts containing cognate and non-cognate *Scots* lexis, as it is hypothesised that cognate lexis may tend to be found in denser contexts.

The linguistic continuum emphasises individual choice from the available linguistic options, but Aitken (1984a: 521) does argue that certain social classes are predisposed to make certain linguistic choices from the cognate vs non-cognate lexis. Broadly speaking, he suggests that middle-class speakers are more likely to use occasional non-cognate *Scots* lexical items. He suggests that working-class speakers are more likely to use more of the cognate *Scots* lexis, especially for content lexis (that is, N, V, Av, Aj (Noun, Verb, Adverb, Adjective) – open class lexis). Consequently section 7.6 examines whether use of cognate vs non-cognate *Scots* lexis varies across the newspapers.

Thus, the present linguistic situation in Scotland presents a large range of choices for individual speakers/writers, and the newspapers, many of which may be stylistically or contextually as well as socially and regionally determined. Not only do individuals have a large range of choices from the available linguistic varieties, but to a great extent those choices will be affected by the status of those varieties – the way they are perceived and the contexts for which they are generally considered suitable. Some *Scottish-English* varieties are considered suitable for a broad range of contexts and text types; others are not.

3.7 LINGUISTIC STATUS

Different ways of conceptualising and even naming *Scottish-English* language varieties can betray interesting differences in underlying ideologies and assumptions about the linguistic status of the varieties (c.f. the different perspectives taken by McArthur (1979; 1987), Görlach (1990) and Strevens (1980) on *Scots, Scottish Standard English* and *Scottish-English*). Additionally, not everyone agrees on the terminology for these varieties and this can cause problems. Macafee (2007) comments that

> [L]inguists have been reluctant to use the term *Scots*, possibly from a fear of seeming to introduce a nationalist bias into their work (if they are Scottish), but also in continuation of a long tradition of writing about Scots as a dialect of English, which is very persistent in the writings of scholars outside Scotland. The result is a great deal of confusion in terminology, and many an awkward circumlocution.

Often the naming strategies adopted are ideological as much as linguistic choices, that is whether individuals believe that those varieties most maximally differentiated from *English*, here (and usually) termed *Scots*, should be collectively considered as forming a separate language from *English*. Alternatively one might argue that *Scots* varieties are merely distinctive dialects of *English*. This is a perennial (and often heated) topic of debate. Arguments put forward for language status for *Scots* include its historical status as the national language of an autonomous state during the late fifteenth and the sixteenth centuries, the breadth and quality of its literature, the fact that it contains within it numerous distinctive regional dialects, even its recognition as a 'minority language' by the European Bureau for Lesser-Used Languages in 2003 (see section 8.2.1). Arguments against include the similarity of *Scots* to *English*, their development from a common ancestor, and the lack of a standard form for *Scots*, though it is not absolutely necessary that a language should have a standard form. There is no easy answer to the question of whether *Scots* should be considered to be a language or a dialect. Languages are sociopolitical constructs and the decision to term a particular variety a 'language' rather than a 'dialect' is often bound up with considerations of politics rather than linguistics.

Present-day *Scots* has a rather ambivalent status depending on the context in which it is being used, and to whom the question of its status is addressed. Many Scots have grown up under an educational system where the use of *Scots* in the classroom was very much discouraged. This led to the well-attested playground-versus-classroom linguistic dichotomy for many (see McArthur 1979: 56; Romaine 1982: 76–7). Not only was the use of *Scots* discouraged, it was also treated as '*bad English*' or 'slang', rather than 'good *Scots*'. Aitken (1982: 33) highlights the distinction often made between 'genuine dialect' (good *Scots*) and the 'disapproved kind of Scots speech' (bad *Scots*) – for example *Glaswegian*. It should be noted that these labels are very tongue-in-cheek and that Aitken himself does not adhere to these value labels, although many laypeople do. Aitken (1981a: 80) coins another term, 'Ideal Scots', which he claims nowadays is an imaginary construct often used by those who claim language status for *Scots*. He describes it as 'consistently fully Scots . . . homogeneous, maximalist, consistent, pure'.

Standard varieties tend to have high status and many (for example McClure (1994: 62) would argue the lack of a standard form of the language has handicapped *Scots*. If the language is to be used solely for personal or literary purposes, then a standard form seems less important. If, however, the language variety is to be used for official, commercial or educational purposes, then the need for a standard becomes clearer. Whilst standards themselves are not necessarily essential accoutrements for a language, the lack of a standard variety for *Scots* implies that the language variety is less important and unfit for official use. This has important implications for its status, the registers in which it is used, and for the use of *Scots* in newspapers, as will be discussed in Chapters 5 and 6.

The problematic status of *Scots* has implications for the registers in which its use is considered acceptable or desirable. A brief glance at the index for the *Scots Thesaurus* shows that *Scots* has become restricted in its domains. There are many words for discussing domestic life, the weather, farming and so on; but virtually none for talking about, for example, politics, technology or official administration. *Scots* has traditionally been stronger in the domain of poetry than prose, but this situation has now intensified. For most people, the use of *Scots* for serious argumentative prose seems odd and contrived. It is much less problematic when used in less formal or humorous contexts. There seems to be a sense that *Scots* could only ever be acceptable for use in serious prose if it discusses something which is archetypally Scottish, such as the state of the *Scots* language, a review of a new work by a Scottish author, the culture of Scotland and so on (c.f. McClure 1979: 47) (section 5.5.1 investigates whether this is the case in the newspaper corpus). However, as will be discussed in Chapter 8, this is something that is slowly beginning to alter, and *Scots* is, in some quarters, being used in new and formal contexts.

The registers of present-day *Scottish Standard English* are much less constrained than those of *Scots*. *Scottish Standard English* is considered suitable for a wider range of domains than *Scots*, and it shares many features with other *Standard Englishes*; thus it is not impossible to use *Scottish Standard English* to communicate in many of the areas such as politics, technology and so on, from which dense *Scots* would usually be debarred. We would therefore expect the newspapers to use more *Scottish Standard English* than they do *Scots*, and this is also tested in section 5.5.1. But why are these two varieties of *Scottish-English* perceived so differently? Perhaps the most salient point is one which is central to most sociolinguistic views of language: *Scottish Standard English* enjoys high status because it is generally associated with a socially and economically powerful social group, the middle classes or above.

3.8 Linguistic Attitudes: Ambivalence and Insecurity

It is often argued that the low status of *Scots* created a climate of linguistic insecurity in Scotland, whereby many people felt their natural language, the tongue they learned and used at home, was considered to be inferior to that used in the education system. The view still prevails to a certain extent, that if you want to 'get on in life' your accent should be modified in a certain way, and your language should be 'good *English*'. Macafee (1994: 188) attests to situations where older members of the speech community have been corrected by their juniors. However, there is a counterbalance to this, in that among the working class such language habits are regarded as pretentious, betraying your roots, and, worst of all, as aping the English. Thus there is covert prestige associated with working-class Scottish speech. It is also considered quite acceptable, indeed in certain contexts desirable, for educated middle-class Scots to use a smattering of *Scots* lexis and idiom (grammar is more problematic), albeit with the safety net of an educated Scottish accent or a thin written context, as a way of claiming linguistic kinship with their fellow Scots. So both *Scots* and *Scottish Standard English* have emblematic status in that they mark out people as belonging, or not belonging, to the Scottish community. By being able to understand the meaning of the *Scots* lexis used in a newspaper, you are meeting the linguistic tariff. You are therefore constructed as belonging to the Scottish linguistic community that is the ideal readership (see section 4.3).

As discussed in section 1.2, problems of definition and awareness have been cited as the reasons why the General Register Office (Scotland) has not yet incorporated a question on *Scots* language usage in the Census questionnaire. Odd as it may seem, comparatively few *Scots* speakers would think of themselves as such. The lack of formal education in *Scots*, its low status, and its problematic definition mean that most *Scots* speakers are much more likely to think of themselves as speaking *English* (or even 'bad *English*'), slang, or a specific local variety such as *Glaswegian*. By contrast, those who write in *Scots* are much more likely to be aware of the fact, and to be using it as a deliberate stylistic or ideological statement. So it would be more accurate to say that people are ambivalent, and indeed often uneducated, about the language varieties they habitually use.

3.9 Linguistic Awareness

This awareness vs lack of awareness also extends to individual *Scots* lexical items. Aitken's (1979) *overt* and *covert* Scotticisms illustrate these differences in the linguistic competence and awareness of individuals. He coins the terms *covert* or 'unmarked' *Scotticism* for peculiarly Scottish usages which Scots are unaware of as being particularly Scottish, and *overt* (or 'marked') *Scotticisms* for those expressions that Scots are aware of and believe to be markedly Scottish which are used as 'a way of claiming membership of the in-group of Scotsmen' (Aitken 1979: 107). So, overt Scotticisms are really a type of *language display* (see section 2.3.1). It is worth noting that, although there may well be general tendencies following class or education in terms of what for individuals are overt or covert Scotticisms, to a certain extent this will be variable, with each person having their own idiolect depending on their background, education, parents, social class and so on. Thus it is very difficult to categorise individual lexical items as overt or covert Scotticisms. For me, the term *camsile* (a sloping ceiling in for example an attic room) was entirely covert until I encountered bemused expressions from my English colleagues. By contrast, I know that if I use the term *dreich* to describe the weather I am patently and, indeed, often deliberately, badging myself as Scottish.

Aitken (1984c: 107) makes some refinements to the above model. He argues for a special type of overt Scotticism, the 'stylistic overt Scotticism', which is 'used for special stylistic effect – as a deliberate deviation from normal style'. As he goes on to explain, these are deliberately *Scots* linguistic choices made by individuals for stylistic reasons. The examples he gives are *aye* (yes), *dinna* (don't), *hame* (home), *hoose* (house) and *ben the hoose* (inside the house). Thus he argues that there are occasions when a Scot will consciously and deliberately choose to use an expression which they themselves realise is markedly Scottish in order to make a particular point, whether that be to demonstrate that they are a 'real Scot', or to introduce an element of humour (also discussed in Aitken 1979).

Aitken (1984c) goes further and argues that some of these marked or overt Scottish expressions are generally only ever used for such stylistic purposes, and are not part of the normal Scottish repertoire for most Scots. These uber-*Scots* lexical items are almost exclusively reserved for overt stylistic use, and tend to be found in the company of *English* rather than *Scots* lexis. This contrasts with the expressions discussed in the previous paragraph which may be used either as a stylistic *coup de grace* or as part of a speaker's normal repertoire of Scottish expressions. These uber-*Scots* expressions, he argues, are 'largely confined to use by "English-speaking" not "Scots-speaking" Scots' (Aitken 1984c: 107). Examples given by Aitken (1984c: 107ff) are: *to keep a calm sough* (keep one's own counsel), *it's back to the auld claes and parritch tomorrow* (or *the morn*) (it's back to the old clothes and porridge tomorrow), *darg* (a day's work), *kenspeckle* (familiar), *thrang* (bustling, crowded) and *stravaig* (wander, roam aimlessly). He argues that the reason why such expressions are more likely to be used by middle-class 'English' (which in my terminology means *Scottish (Standard) English*) speaking Scots is that such people are more likely to have been exposed to Scottish literature or are more likely to be interested in more archaic lexical forms. Some of these lexical items form part of the search list used to interrogate the newspaper data, and will therefore be returned to in section 6.1.1, where Aitken's hypothesis will be tested.

3.10 IMPLICATIONS FOR SCOTTISH NEWSPAPER TEXTS

What are the implications of all this for the newspaper texts? Newspapers (whether they are broadsheet or tabloid) are a fairly formal, public discourse. Thus there is an expectation that they will be mostly written in a standard variety. (See discussion in section 4.5ff.) *Scots*, given its low status, lack of an agreed standard form, and prevalence in the spoken mode seems unlikely to be used by the newspapers in significant quantities. It is anticipated therefore that the newspapers are more likely to use occasional items of *Scots* lexis in thin contexts rather than sustained passages of dense *Scots*. So newspaper language would generally be expected to tend more towards McClure's 'thin Scots' (1979: 30), or even *Scottish Standard English*. Sections 2.4.4 and 3.3 argued that in the written mode, for the majority of Scots, thin *Scots* is easier to identify with, and therefore more powerfully symbolic than dense *Scots*. Because many written varieties of *Scots*, such as *Lallans*, are the preserve of the well-educated or enthusiastic few, it is unlikely that the newspapers would risk excluding readers by regularly including dense *Scots* in their articles, though they may make an exception if it is used actually to discuss *Scots* language. If newspaper language veers towards the *Scots* end of the continuum at all, it is likely to be in a limited fashion or restricted to certain types of subject matter.

We would expect newspaper language to be constrained by considerations of appropriacy (see discussion in section 4.6ff.), which might mean that not only is *Scots* lexis limited in terms of density, but that where it does occur, it is likely to be restricted to certain parts of the newspaper such as feature articles, where problems of register are less of an issue.

Even the type of *Scots* lexis used by the newspapers might be subject to restrictions, and the reasons for this are considered in more detail in the next chapter. We would expect to find cultural Scotticisms, for example *rector* for a *school headteacher*, *kirk* rather than the *English church*, or a verdict of *not proven*, and probably also functional Scotticisms, as these are unlikely to be perceived as inappropriate uses of Scottish terms. However, there may be varying restrictions operating on open vs closed class *Scots* lexis, cognate vs non-cognate *Scots* lexis, shibboleths and uber-Scotticisms, and these hypotheses are tested in the data chapters.

We would also expect that newspapers would use language that is 'current'; that is the *Scots* lexis used will not include many archaic or obsolete words. There would be little reason for newspaper language to contain such words and they are much less likely to be used for stylistic effect in a newspaper than they are in poetry. More importantly, such lexis would probably impede comprehension and thus alienate readers. This hypothesis is tested in section 6.1.1.

We would expect the language used by newspapers to be easily recognised by speakers from all over Scotland and not be especially localised. This is very important if the newspaper seeks to be national rather than local or regional. External commercial pressures (that is newspaper owners want to be able to sell newspapers all over Scotland) may therefore have an effect on linguistic choices.

These hypotheses will be tested in Chapters 5 and 6, but before analysing the language of the Scottish newspapers themselves, it is necessary to consider the relationship that exists between these newspapers and their readers.

Further Reading

1. The historical development of the *Scottish-English* varieties is complex and Macafee (2007) and McClure (1994) are useful preliminary further reading.
2. Corbett et al. (2003) give an accessible introduction to *Scots*, its history, its phonology, grammar and lexis. Jones (1997) is a much more detailed but consequently less accessible account. See also Aitken (1979; 1984a) and McClure (1979; 1994) for good overviews. A brief overview is given in Douglas (2006).

3. Both *Scots* and *Scottish Standard English* have different phonological systems from that of *English*. For example, both *Scots* and *Scottish Standard English* are well-known for features such as differences in vowel distribution (a detailed analysis of which can be found in Aitken (1981b)), rhoticity and particular word stress patterns. See Stuart-Smith (2003; 2004) and Johnston (1997) for good overall descriptions. Aitken (1981b) contains the original description of the Scottish Vowel Length Rule and Scobbie et al. (1999) provide some suggested modifications for certain Scottish speakers.

4. Further reading on the grammatical characteristics of *Scottish-English* varieties can be found in Miller (1993; 2003), Miller and Brown (1982), and Macafee (1992; 2007).

4

Newspapers and their Readers

This chapter begins by outlining the situation as regards Scottish newspapers and their readers. It then examines the nature of the relationship that exists between newspapers and their readers more closely and queries how a sense of shared community consciousness between newspaper and reader is created. It introduces the concept of the 'ideal reader', before going on to consider how newspapers seek to align themselves with their readerships, and the various strategies open to newspapers seeking to align themselves with a Scottish readership. How do these newspapers foster their Scottish identity and what effects might this have on the language they use? The chapter concludes by examining the role of the press as gatekeepers and assessing the impact of appropriacy constraints on the language that they use.

4.1 READERSHIPS

Newspapers need readers – an obvious statement perhaps, but nevertheless crucially important. They rely on developing a core loyal readership who will continue to buy the same newspaper day after day, year after year. Newspaper readers, not editors, have the ultimate power of veto. If they do not like what the newspaper contains, or its political or ideological viewpoints, or even the language it uses, they can choose not to buy it. Ultimately newspapers are driven by commercial forces; they have to sell to survive. So keeping their readers happy and, indeed, just keeping them as readers, is essential.

Although there are increasingly tales of doom and gloom surrounding the newspaper industry (c.f. Reid (2006) and discussion in section 8.3ff.), Scotland has traditionally had a comparatively healthy newspaper industry with a 'generous choice of newspaper titles' (Meech and Kilborn 1992: 255) and its own well-established national press. Readers can choose from homegrown or indigenous newspapers such as *The Herald*, *The Scotsman* and the *Daily Record*; explicitly Scotticised editions of UK titles such as the

Scottish Express and *The Scottish Sun*; and UK titles such as *The Times* or *The Independent* which contain varying amounts of targeted Scottish content in the editions sold north of the border. Of course, this range of choice also means that there is often a battle for readers, something that is discussed further in Chapter 8.

Scotland boasts high newspaper circulation and readership figures for its population size. Using Audit Bureau of Circulation (ABC) average circulation figures for the period 31 July 2006 to 27 August 2006, Scotland accounted for 12.9 per cent of the total UK circulation figures for national newspapers, well ahead of the rest of the UK and higher than would be expected given its proportionate population size. (Scotland accounts for only approximately 8.5 per cent of the UK population, based on mid-2005 population estimates: (Office for National Statistics).) It is worth remembering that these are circulation, not readership, figures; one newspaper bought may be read by multiple individuals. It has been alleged that Scotland's adult readership is 10 per cent higher than that south of the border, and, outside China, 'the highest in the world' (Davidson 2004). Figures for readerships of local and regional newspapers are also significantly higher in Scotland than anywhere else in the country. In 2003, the overall average readership figure in Scotland was 93 per cent compared with a UK average of 84.5 per cent (National Newspaper Society). So on the whole, Scotland is a proportionately heavier consumer of newspapers than is the rest of the UK, and in May 2008, had seventeen daily titles competing for a share of the market (*Morning Extra*, 16 May 2008).

4.2 IMPORTANCE OF A SHARED COMMUNITY CONSCIOUSNESS

Newspapers rely on creating a shared community consciousness with their readerships. It is important that readers feel that the newspaper they read is their newspaper, which concurs with their world-view, reports on matters of interest to them, and is written for people like them. Scotland's indigenous national press has a distinctively Scottish identity and is designed to appeal to a largely Scottish readership.

Most readers will, at some time, have encountered the frustration of reading a newspaper that seems to have been written for a community that is not their own – for example my frequent frustration with *The Times* (London) because it lists only London-based concert and theatre events and therefore seems to be written for an entirely London-based audience. Scottish newspapers are aimed at a predominantly Scottish readership. Rosie et al. (2004: 437) found that English migrants to Scotland noticed a difference of agenda and content in Scottish newspapers from those they were used to in England. Migrants commented on the Scottish newspapers' localism and the overt flagging of news as 'Scottish', and also on the Anglo-centrism of the UK press. Kiely et al. (2006) discovered that some English migrants to Scotland found their attitudes to the newspapers they habitually read altered when they moved to Scotland; many of them began to find the UK titles very Anglo- and especially London-centric, and perhaps naturally, some felt that the Scottish newspapers were now of more relevance.

Scottish newspapers have a powerful and 'exclusive' relationship with their readers based largely on a sense of shared Scottish community and national consciousness. Scottish readerships want newspapers that relate to them. Kiely et al. (2006: 473) note that 'newspapers have long been seen as binding people into "national" political and cultural agendas, thereby helping to create and sustain a strong sense of national identity'. They suggest that Scotland, with its distinctively Scottish press and broadcast media, makes an interesting test case for questioning assumptions about the links between national identity and media consumption (Kiely et al. 2006: 475) (see also McCrone 2001: 44–5). Section 2.4.2 considered the importance of the 'imagined community' (Anderson 1991) for group identities. Anderson (1991: 35–6) sees the newspaper as a socially unifying force within the national imagined community, and emphasises the historical importance of the print media in raising national consciousness: 'these fellow readers, to whom they were connected through print, formed in their secular, particular, visible invisibility, the embryo of the nationally imagined community' (Anderson 1991: 44). The picture he paints is one where the very act of reading a newspaper makes the individual part of society, or of a group within society, as the reader is aware that there is a larger body of readers who presumably share similar attitudes and aspirations to themselves. Anderson uses the metaphor of the Catholic mass by describing readers as 'communicants' (1991: 35–6), and the act of reading as the ceremony, a picture which stresses the symbolic solidarity that newspapers can engender.

As Rosie et al. (2004: 438) argue, this premise assumes that newspaper readers are actually imagining themselves as part of this wider, nationally constructed group as they read, potentially a problematic assumption. According to Anderson (1991), the readers are constructing themselves as part of the same national group by their act of newspaper reading. In *Banal Nationalism*, Billig (1995) approaches the question from the opposite direction, suggesting that it is the newspapers that construct the readers as part of a shared national community, and pointing to aspects of newspaper content, organisation and textual features such as deictic reference as accomplishing this (see section 4.4.5.1). Billig's approach, though flawed (he 'banally' makes the mistake of assuming that there is a homogeneous 'British national press' and readership (c.f. Rosie et al. (2004)), seems, perhaps, more plausible, and has formed the basis of numerous further studies such as Law (2001). Billig's approach is useful insofar as it stresses the importance of textual as well as content analysis of the newspaper texts.

Kiely et al. (2006: 473) complain that 'the relationship between national identity and how people perceive and consume print and broadcast media is one of the central but largely untested assumptions of studies of nationalism', but their recent survey, although by no means conclusive, did find 'a clear but weak relationship between claimed newspaper readership and preferred national identity' (2006: 479) (see also Rosie et al. (2004: 437)). Readership of UK broadsheets was higher among those individuals who prioritised a British identity, readership of UK tabloids was stable across identity categories, readership of the *Daily Record/Scottish Mirror* was highest in those prioritising a Scottish identity, and readership of Scottish broadsheets was slightly higher among those prioritising British identity. (Kiely et al. (2006) point out that the *Daily Record* and *Scottish Mirror* data have been combined as, prior to 2003, they were coded together in the *Social Attitudes Survey*. However, they argue that the 2003 data suggest this category consists primarily of *Daily Record* readers.) Kiely et al. (2006: 488) argue that, although the preference Scottish nationals often show for Scottish newspapers may be based largely on habit (or Bourdieu's (1997) 'habitus'), nevertheless 'a sense of Scottishness is important'. It is a truism to say that the newspaper(s) people buy say(s) quite a lot about the types of people they are and aspire to be, but arguably there is a definite sense of Scottish solidarity in buying a Scottish newspaper. On a more general note, Hall (1978) emphasises that all newspapers construct their readers as part of the same society with shared cultural knowledge, and they emphasise consensus. He argues that events covered in a newspaper have to be interpreted 'to mean' within the known context of the society addressed. In order to do this effectively, newspapers need to have a pretty good idea of who their readership is. This brings us to the concept of the 'ideal reader'.

4.3 THE IDEAL READER

Fowler (1991: 232) talks about newspapers as constructing the ideal reader or an 'implied addressee', and, of course, it is generally accepted that newspapers, which usually have identifiable political and social positions, are written with a target readership in mind. Thus it can be posited that a *Guardian* reader is likely to be politically left-of-centre, middle-class and perhaps employed in education; the typical *Sun* reader is likely to be youngish, male and working-class. The fact that it is possible to identify such reader 'types', means that newspapers must be able to construct their ideal readers as belonging to particular social and political groups.

Fowler argues that the real reader (that is the person who actually buys the newspaper and keeps sales figures and hence advertising revenues up) will be in sympathy with the ideological position of their chosen newspaper, and that it is important that readers feel comfortable with the ideological position offered. If the newspaper is to make its readership 'comfortable', it is essential that target readers are made to feel 'at home'. Newspapers achieve this by aligning themselves with their readers. For newspapers competing for readers in the Scottish market there is an additional level on which they can, and I would argue must, relate to their readerships. For the Scottish press, being able to tap into a Scottish identity is crucial. Scottishness sells. Scottish newspapers must appeal to a Scottish audience in order to survive. The key thing which they share with their readers is their Scottishness (complex though this concept is), and thus this is often exploited to create a feeling of newspaper-reader solidarity.

4.4 ALIGNMENT WITH READERSHIP

There are various ways in which this alignment with the readership and building of a sense of shared community consciousness can be achieved. It may be seen in the opinions espoused in the editorial sections (with which the majority of readers are expected to agree), or in the invitations to contribute to the letters pages (a discourse community feedback mechanism for Bex (1996) – see discussion in section 2.3) or to compete with other readers to win the crossword, Sudoku or other competition prizes. The organisation of the newspaper can also indicate the target readership, as the ordering of particular news items into sections on local, national and international news situates the reader within a specific readership community. What goes into the local, regional or national news sections indicates where the newspaper geographically situates itself and its readership. The coverage of local or regional news adds to a sense of a shared, but geographically limited readership. Even components such as the small ads and the television/radio pages can contribute to this sense of shared but circumscribed community – for example different regional TV listings (Grampian, Yorkshire etc.) in different parts of the country.

4.4.1 Scottish branding

Declaring your newspaper as being aligned with a particular readership is another common strategy in Scotland. Having an identifiably Scottish identity is so important for newspapers competing in the Scottish market that many of them self-brand as such. Obvious branding strategies can be seen in newspaper titles and/or the use of slogans which emphasise Scottishness. Clearly titles matter. *The Scotsman* is self-evidently a Scottish paper and *The Herald* dropped *Glasgow* from its title in 1992 (although it still appears in the masthead) in a bid to broaden its appeal. Note that we must be careful to distinguish between those newspapers which are indigenously Scottish, that is, written, produced and rooted in Scotland such as *The Herald*, *The Scotsman* and the *Daily Record*, and those which are the Scottish editions of UK titles claiming Scottishness such as *The Scottish Sun*, the *Scottish Daily Mail* and the *Scottish Express*. Generally UK titles brand their Scottish editions as such by adding 'Scottish' to their titles. However, Law (2001: 306) makes the interesting observation that the premodifying 'Scottish' is always rendered in a smaller font than the rest of the title. The increasing attempts by such newspapers to appeal to the Scottish market can be seen both in the growth of their Scottish editions and in specially targeted newspaper supplements (see further discussion in section 8.4ff).

Law (2001: 306–7; 2003: 113–14) discusses the prevalence of slogans that appeal to a sense of Scottishness such as 'Scotland's Champion' (*Daily Record* 1995–9), or 'Scotland's National Newspaper' (*The Scotsman*). There are claims of Scottish authenticity (*The Scottish Sun* is 'Dedicated to the people of Scotland'; *The Scottish Mirror* is 'Printed in Scotland'; *The Scottish Express* is 'Printed and published in Scotland'). There is also the use of iconographic Scottish symbols such as the thistle (*The Scottish Sun*, *The Scotsman*), the Saltire (the *Scottish Express*) and the lion rampant (the *Daily Record*, the *Scottish Express*) in newspaper mastheads (see also Meech and Kilborn 1992; Douglas 2000; 2002).

4.4.2 A visible presence

Having a visible presence in one of Scotland's two main cities, Edinburgh or Glasgow, is also important (and this arguably affects newspapers' deictic centres; see discussion in section 4.4.2). Both Scottish broadsheets included in the study occupied famous landmark buildings that still bear their name before moving to more modern premises, *The Herald* in Glasgow and *The Scotsman* in Edinburgh. The *Daily Record* also has a very visible presence in

Glasgow. It would appear that even in these days of modern technology, where news is often distributed all round the world by the large news agencies, a tangible and visible presence within Scotland is very important. A case in point is *The Scottish Sun*, which moved its printing operation to Kinning Park in Glasgow, and *The Times* which has moved its Scottish edition printing operation to Eurocentral (see section 8.4).

4.4.3 Rootedness of journalists

Another important point is that of the nationality or rootedness of the journalists. Of course, Scottish newspapers do not employ only Scottish journalists, or editors for that matter. Nor do people necessarily have to write in a way that betrays national origins. Many journalists move around the country in the course of their careers, often starting out working for a local newspaper before progressing to one of the nationals, and they may switch between a variety of newspapers in the course of their careers. It is also perfectly possible for non-Scots (outgroup members) to use elements of *Scots* lexis, perhaps as a deliberate way of negotiating group membership, or alternatively because they have been conditioned into the use of certain items of lexis by others around them. For example, what I termed a *burn* (small stream) in Scotland, I am perfectly happy to call a *beck* in Yorkshire, because that is what people around me call it. Such outgroup use of a variety to negotiate group membership, does, however, have to be treated with caution. For me to attempt to mimic a broad *Yorkshire* dialect or accent, would, I suspect, be much less well received. These caveats aside, the nationality or rootedness of journalists is potentially very significant in the Scottish nationals, depending on which part of the newspaper they contribute articles to. For international or British news stories, the nationality of the journalist is unlikely to be foregrounded. However, as will be discussed in sections 5.3 and 5.4, in certain parts of the newspaper, especially in feature articles such as the 'Diary' or feature columns, the very Scottishness of the journalist seems to be foregrounded, and this may extend to their linguistic choices. A similar situation applies, though perhaps to a lesser extent, with some of the sports pages.

4.4.4 Including Scottish content and viewpoint

If trying to appeal to a Scottish readership, logic dictates that ensuring coverage of Scottish content and/or viewpoints is crucial. All news stories are at some stage selected for inclusion in the newspaper, and told from some viewpoint, and it is to be expected that journalists writing for the

Scottish press (as for other localised readerships) will tend to try to find points of relevance for and connection with their readers. Those stories that are selected for inclusion or omitted from a newspaper may reveal a great deal about that newspaper's predilections and underlying ideological stance. Galtung and Ruge (1973) introduce the useful criteria of *proximity* and *relevance* which can be applied to a consideration of the newsworthiness of any story to its readership. The *proximity* criterion says that stories which are geographically or culturally closest to the readership have more news value than ones that are further away. The *relevance* criterion applies where the news event has some impact on the readers' own lives or is close to their experience. Scottish newspapers therefore need to convince their ideal readerships that they are part of a shared Scottish culture and experience. This may be done in a variety of ways.

Most obviously this means giving proportionately more coverage to Scottish stories such as Scottish sport, politics and government issues, the Scottish courts and so on, and taking account of Scotland's distinctive history and culture (Tunstall 1996: 64). For indigenous Scottish newspapers, this is a fairly natural process. However, the Scottish editions of UK titles are increasingly making attempts to tailor their content to a Scottish audience (see discussion in section 8.4). Tunstall (1996: 211) notes that one of the most heavily regionalised parts of the newspaper is the sports pages, with the tabloids placing particular emphasis and resources in this area, and, as discussed in section 2.4.1, sport is a well-known and powerful focus of national identity. Certainly, localised sports pages and letters columns are often substituted in the UK titles for a north-of-the-border audience in their Scottish editions. The significance of sport in fostering a sense of national and/or local identity should not be underestimated. The *Daily Record* brands itself as 'Number One for Scottish Sport', and, of course, there are separate Scottish and English football leagues.

Alternatively, the establishing of a common culture may be achieved by highlighting or seeking out a peculiarly Scottish news angle on what is essentially a UK story. Rosie et al. found that 'most newspapers in Scotland go to considerable lengths to explicitly flag newsworthy stories, persons, or institutions wherever possible as "Scottish"' (2006a: 337; see also 2004). Kiely et al. (2006) point to advances in print technology over recent years which now make it much easier to customise editions to the target readership (see also discussion in section 8.4ff). These innovations are particularly important for UK newspapers trying to 'put a kilt on their Scottish editions' of British titles (Kiely et al. 2006: 475). Conventionally, the phrase 'putting a kilt on it' is used refer to the journalistic practice of putting across a peculiarly Scottish viewpoint in a news story, and thereby making it more relevant to a Scottish audience. The phrase is rejected by some journalists who prefer to see that they are making stories relevant to the newspaper's audience rather than simply tartanising them (Kiely et al. 2006).

4.4.5 Alignment via language

More subtle indicators buried in the language may also show how newspapers seek to align themselves with their readers. The analysis of any piece of language can reveal a great deal about underlying ideological stances, and newspaper language is no exception. Even the presentation of facts, which forms a large part of the newspapers' remit, has to be mediated through language, and language itself inherently involves choices. These linguistic choices can reflect different underlying ideologies. As Fowler (1991: 4) argues, '[T]here are always different ways of saying the same thing, and they are not random, accidental alternatives. Differences in expression carry ideological distinctions.' Reah (1998: 55) makes a similar point. As with all newspapers, Scottish newspapers will attempt to establish common ideological ground between themselves and their readers. Two key ways in which this can be achieved are: firstly by features in the language that explicitly situate the readership (the deictic elements and 'flags' discussed in the next section) and secondly by the use of identifiably Scottish language (c.f. discussion of the use of *Scots* lexis by the newspapers in the data chapters).

4.4.5.1 Using deictic expressions and 'flags'

Expressions in the newspapers like *the Mirror's loyal readers* or deictic elements such as the use of the inclusive pronouns *we* and *our*, can be very revealing. Deixis gives information on spatio-temporal point of view and it can usefully be analysed to work out how writers situate themselves, and also how readers are being situated, with respect to the text. Generally three types of deixis are considered: spatial or locative deixis (for example *here, in Scotland*) temporal deixis (for example *now, then*) and personal deixis (for example *we, us, they, our*). Most of these examples are fairly obvious, but deixis can be more subtle (for example *Sassenachs, fellow Scots, as Brits*) and it is, of course, context dependent. By analysing the deictic expressions in a text, it is possible to get a good idea of where writers situate themselves in terms of place and community, and also where they situate their readers. Do they share the same context, and if so what is it and what are its boundaries? Wodak et al. (1999) focus on personal, spatial and temporal reference points as useful indicators of writer/speaker viewpoint in their critical discourse analysis of the discursive construction of national identities. Arguably, deictic expressions can contribute effectively to the fulfilment of both the *proximity* and *relevance* criteria.

As Rosie et al. (2006a: 329) note, 'Billig's (1995) *Banal Nationalism* argued that newspapers "nationalise" news through the routine use of deictic language, "flags" (explicit references to, and markers of, the nation), and assumptions about the spatial location of both reader and news agenda.' Interestingly, Billig argued that the absence as well as the presence of specific locative pointing devices could be effective in establishing context, and *The Herald*'s in-house style guide ('News subs do it in style') specifically warns against the overuse of locative phrases: 'The word Scots is being used unnecessarily in more and more intros, particularly freelance copy. The *Herald* is a Scottish newspaper and does not need to tell its readers that an event has happened in Scotland' (cited in Higgins 2004: 634–5).

Law (2001) analyses what he terms the 'deictic centres' of a range of newspapers sold in Scotland to see where they locate themselves and their readers. Although Law (2001; 2003) argues for some revision of Billig's theory in the Scottish context, he essentially adopts and develops Billig's approach by analysing the 'wee words of nationalism' (2003: 111–12) which are essentially deictic elements such as *we, us, here, there* as well as explicit references to *Scotland* or *Scottish* in trying to establish just where the proximal and distal reference points lie. Law (2001) plots the results for 'indigenous' Scottish newspapers (*The Herald, The Scotsman,* the *Daily Record*), what he terms 'interloper' newspapers such as *The Scottish Sun* and the *Scottish Express*, which although UK titles are trying to claim Scottish authenticity, and Anglo-centric newspapers such as *The Times* (c.f. with Rosie et al.'s (2004) study of the extent of Scotticisation of the press discussed in section 8.4). Unsurprisingly the indigenous Scottish newspapers demonstrate near-identical Scottish deictic centres, the interlopers have adopted deictic centres proximal to a Scottish viewpoint, and the Anglo-centric newspapers have distal relationships to the Scottish deictic centre which sit alongside their near identical British, or more interestingly, given their claim to be British or UK-based rather than solely English, English deictic centre.

However, it must be remembered that deictic expressions are context dependent, and as Rosie et al. (2004) argue persuasively, deictic terms, by their very nature, can be polyvalent and/or ambiguous. There can also be a multiplicity of deictic centres or, as Petersoo (2007) has it, 'the "we" wanders' (cited in Rosie et al. 2006a). Take, for example, the terms *we* or *us*. The implied *we* or *us* may well shift from *we* the implied readership, to *we* the Scots, to *we* in the UK, *we* in Scotland and in the UK as a whole and so on, either within or between newspaper articles. At times, it may be impossible to decide on precisely to which bounded community any given *we* relates, and much of the contextual inference will depend on the reader. As Rosie et al. (2004) suggest, this is not necessarily due to sloppy journalism, but rather is merely a reflection of the ambiguous and polyvalent political and constitutional situation that exists in the UK. Law (2003: 117) concedes that 'newspapers are not simply unilateral textual devices, repetitiously imparting national identity by means of encoded devices. Rather, they are better understood as "dialogical performances in print", engaged in an open-ended time-space/insider/outsider dialectic.'

4.4.5.2 A dialogue between newspapers and readers

This notion of an ongoing dialogic construction of national identity by newspapers and readers ties in well with constructive theories of identity discussed in Chapter 2, especially Bakhtin's dialogic construction of identity (Bakhtin 1981). Scottish readers are not merely the passive recipients of a newspaper's concept of Scottishness. The Scottish identity which newspapers project must be accepted by, and negotiated with, their readers. There is an unspoken dialogue between the newspaper and its readers, with the readers involved in a dialogic negotiation which constructs and maintains a shared Scottish identity and ultimately sets the boundaries within which the newspaper operates. The reader is involved in the negotiation of significance and meaning, and I suggest that this negotiation process is at least partly responsible for readers feeling that it is 'their newspaper'. They are partners in a collaborative effort to make sense of the world. Being a reader is not just a passive process. Similarly, the elements of Scottish language used by the newspapers to bolster their Scottish identity (as discussed in the next section) are, in effect, negotiated with their readers.

4.4.5.3 Using identifiably Scottish language

Having accepted that language can be used to construct or maintain identity (depending on your viewpoint; see section 2.2), it is reasonable to suggest that newspapers wishing to align themselves with their readers, and to have their readers identify with them, may exploit this feature of language. In other words, Scottish newspapers also have the option of using Scottish language to authenticate their Scottishness and better relate to their readers. They can use Scottish linguistic features (for this study specifically *Scots* lexis) as a way of promoting their Scottish identity and relating to their largely Scottish readerships. Crucially though, that use of *Scots* lexis has to be negotiated with their readers.

4.4.5.4 A negotiated language

Newspapers will use language with which their readers are familiar and comfortable, and to which they can relate. Anderson's (1991: 63) assertion that 'the very conception of the newspaper implies the refraction of even "world events" into a specific imagined world of *vernacular readers*' (my emphasis) implies that the newspaper presents an account of world events in the native regional or local language of its readers. However, it is important to realise that this does not necessarily mean that the newspaper language will be exactly the same as that used by its readers. In the case of a national newspaper, read all over Scotland, albeit with strongholds in particular geographic locations, that would be impossible to achieve. Each Scottish reader's language will be individual to them (that is an idiolect), having been moulded by a variety of factors such as their education, forms used by their parents and peers, geographical origins, social class and related social aspirations and so on, and this would be impossible for the newspapers to replicate for each individual reader. Rather, the newspapers will develop and use a common discourse which will be related but not identical to the language of their ideal readers. Hall argues that the language they use will be

> the *newspaper's own version of the language of the public to whom it is principally addressed*: its version of the rhetoric, imagery and underlying common stock of knowledge which it assumes its audience shares and which thus forms the basis of the reciprocity of producer/reader. (Hall 1978: 61; also quoted in Fowler 1991: 48)

Fowler (1991: 48) argues that newspaper language is not 'an objective rendering of the speech of its readers' – that it is not intended to be a slavish reproduction of 'authentic vernacular', rather it is a representation of a style of language with which the readership is comfortable. Cameron (1995: 46) makes the same point. So Glaswegian readers of the *Daily Record* will not expect or even want to see broad *Glaswegian* used as the main discourse variety of their newspaper. Fowler (1991) underlines the notion of *reciprocity* between writers and readers. This concept of *reciprocity* underlines the negotiation of a language style between the newspaper and its readers. Producers and consumers of the press are bound together in a mutual relationship, where what is permissible and/or desirable has been negotiated with both parties. This has important implications for the appropriacy constraints and the press' gatekeeping functions discussed in the next section.

4.5 THE PRESS AS GATEKEEPERS

Cameron (1995: 34–8) discusses at length the function of the press as guardians or 'gatekeepers' of the language and, as she notes, the press often plays a significant part in constructing and maintaining the notions of linguistic standards. Cameron argues that there are strong stylistic expectations of what is considered to be appropriate form in print journalism. Bell (1991: 82) notes that an important function of copy-editing is to ensure the language used by the newspaper adheres to 'language standards' and the wider 'speech community's prescriptions'. There is pressure on journalists from both editors and readers to write using *Standard Written English* grammar, given the general expectation that formal written prose should follow these standard grammatical conventions, especially if writing serious articles in the broadsheet press. Whilst newspapers are not at the extreme or 'frozen' end of the formality spectrum, as are certain types of bureaucratic institutionalised prose, they are often expected to 'uphold certain linguistic standards' or to practise 'verbal hygiene' (Cameron 1995: 58). Cameron argues that this is not just a perception which readers have of newspapers, but is also a role which newspapers may see themselves as fulfilling. Her discussion focuses particularly on *The Times*, but the general precept has wider applications in the press. She argues that copy-editors are powerful gatekeepers, and that they form an elite group (c.f. Cooper 1989: 135) which imposes its notions of correctness onto not only those who write for the publication in question, but also, by extension, onto those who read the publication. For most readers, newspapers and the language they use are imbued with a sense of correctness. These notions of correctness and the newspapers' gatekeeping function mean that there are fairly well-defined and rigid expectations about the types of language it is acceptable or appropriate for newspapers to use.

4.6 THE APPROPRIACY PACT

Fairclough (1995) introduces the concept of *appropriacy* in a discussion of the mores of education to describe the way in which certain language varieties are generally considered more or less appropriate for use by schoolchildren depending on context. Thus, for example, *Standard Written English* would generally be deemed the appropriate variety for formal written prose, whereas non-standard dialect forms might be considered to be more appropriate for use in the home, or in creative writing. Fairclough (1995) is heavily critical of the notion of appropriacy in the educational context. Nevertheless, the concept of appropriacy is useful for discussion of language in the broader context, as it is clear that certain language varieties are considered appropriate or inappropriate for use in particular text types. The newspapers are no exception. Fowler (1991: 42) in his study of newspaper language notes that 'it is obligatory to select a style of discourse which is communicatively *appropriate* to the particular setting' (Fowler 1991: 42, my emphasis). He goes on to argue that

> the newspaper and its readers share a common 'discursive competence', know the *permissible* statements, *permissions* and *prohibitions* . . . Newspaper and reader *negotiate* the significance of the text around the *stipulations* of the *appropriate discourse*, a mode of discourse 'cued' for the reader by significant linguistic options. (Fowler 1991: 44, my emphasis)

Once again we are talking about a negotiation process between newspapers and readers, but this time about a negotiation process with clearly defined rules. As Cameron's (1995) discussion suggests, newspapers are examples of a particular type of institutional discourse, and as such their language will tend to conform to the prevailing institutional and societal norms. (See also Hall (1978: 58).) They are therefore more likely to uphold than to subvert hegemonic norms, and, as discussed by Cameron (1995), the media itself is an institution which exerts powerful hegemonic influences on language. It is a very public discourse form, and as such is much more open to criticisms about its linguistic practices. Many newspaper letters pages include readers' complaints about the newspaper's use of language – 'ungrammatical', 'newfangled', 'incorrect English' and so on.

Newspapers are not written by individuals. Each article will have to go through various editorial stages, and thus, to an extent, newspapers are written by committee. As such, it is not surprising that they tend to conform to the prevailing linguistic hegemony. Usually, the more people who are involved in its production, the more normalised will be the discourse. The print medium means that any idiosyncratic choices would be preserved for all to see, and this also tends to engender standard forms. And, as Cameron (1995: 58) notes, newspapers see themselves as arbiters of style.

4.7 GATEKEEPING, APPROPRIACY AND USE OF SCOTS LANGUAGE

As outlined in section 3.7, *Scots* has some status problems. Its low status and its lack of an agreed standard variety inhibit the registers for which it is considered suitable. Indeed, it can be argued that choosing to write in *Scots* rather than *English* automatically lowers the register of a text. Therefore

Scots is usually considered suitable or appropriate only for humorous or informal contexts, seldom for serious discursive prose. Following Fowler (1991), the status, or rather lack of status, of *Scots* language in the newspapers reflects the views of, and has been negotiated with, the readership. *Standard Written English*, on the other hand, is universally considered entirely appropriate for serious discursive prose, and *Scottish Standard English* occupies a similar position. Law's (2003: 108) observation that 'since newspapers in Scotland are in fierce daily competition with each other it cannot be envisaged that they will risk experimenting with unfamiliar written styles when such demand plainly does not exist among their consumers' echoes McClure's comment that

> one only has to imagine a quality newspaper, containing reports and analyses of local, national and world politics, editorials, sports commentaries, reviews of books, theatre and broadcasting, and the other regular features of *The Scotsman* or *The Herald* written entirely in Scots, to realise how far it is from the *ausbau* level of a world language. (McClure 1997: 19)

Therefore, as outlined in the previous chapter, it is expected that the Scottish newspapers will use far more *Standard Written English* or, depending on context and subject matter, *Scottish Standard English* than broad *Scots*. As suggested in the previous chapter in section 3.10, it is also anticipated that any passages of dense *Scots* will be confined to certain types of article (for example features) and certain types of subject-matter. Chapter 5 investigates whether these hypotheses are correct.

But what about a standard *Scots*? If the newspapers are going to use at least some *Scots*, albeit perhaps more likely to be the occasional item of lexis in *Scottish Standard English* rather than prolonged passages of dense *Scots*, is it necessary or desirable that they should use standardised forms? Indeed, is such a thing even possible given the previous discussion on standards (or the lack thereof)? As discussed in section 3.7, present-day *Scots* has no adequate standard form, and no recommendations for the development of a standard form or orthography for *Scots* have been widely agreed. Cameron's (1995) observations on the role of the press in maintaining standards suggest that the Scottish press could have a powerful role in the development of a standard *Scots*. However, this is unlikely to be achieved unless deeply ingrained attitudes to *Scots* are changed and editors, journalists and readers see this as important. The extent to which a standardised form for *Scots* does exist in the Scottish newspapers can be gauged in some measure by the degree of variation the newspapers allow in the orthography of *Scots* lexical items, and this is investigated in section 5.8.

4.8 Conclusion

Newspapers want to create a sense of shared community consciousness, and in the case of Scottish readerships, a shared Scottish identity with their readers. They have various strategies for doing this, a key one of which is the use of Scottish language (c.f. section 2.4.3). Newspapers may well attempt to use the vernacular of their perceived readership, but they are engaged in an ongoing negotiation of acceptable language styles with their readerships. The language thus negotiated will play a part in the construction and maintenance of Scottish identity, itself a complex multifaceted phenomenon. The use of *Scots* lexis in the newspapers is as much for symbolic purposes, language display and stylistic considerations as it is for communicative import. Therefore it does not really matter whether or not the *Scots* used by the newspapers is particularly 'authentic' (whatever that may be) or clichéd; what matters is that readers should be able to recognise it as being Scottish, and therefore be able to identify with it, but also that they should find it acceptable. Following Anderson (1991), it should be recognisable as their vernacular but it must be a representation of that vernacular with which they feel comfortable and which they consider to be appropriate. The following data chapters investigate just what that acceptable vernacular looks like.

Further Reading

1. General works on media studies such as Tunstall (1996) and Bell (1991) provide good background information on the press.
2. Smith (1994), although now somewhat outdated, gives a useful overview of the key motivating forces and politics behind the Scottish press, and focuses particularly on the coverage of the independence question. Although not written from a linguistic viewpoint, it gives good background information on the powers behind the newspapers. Reid (2006), former editor of *The Herald*, gives more and updated behind-the-scenes insights.
3. Fowler (1991) is an accessible introduction to analysing the language of newspapers. Cameron (1995) is a very readable account of the gatekeeping role of the press. Both Fowler (1991) and Cameron (1995) are written from critical theory perspectives.

5

A Limited Identity

Having outlined the key theoretical constructs on which this study is based in Chapters 1–4, this chapter begins the detailed analysis of the newspaper corpus. It uses quantitative and qualitative analytical techniques to discover whether there are indeed appropriacy constraints operating on Scottish newspapers which affect where and in what quantities *Scots* lexis is used. If so, this would suggest that there are limitations operating on the linguistic construction of identity. In addition, it considers whether the *Scots* words and phrases found occur in passages of dense or thin *Scottish-English*, and also whether the items found tend to be non-cognate or cognate lexis. The previous chapter suggested that newspapers are expected to uphold certain standards, and hence institutional expectations may mean that the newspaper needs to distance itself from the use of *Scots*. Thus the extent to which *Scots* lexis is restricted to direct speech contexts and regular feature columns is also investigated. Status constraints mean that *Scots* is often thought to be preferred for use in humorous rather than serious contexts. Does the newspaper data exhibit this pattern of usage? The final section of this chapter looks for evidence of the Scottish newspapers' potential role as a force for standardisation in their spelling conventions for *Scots* lexis.

5.1 THE OVERVIEW

Before answering these questions, it is useful to get an overview of the usage of *Scots* lexis by the newspapers. As outlined in section 1.4.1, the collection methodology was for a full year's data in each case and it was posited that there might be specific points in the year, for example around Burns Night or Hogmanay, when the use of *Scots* lexis was more frequent. Analysis of the data proved such concerns to be unfounded. As Table 5.1 shows, there were peaks in certain months in some newspapers but no clear patterns could be discerned within or across newspapers.

Month	Herald (1995)	Herald (2005)	Scotsman (1995)	Scotsman (2005)	Record (1995)	Record (2005)	Sun (1995)	Sun (2005)	Times (1995)	Times (2005)	Total Scots tokens
Jan.	745	359	500	336	213	486	3	283	35	64	3,024
Feb.	596	304	250	275	217	501	9	253	19	156	2,580
Mar.	723	265	343	218	206	529	7	359	30	96	2,776
Apr.	546	234	137	214	225	450	11	240	27	134	2,218
May	717	296	128	232	241	385	15	356	25	112	2,507
June	807	266	341	217	239	436	5	168	28	66	2,573
July	631	253	305	241	166	408	7	240	31	81	2,363
Aug.	597	338	359	196	213	476	3	279	36	82	2,579
Sept.	996	326	308	185	254	454	8	275	9	133	2,948
Oct.	586	353	232	167	210	440	14	375	19	110	2,506
Nov.	1,247	281	294	137	192	397	18	217	39	102	2,924
Dec.	794	351	295	207	241	466	6	281	19	88	2,748
TOTALS	8,985	3,626	3,492	2,625	2,617	5,428	106	3,326	317	1,224	31,746

Table 5.1 Scots tokens by newspaper and by month

Newspaper	Total articles	Total word count	Scots token totals
Herald (1995)	3,049	2,560,067	8,985
Herald (2005)	1,667	1,193,251	3,626
Scotsman (1995)	1,366	1,006,644	3,492
Scotsman (2005)	1,079	861,330	2,625
Daily Record (1995)	1,535	753,938	2,617
Daily Record (2005)	3,273	1,585,852	5,428
Sun (1995)	77	32,774	106
Sun (2005)	1,798	835,992	3,326
Times (1995)	177	141,430	317
Times (2005)	693	496,392	1,224
TOTALS	14,714	9,467,670	31,746

Table 5.2 Overall corpus composition: article, word count and *Scots* token totals

As shown in Table 5.2, the test word-list yielded a total of 14,714 newspaper articles for the 1995/2005 corpus (6,204 articles in the 1995 corpus, and 8,510 in the 2005 corpus). Each of these articles contained at least one item of search lexis, but, of course, many contained more. Once the secondary searches were run on these articles using the comparative word-lists methodology, the resulting confirmed count of occurrences (that is tokens) of *Scots* lexis in the corpus came to 31,746. Thus, on average, each article contained just over 2 tokens of identifiably *Scots* lexis. Of course, such averages conceal local patterns and can only ever give a general indication. The most densely *Scots* article in the corpus contained some 656 *Scots* lexical tokens and will be discussed further in section 5.5.1. As Table 5.2 shows, the overall corpus size was just under 9.5 million words. Thus, in the corpus as a whole, the ratio of identifiably *Scots* lexis to non-identifiably or non-*Scots* lexis was approximately 1:298. This was reasonably constant across the different newspapers. The highest proportions of *Scots* lexis were found in *The Sun* (2005) 1: 251 (an unexpected result discussed further in section 8.9); the lowest in *The Times* (1995) 1: 446. Figure 5.1 shows values for individual newspapers.

So clearly we are not talking about huge quantities of *Scots* lexis, and some corpus experts may be tempted to dismiss such figures as accidental or anomalous. However, this can be challenged on two grounds. Firstly, as discussed in section 3.1, the methods used pick up only those items of lexis that are identifiably *Scots* (both non-cognate and cognate items) and

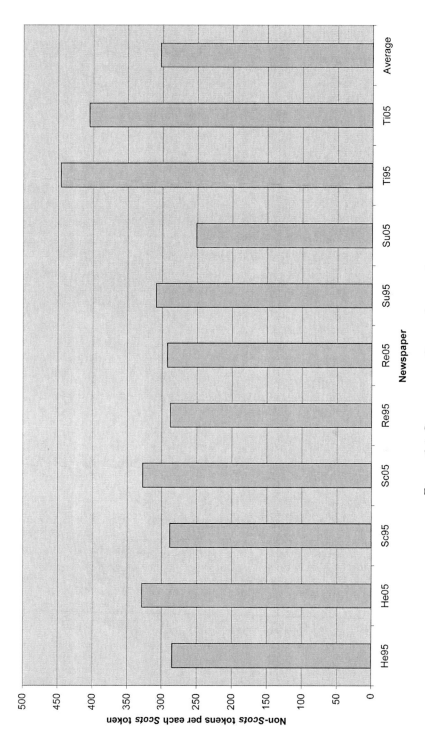

Figure 5.1 Scots to non-Scots token ratios

uncontroversially not *English*. The methodology therefore conceals the considerable quantities of common-core lexis in the corpus. This is unavoidable and arises due to the close linguistic interrelationship of *Scots* with *English*.

Secondly, the very fact that the *Scots* lexis is there at all, albeit in small quantities, is significant. In corpus-based work we can often get too 'hung-up' on the figures and notions of statistical significance without considering whether this is the whole story. Quantitative analysis of corpus data can take us only so far; qualitative analysis is an essential complement. Attestation of linguistic forms is sadly often overlooked or masked by large-scale corpus analysis, and yet it can be important, particularly for varieties such as *Scots* which have problematic status and a cognate and slippery style-drifting or even code-switching relationship with the hegemonic norm (in this case *Standard Written English* or *Scottish Standard English*). Dictionaries, even the well-respected ones such as *OED*, sometimes have to rely on scantily spread attestation evidence for certain dates, meanings or provenances when compiling their entries and yet their authority or reliability is seldom questioned. Arguably the low frequencies of usage of lexical items from lesser-used or heteroglossic varieties such as *Scots* is a similar case, and perhaps this is something to bear in mind when analysing corpora which include such forms. Given the public audience, formal register and gatekeeping function of the newspaper genre, the significance of the presence of **any** *Scots* lexis in the newspapers, even in low quantities, should not be underestimated. As discussed in section 3.3, the preconditioning effect of factors such as the education system and even spell-checkers with their emphasis on *Standard Written English*, combined with the heavy editing regime of newspaper writing, means that the use of *Scots* lexis in the written mode can never really be an unconscious or accidental act. So someone somewhere is choosing to include these items of *Scots* lexis. Yes the corpus data suggest that the usage of *Scots* lexis is limited, but this is what was anticipated anyway. What is more important is that it is there at all! Having got over this understandable quantification hang-up, attention now moves to the more interesting consideration of where the *Scots* lexis appears, in what contexts and with what significance.

5.2 WHERE DO WE FIND SCOTS LEXIS?

This section considers whereabouts in the newspapers *Scots* lexis is found. Section 3.7 discussed the generally low status of *Scots* and the fact that it is usually considered more suitable for use in domestic or low-key settings, whereas *Scottish Standard English* enjoys much higher status and is likely to be acceptable for use in a much broader range of contexts, including high-status visible public discourse. Section 4.6 raised the notion of appropriacy and asked how this might affect linguistic choices across newspaper article types. Bex (1996) argues that texts are produced according to the norms of the discourse community, and crucially for the argument pursued here, according to the functions they are expected to perform within that community. Thus it can be predicted that the generally low status of *Scots* and its usual restriction to literature, the homely and domestic, or use for humour would preclude its use in serious news articles but might allow limited use in feature articles where its potential for constructing Scottish identity is not threatened so seriously by considerations of 'correctness'. Macafee (1983: 139) claims that 'the Scottish press regularly admits dialect in certain specialised areas, particularly cartoons and anecdotes with dialogue. Feature and sports writers also often flatter their readers by using dialectal items for key terms.' This section asks whether this claim is accurate. Is identifiably *Scots* lexis concentrated in certain parts of the newspaper and in certain types of article and/ or restricted to certain journalists?

5.2.1 Methodology

In a corpus of this size, the analysis of article types could be based only on the classifications assigned to individual articles by the original resource producers. Unfortunately, not all newspapers gave full data, not all articles were thus classified, and, due to different classification systems, results were not comparable across newspapers or indeed across the 1995 and 2005 parts of the corpus. It was therefore necessary to consider each newspaper individually, and then to look across newspapers to see whether any general trends could be discerned. The analysis of journalist bylines provided a useful counter-check to the article/section type analysis as journalists characteristically tend to write certain types of articles in particular parts of the newspaper, for example sports columnists vs political correspondents. Due to the unwieldiness of the newspapers' and *LexisNexis'* bundled search engines, the very large quantities of data involved, and inconsistencies in naming practices, it was impossible to ascertain the overall proportions of article types in each newspaper over the period of a year. Therefore, unless stated otherwise, the figures given are quoted relative to the corpus collected using the search list, not the whole of the contents of the 1995/2005 newspapers.

5.2.2 Most Scots article types and journalists

In *The Herald* (1995) corpus data, the most common type of article represented was the feature article, accounting for 46 per cent of all articles saved, followed by the sports pages, 'The Diary' (a humorous feature column), 'The Weekender'/'Weekend Extra', the 'Education' and 'Schools' pages, and 'The Farmers' Diary' as the most likely places to find *Scots* lexis. Analysis of the 2005 *Herald* corpus data showed that 38 per cent of articles saved were classified as features articles (again the most frequently occurring article type in the corpus), and 21 per cent as sports articles. *The Herald*'s 'Weekender' and 'Weekend Extra' sections were well represented in the 1995 data (figures for the 2005 data were unavailable), accounting for 248 and 43 stories respectively (a total of 9 per cent of all 1995 *Herald* articles saved in the corpus), a figure that is noteworthy when it is remembered that these newspaper sections appear only in Saturday editions of the newspaper, whereas most other sections are represented across the week. Due to the nature of the data, figures for *The Scotsman* and the *Daily Record* were impossible to derive by article/section type, but similar patterns could be discerned by analysis of byline information across the newspapers. A summary of the results of the search for the most '*Scots*' journalists is given in Table 5.3.

In *The Herald* (1995), the most prolifically *Scots* journalist by number of newspaper articles saved was Tom Shields writing in 'The *(Herald)* Diary' and some sports articles, who contributed 136 stories (80 per cent of all the stories he wrote that year) to the 1995 corpus. He was closely followed by the columnist Jack McLean, who contributed 107 articles to the corpus (89 per cent of his total 1995 output). So both these journalists were habitually using *Scots* lexis in the majority of their articles. In *The Herald* (2005), Ken Smith and David Belcher, the new co-authors of 'The *(Herald)* Diary', were by far the most prolifically *Scots* lexis-using journalists.

In *The Scotsman* (1995), by far the most '*Scots*' journalist was Fordyce Maxwell (122 articles) erstwhile author of 'The *(Scotsman)* Diary'. Other journalists who featured quite prominently in articles saved from *The Scotsman* (1995) were the sports writers Graham Law, Mike Aitken and Hugh Keevins. In *The Scotsman* (2005), Robert McNeil, Simon Pia, Jim Gilchrist and Fordyce Maxwell were all heavily represented. Robert McNeil was writing mainly TV reviews, Simon Pia was the new author of 'The Diary' – now renamed as 'Simon Pia's Diary', Jim Gilchrist was writing feature-type articles, and Fordyce Maxwell, though seldom writing 'The Diary', was still writing feature-type articles. Thus again 'The Diary' and other features and sports stories were heavily represented.

Patterns were slightly different in the *Daily Record*. John Millar, who wrote TV reviews and features, had most articles, closely followed by Joan Burnie, who wrote human interest stories and the agony column, and Bill Leckie, who mostly wrote sports articles. Interestingly, initial analysis of the

Newspaper	Journalist	Article type	Stories	Types	Tokens
Herald (1995)	Tom Shields	Diary, sports	136	603	730
	David Belcher	Entertainment reviews	110	258	291
	Jack McLean	Feature column	107	512	710
	Derek Douglas	Sports	70	86	90
Herald (2005)	Ken Smith, David Belcher	Diary	159	686	762
Scotsman (1995)	Fordyce Maxwell	Diary	122	607	714
Scotsman (2005)	Robert McNeil	TV reviews	156	596	686
	Simon Pia	Diary	117	372	414
	Jim Gilchrist	Features	57	111	119
	Fordyce Maxwell	Features	29	117	132
Daily Record (1995)	John Millar	TV reviews, features	88	115	138
	Joan Burnie	Agony column, human interest	75	143	196
	Bill Leckie	Sports	63	130	167
Daily Record (2005)	Tam Cowan	Sports, features	197	368	416
	Joan Burnie	Agony column, human interest	164	205	224
	Paul English	Features	124	250	304

Table 5.3 Most 'Scots' journalists

1995 *Daily Record* data based on the data source's own classification suggested that there were substantial numbers of news articles (of the order of approximately 20 per cent) among the data. Given the patterns noted in the other newspapers and the expectations raised by considerations of appropriacy, this seemed odd. However, further analysis revealed that what the *Daily Record* classified as 'news' was often far removed from the hard news category of the broadsheets and more akin to features reporting there. In the 2005 *Daily Record* data, Tam Cowan, author of sports and feature articles, Joan Burnie, authoring the same types of articles as in 1995, and Paul English, features writer, were the most prominent journalists. Again, features (though often of a rather different type from those in *The Herald* and *The Scotsman* – for example the agony column) and sport articles predominated.

Comparison with *The Sun* (2005) and *The Times* (2005) shows similarities, but also often additional flagging of Scottish content. (C.f. discussion in section 8.4.) (Data were unavailable for *The Sun* (1995) and *The Times* (1995).) In *The Sun* (2005), the most heavily represented article types were opinion, the interestingly named and self-evidently Scottish in angle 'Scotcha', and football reports. In *The Times* (2005), the most heavily represented article types were features (some in 'Times2'), sport (sometimes 'Sport; Scotland') and 'Home News; Scotland'.

Even allowing for the caveats about the comparability of the different datasets, it is clear that feature-type and sports articles were the most likely to use *Scots* lexis, and that (where this information is available) specialist feature-type sections were the most likely location of *Scots* lexis in the newspapers. Analysis of the newspaper data shows clear evidence for the claims made by Macafee (1983: 139) and Tunstall (1996: 211) (see above at sections 5.2 and 4.4.4 respectively) that features and sports writing are both heavily regionalised, as this is where the greatest numbers of newspaper articles containing *Scots* lexis were found.

Scots lexis was much less likely to be found in (hard) news articles. These tendencies are also borne out by analysis of article page number data. This revealed that, as expected, the use of identifiably *Scots* lexis on page 1 was fairly infrequent; across the corpus as a whole, only 183 stories – that is 1.2 per cent of the corpus articles (accounting for 253 tokens – that is 0.8 per cent of all *Scots* tokens) had *Scots* lexis on page 1. The expectations associated with the use of *Scots* impact, not only on the types of articles in which *Scots* lexis is considered suitable for use, but also on their relative prominence in the newspapers. In most newspapers, especially the broadsheets, feature articles are much more likely to be found in specialised sections or in regular slots in pages towards the middle or back of the newspaper. It would seem inappropriate or non-authoritative to most Scottish newspaper readers if front-page news coverage were to be written in broad *Scots*. *Scots* is generally perceived as largely being confined to home life, the private or personal, to comedy or to sentimental literature, and thus a significant presence on the front page in most serious news articles would seem extremely odd. However, as discussed in section 8.9 re coverage of the Dunblane massacre, occasional items of *Scots* lexis are sometimes used in a news story in exceptional circumstances as a way of enhancing the local salience of the news story. Further investigation is necessary, but personal observation suggests that this is particularly likely to be the case where some Scottish tragedy is covered. For example, something similar seemed to happen in TV reporting (I have not yet checked newspaper coverage) of the unexpected death of Donald Dewar, Scotland's initial First Minister for the new Parliament.

5.3 Why is Usage of Scots Lexis Restricted to these Areas?

Why should *Scots* lexis be more commonly found in the feature-type articles, in specialised newspaper sections and often tied to particular journalists? The answer probably lies in the different functions of news articles and feature articles, and the language used may vary according to the function the articles are expected to perform (c.f. Bex's (1996) discourse communities). News-type articles are written primarily to convey information. They are ostensibly unbiased reports of factual events and the personality of the news reporter is usually not foregrounded. To do so would be to suggest an element of personal opinion, and this would run contrary to the general ethos of the news article. News articles are generally written in a fairly impersonal style, which suggests that what is contained therein is not the product of one individual's thoughts, but is, rather, an objective account of the facts. By contrast, the primary function of the feature article is to entertain, although many feature articles also seek to inform, for example articles on education, cooking or gardening. Feature articles often highlight the persona and opinions of the writer (see discussion of journalists in section 5.4), and thus, as a personal opinion is being expressed (although obviously the general ethos and ideological viewpoint of the newspaper will also have an effect), there is less problem with using *Scots* lexis. The register of the text is more personal and less formal, so using *Scots* lexis is less problematic. Feature articles and news articles are read in quite a different way, and are perceived differently in the minds of readers. Bell (1991: 14) notes that 'in features, journalists are allowed more liberty of style, and many features are written by non-journalists'. It should of course be remembered that, although feature writers may have more autonomy over the content of their articles than news reporters, they are still subject to the rigours of copy editors and thus it is highly unlikely that any article will be entirely the work of one person. Nevertheless, feature writers are allowed to be, and probably also encouraged to be more individualistic and idiosyncratic in their style, and for some of them, that will include using *Scots* lexis.

5.4 A Humorous Language?

Feature articles, especially the 'Diary' columns in both *The Herald* and *The Scotsman* are often humorous and, as discussed in section 3.7, there is a strong association and tradition of *Scots* and humour. In this study, 10 per cent of all the feature articles saved in the corpus were taken from 'The (*Herald*) Diary' as written by Tom Shields. Much of Scotland's popular culture uses Scottish language for humorous purposes, probably the best known proponent being the comedian Harry Lauder (1870–1950), but there has been a long tradition of others, for example Rikki Fulton, Jimmy Logan and Billy Connolly. And as noted in section 2.4.5, humour is one of the central characteristics associated with the Scottish Kailyard stereotype. The association of *Scots* language with humour is something that is often lamented by Scots language activists who argue it denigrates the status of the variety, devalues it, and debars it from use in other, more serious contexts. However, I would suggest that the demonstrable association of *Scots* lexis with humour in the newspapers is not necessarily, as might be assumed, a bad thing. The use of *Scots* lexis in features such as the 'Diary' or Jack McLean's former column in *The Herald* helps to create a sense of solidarity, as the reader often needs ingroup knowledge of the *Scots* lexis or other types of shared knowledge to 'get' the joke.

For example, *The Herald*'s article 'Genteel Disclosure in Govan Gents' (31 January 1995) is a humorous story narrated by a Rab C. Nesbitt-type character who speaks something akin to *Glaswegian* urban colloquial *Scots*. It narrates a fictional conversation between the Rab C. Nesbitt character and a posh civil servant from Edinburgh, which takes place in a gents' toilet. A fair proportion of the lexis for example *semmit* (vest), *tumshie* (idiot or turnip), *buroo* (Unemployment Benefit Office) is of localised Scottish provenance and therefore inaccessible to the outsider. By being able to meet the linguistic tariff raised by the *Scots* lexis, the ingroup reader is constructed as part of the wider Scottish community. There is also appeal to localised shared knowledge, for example the rhyming slang in *yi made a right St Rollox o' it* (St. Rollox was a locomotive works outside Springburn (Glasgow)), more word play in the extract '*I was born in Mafeking Street.*'

'An' I wis born in mine' sez I, fair let doon (Mafeking Street is an actual street near Glasgow's Ibrox Stadium), and a reference to Burns' poem 'Tam O'Shanter' in see that bit aboot gatherin' her brows and nursin' her wrath. Funny the things that creep into yir thick skull when yir stoatin' along the road in the direction o' her indoors. All these references delimit the ideal readership.

Munro (2002), summarised and quoted here from 'Scots Language and Comic Performance' (n.d.) argues that the use of Scots allows comic performers to 'manufacture a collective cultural identity with their audience', thus creating an 'us' and 'them' situation where those who lack the necessary linguistic skills to 'get' the joke (some of whom may be members of the dominant English-only speaking hegemonic group) are excluded from the discourse community. Hence, she argues, the expected power and dominance of the hegemonic group is subverted, often without its members realising it. This adds to the comedic effect and strengthens ingroup identity for the Scots-speaking/comprehending discourse community. It can therefore be suggested that the use of Scots language for humour, as in the humorous feature columns, plays a significant role in strengthening ingroup identity.

Humorous feature columns often seem to function mainly as platforms from which the individual columnists pronounce their general views on the world. In such cases, the individual voice of the feature columnist may well be more a dramatic persona than a true representation of the columnist's character; there is no necessary correlation between the persona projected in the newspaper, and the real person behind the article. Indeed, in the case of Scottish newspaper columns, there often seems to be a deliberate heightening of the Scottishness and local provenance of the columnist as a way of making contact with the reader. Jack McLean, for example, was well known for writing about his adventures in pubs on the south side of Glasgow. Tom Shields' 'Diary' in The Herald (1995) and Maxwell's and Pia's 'Diaries' in The Scotsman give amusing anecdotes on local events, personalities and organisations. These columnists are expected to be humorous or slightly outrageous in the things they say, and therefore these parts of the newspaper are read in a different way from the news articles or other more serious matter. The use of Scots lexis and other Scots features in such columns helps to create this impression of anti-establishment and personal opinion writing.

So what conclusions can be drawn about the distribution of Scots lexis in terms of journalists and article types? As has been argued, the use of Scots lexis can encode certain registers and values into the message. Scots lexis is generally restricted to certain parts of the newspaper, and is commonly used for humour. Reah (1998) argues that newspaper language reflects the views of its readership, and reinforces their attitudes, so her argument suggests that *Scots* lexis is restricted to such areas because these are the only places where it is deemed acceptable by the readers. Unless the majority of readers change their attitudes, *Scots* lexis is extremely unlikely to move into other areas of the newspaper.

It is interesting to note in passing Marshalsay's point that the very successful Scottish comedian, Harry Lauder, sang his songs in *English*, 'using the occasional Scots word for spice' (1992: 18). She argues that he realised early in his career that using broad *Scots* dialect in his songs would be a bad idea as a significant proportion of his audience would fail to understand it and hence be alienated by it. Instead he preferred to use songs written in very thin *Scottish-English* which used only the occasional item of *Scots* lexis (a type of language display) and rendered them in a clearly enunciated Scottish accent.

5.5 HOW SCOTTISH IS TOO SCOTTISH?

This preference for thin and tokenist *Scots* is something which pervades popular culture, and the next section assesses evidence of this tendency in the Scottish newspapers. It considers 'How Scottish is too Scottish?' That is, are thin or dense language contexts preferred in the newspapers, and also are the *Scots* lexical items used more likely to be open or closed class items?

5.5.1 Thin and dense Scots

Chapter 3 considered the range of varieties that exist along the *Scottish-English* linguistic continuum, and following McClure (1979: 30) suggested that texts could be classified as dense (towards the *Scots* end of the continuum) and thin (the 'limiting case' being *Scottish Standard English*). Thus a quantitative distinction can be made between those texts which contain a significant proportion of identifiably *Scots* lexis and those which contain comparatively little. As discussed in section 3.2.2, it is quite possible, indeed often usual, for texts to code-switch between the thin and dense ends of the linguistic continuum. Section 2.3.1 introduced the concept of language display ('a type of borrowing/code-switching for special purposes' (Eastman and Stein 1993: 188)). Crucially, such borrowing or code-switching is a limited departure from the expected linguistic norm. It was therefore anticipated that the newspapers would prefer thin rather than densely *Scots* texts, that is, use occasional items of *Scots* lexis rather than sustained passages of *Scots*. So not only is *Scots* lexis constrained in terms of where it occurs, but it is also likely to be limited in terms of quantity and density.

'Scotsness' densities were calculated for each of the newspaper articles in the corpus. Using the full word-list, two Scottishness quotients were devised on purely quantitative grounds: the first was calculated based on the overall occurrences of identifiably *Scots* lexis in each newspaper article as a proportion of the overall article word count; the second calculated the number of sentences containing at least one item of *Scots* lexis against the overall article sentence count. Although not foolproof (there are limitations related to article length, for example, due to the well-attested sensitivity to corpus size), using these measures in tandem gives a fairly crude but nevertheless useful quantification of how densely *Scots* any given article is, though clearly it only deals with part of McClure's (1979: 30) criteria for thin/dense *Scots* (see section 3.4). That is, it covers the 'distinctively Scots words', idiom and distinctive *Scots* orthography criteria, but does not deal with the *Scots* grammar criterion. Using this methodology, it was possible both firstly to quantify the extent to which the language of the newspaper articles was markedly *Scots*, and secondly to identify the most densely *Scots* texts.

Analysis of the data proved that the vast majority of *Scots* lexis used in the newspapers did indeed occur in thin rather than dense contexts. As noted in section 5.1, on average, each newspaper article contained only two occurrences of *Scots* lexis, although this varied a little between newspapers. This very low density of *Scots* forms is what would be expected in a public discourse type like the newspapers anyway. Generally newspapers are written in *Standard Written English* and a simple comparison with other newspapers around the world illustrates just how usual this pattern is. A search on the *Singlish* emphatic discourse particle, *lah*, in *The Straits Times* during 2005 yielded only 138 occurrences, the vast majority of which were in direct speech contexts. A search on *dunny* (toilet) in *The Sydney Morning Herald* over the same period yielded 49 results, compared with 5 incidences in *The Times* (London). So all these newspapers are generally written in *World Standard English*, but clearly there are also some isolated examples of more localised lexis. In fact, the analysis of *lah*, a very commonly occurring *Singlish* particle which might usefully be compared with the very commonly occurring *Scots* adjective *wee* (small), perhaps suggests that the Scottish newspapers are doing rather more of this emblematic marking of national identity than some of their global counterparts, though much more exhaustive research would need to be carried out to ascertain if this is indeed the case.

Analysis of text densities by expressing the total of distinctively *Scots* lexis as a proportion of the overall article running word count also bore out this conclusion. The highest proportion was 44 per cent but this was a fairly isolated occurrence. Of the 14,714 newspaper articles in the corpus, only 32 had *Scots* lexical densities in double figures. Even allowing for the non-inclusion of common-core lexis, this figure is low. Thus we can confidently say that very few of the newspaper articles were written in anything approaching dense *Scots*. Those few examples that did occur tended to be written not by journalists but by language activists (see Bell's (1991: 14) comment, quoted in section 5.3), and had headlines that clearly indicated their pro-*Scots* language content:

'Burns' nationalism'
'Heist yer gless tae oor Naitional Bard'
'Scots language'
'Ca' the Yowes to the Knowes: The Life and Times of . . .'
                                        (*The Scotsman* 1995)

'The cultural deficit is much more serious'
'Let us speak in tongues'
'Time tae cure oor cultural cringe aboot native tungs'
'Braidth o vision in baith Scots an English'
                                        (*The Herald* 1995)

Such articles were predominantly found in the quality press, and were in features, letters pages or the education sections. The only tabloid article with significant proportions of *Scots* lexis was 'A daughter's lament for mum' (where the phrase *ma (moanie) maw* accounts for 19 of the 27 *Scots* lexical occurrences (tokens) (the others being *ye, yer, sae, tae, wee*) (*Record*). Interestingly the top ten most Scottish stories in terms of density of *Scots* lexis were drawn, in the main, from the 1995 corpus (the notable exception being a 2005 *Times* article with the headline 'Scots wa' hae . . .'. (See Chapter 7 for more detailed examination of comparison between 1995 and 2005 data.)

The articles containing by far the highest number of occurrences of *Scots* lexis were the aforementioned 'Let us speak in tongues' (*Herald*, 25 November 1995) with 285 *Scots* tokens, and 'Time tae cure oor cultural cringe aboot native tungs' (*Herald*, 12 September 1995) with 656 *Scots* tokens, both written by John Hodgart, author, former principal teacher of English and Scots language activist. He submits only two articles to *The Herald* in 1995, but these contain a combined total of 299 *Scots* lexical types and 941 tokens. Their Scotsness ratios (that is percentage of identifiably *Scots* lexis) are respectively 96.30 per cent and 88.24 per cent in terms of sentences containing identifiably *Scots* lexis, and 26.46 per cent and 29.46

per cent in terms of words. Closer examination of the articles shows they are written in sustained and fairly formal dense *Scots*.

Such articles show *Scots* being used in a very public discourse to discuss serious topics. However, *Scots* is only ever used in this way in the newspapers to discuss Scottish topics such as the state of the language, Scottish literature and so on. The newspaper data therefore uphold McClure's observation that

> Such few attempts at non-literary prose as have appeared in Scots are – again with no exception known to me – discussions of Scots writers, comments on the use of the Scots language, suggestions for Scots spelling reform, or similar Scottish topics. (McClure 1979: 47)

Indeed, it was found that some of the articles discussing *Scots* language complained about, or defended the use of, particular orthographic forms for certain *Scots* words. Clearly there are unspoken appropriacy rules operating which allow *Scots* in these very restricted contexts, but would presumably rule out the use of dense *Scots* in an article covering the Chancellor's budget speech.

On the whole, the language contexts for *Scots* lexis in the newspapers tend very much towards the extreme thin end of the linguistic continuum with very few texts being written in sustained *Scots*. Why should this be the case and what is the effect on the linguistic construction of Scottish identity?

This study argues that, though the newspapers can exploit *Scots* lexis in their construction of a Scottish identity, the fairly limited use of items of *Scots* lexis and idiom is more likely to function as a focus for Scottish identity for most readers than is broad *Scots*. The issue is one of quantity or density, particularly in the written mode. So, for example, *the best laid plans o' mice, men and homebuyers go desperately agley* (Herald 1995) or *It looked like it was going to be a typically dreich Scottish Hogmanay as the celebrations began in George Square on Saturday night* (Herald 2005) are, for most Scots, easier to identify with than *Born in 1759 and deein in 1796, Burns leeved at a time whan the Scottish estaiblishment an poleeticallie acteeve clesses hid gien up their Scots identitie in a muckle breenge tae be 'British' – a concept whilk wisnae echoed sooth o the mairches* (Scotsman 1995). Although it might have initially been imagined that less densely *Scots* texts would be less effective linguistic constructors of identity, given most Scots' inexperience of written *Scots* and its problematic status, the reverse is more likely to be true. Thin texts punctuated by the occasional item of *Scots* lexis are more likely to be understood, and to be acceptable to readers, especially given the gate-keeping status accorded to newspapers by their readers outlined in section

4.5. Whilst densely *Scots* texts can arguably construct Scottish identity by virtue of their distinctive and marked Scottishness, it is an identity less accessible and often less acceptable to the majority of Scots than that constructed by thinner texts. For most Scots, the linguistic tariffs raised by very dense written *Scots* texts (particularly of the formal *Scots* as evidenced in the Hodgart articles) are too high, and therefore individuals may feel excluded from that particular discourse community. Texts towards the thin end of the *Scottish-English* continuum are probably much more effective for the construction and maintenance of Scottish identity than are more dense *Scots* texts. Linguistic tokenism it may be; nevertheless, it works.

5.5.2 Open vs closed class lexis

So it can be demonstrated that *Scots* lexis in the newspapers is restricted in terms of its distribution, quantity and density. This argument, however, can be taken one stage further by suggesting that not only is the quantity of *Scots* lexis used important, but also that the type (or class) of *Scots* lexis used is highly significant. As discussed in section 3.5, it is hypothesised firstly that the frequency of occurrence of open vs closed class lexis is likely to be significant, with open class lexis more frequently used in language display than closed class lexis and also more likely to be found in isolation in 'thin' contexts. Conversely it is hypothesised that closed class lexis will tend to be found in more dense contexts. Secondly, it is anticipated that the presence or absence of identifiably *Scots* closed class lexis may be used as an indicator of the overall density and register of the text. Both the original 440 test word-list list and the resulting word-list (after comparing the word-lists) of 1,519 lexemes included a mixture of open and closed class lexis, thus allowing both these hypotheses to be tested. Note that some items could be classified as open or closed class depending on part of speech and context, for example *outwith* can be a preposition (closed class), adverb or adjective (both open class). So, what was the frequency of usage of open vs closed class *Scots* lexical items and did it bear out these hypotheses?

As Figures 5.2 and 5.3 demonstrate, there is clear evidence that open class *Scots* lexis predominates in the newspaper texts both at the level of lexemes and tokens. What are the likely explanations for this phenomenon? The first explanation centres on notions of correctness. In the written mode, particularly in fairly formal or public discourses such as newspaper articles, there is strong pressure to conform to the norms of *Standard Written English*. And, as Cameron (1995) notes, (see discussion in Chapter 4) press and readers share an expectation that newspapers should use standard forms and be arbiters of 'good style'. The emphasis is on 'correctness' and it is likely to focus more on grammar than on individual items of lexis, although it must be noted that there is also some pressure to use a standard lexicon. Any obviously non-standard (*English*) grammar would probably have to be justifiable in the context of the newspaper article (for example, perhaps being used in humorous anecdotes, to represent individuals' speech and so on), and is unlikely be used for extensive passages of serious prose. Non-standard syntactic and/or morphological features are likely to be regarded simply as 'bad *English*' (c.f. Cheshire and Milroy's (1993: 15) discussion of attitudes to regional *English*). The use of non-standard content (that is open class) lexis is likely to be regarded more leniently, perhaps as adding authenticity, local colour or a touch of the exotic, for example *a weel-kent face* rather than 'a well-known face', without compromising on standards. Because closed class lexis forms what is sometimes called the 'grammatical glue' of language, there are likely to be greater appropriacy and register constraints placed on it.

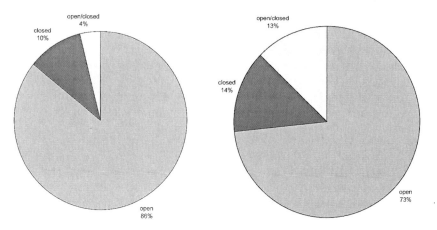

Figure 5.2 Open vs closed class: lexemes *Figure 5.3* Open vs closed class: tokens

The second explanation relates once again to the concept of language display. Perceptions of and attitudes towards content and non-content lexis affect not only the contexts in which open class and closed class *Scots* lexis are used, but also their capacity and desirability for use in overt language display. For language display purposes (Eastman and Stein 1993), it is much more likely that, for example, a *French* or *German* noun would be incorporated into *English* discourse to demonstrate one's knowledge, rather than that the occasional *French* or *German* definite article or preposition would be used as the act of display alongside *English* open class items. Thus it can be argued that, for many Scots (probably especially middle-class Scots), open class *Scots* lexical items are much more salient and acceptable for acts of overt language display than closed class lexical items. Whilst items of *Scots* open class lexis can easily be used stylistically as an act of language display, closed class *Scots* lexis is likely to be precluded for language display, unless confined within the 'safe' limits of a formulaic fixed expression such as those discussed in the next chapter. The use of closed class *Scots* lexis outwith formulaic fixed expressions is likely to be avoided.

The top ten most frequently occurring *Scots* words in the corpus were a fairly evenly split mixture of open (o) and closed (c) class forms: 7,269 x *wee* (o), 1,288 x *outwith* (o, c), 843 x *aye* (o, c), 736 x *ned/s* (o), 689 x *canny* (o), 512 x *tae* (o, c), 475 x *ye* (c), 349 x *auld* (o), 319 x *ma* (o, c), 280 x *nae* (o). Note that, although all of these are accepted items of *Scots* lexis, some of them do have a currency outside Scotland (for example *canny*, *wee*). The data showed that, even though the overall quantities of closed class lexis were lower than those for open class lexis, in quite a few cases, the actual frequencies of occurrence noted for certain items of closed class lexis were quite considerable. Two observations should be made in light of these results. Firstly, in any corpus it would be expected that the frequencies of individual closed class lexical items such as those listed above would be higher than the frequencies for individual items of content lexis – there is always plenty of grammatical 'glue' in texts (see Sinclair 1991: 100). Secondly, in some cases, these high frequencies were due to particularly high usage in one or two articles, such as some of the *Scots* language articles discussed previously in section 5.5.1. However, analysis of the language contexts for open vs closed class data did suggest that the hypothesis that closed class lexis tends to favour more dense contexts was correct. The average *Scots* lexical density surrounding closed class lexis was 3.12 per cent. For open class lexis this drops to 1.8 per cent. Although a fairly crude measure, this does suggest that there are clear differences in the language varieties of the contexts of open versus closed class lexis in the newspaper data. On the basis of the data collected by this study, closed class lexical items are more likely to be found in denser contexts than are open class lexical items. The data also show that the use of closed class *Scots* lexis is more likely to be restricted to use in dense *Scots* contexts, and seldom extends to thinner contexts.

5.6 How Different does it have to be from English?

This section considers how distinctive the *Scots* lexis adopted by the newspapers is, that is whether it is cognate or non-cognate lexis (see section 3.6 or Glossary for definition). It seeks to identify whether there are any differences in terms of usage, quantity and context between cognate and non-cognate

Scots lexis (for example, *hame/home* vs *bairn/child*) in the newspaper texts. Does the hypothesis outlined in Chapter 3 that non-cognate lexis is likely to be more acceptable/desirable for language display mean, firstly, that there is more cognate than non-cognate *Scots* lexis in the newspapers, and secondly that cognate and non-cognate lexis occur in *Scottish-English* contexts of differing densities, with cognate lexis more likely to be found in denser contexts and non-cognate lexis favouring thinner contexts? Figures 5.4 and 5.5 show the results obtained for lexemes and tokens respectively.

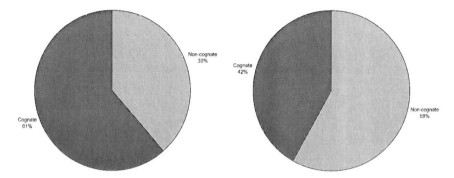

Figure 5.4 Cognate vs non-cognate: lexemes   *Figure 5.5* Cognate vs non-cognate: tokens

As Figure 5.4 illustrates, in terms of *Scots* forms (lexemes), cognate lexis predominates in the newspapers. However, the picture alters when considering actual lexical frequencies (tokens), as illustrated by Figure 5.5. Here non-cognate items are in the majority. Therefore, whilst, on average, each non-cognate *Scots* form (lexeme) generated 32 actual occurrences (tokens), each cognate form generated less than half as many with on average only 14 occurrences. In terms of overall lexical frequencies then, non-cognate *Scots* lexical items predominate in the newspaper corpus. This is what might have been anticipated anyway given their less problematic salience for language display purposes.

5.6.1 Cognate/non-cognate lexis and density

How does the use of cognate and non-cognate items relate to density? It was hypothesised that cognate lexis may tend to be associated with more densely *Scots* contexts, and that conversely, non-cognate lexis (as self-evidently *Scots* and not 'Scotticised English') may be more salient for language display in thinner contexts. Across the corpus (1995/2005), there were some differences in the density of the surrounding contexts of cognate and non-cognate items. Non-cognate items were found in contexts with an average *Scots* word density of 0.63 per cent; cognate items in contexts with an average density of 1.39 per cent. Clearly these density figures are low (as was noted earlier, newspaper contexts are generally towards the extreme thin end of the continuum). Nevertheless, there does appear to be an association of non-cognate lexis with less dense contexts than those of cognate items, cognate items generally occurring in contexts that are, on average, twice as dense as those for non-cognate lexical items. So the hypothesis raised in section 3.6 seems to be correct.

It can be suggested that non-cognate lexis has proportionately more contexts towards the thinner end of the *Scottish-English* continuum because these items are sufficiently distinct from *English*, not to be confused with it. Stylistically they therefore function as overtly distinct *Scots* lexical items, and as such are highly salient for language display in thinner contexts. Cognate lexis, having readily accessible *English* phonological and ortho-graphic cognates, may seem less acceptable in formal thinner written contexts, precisely because it can be perceived as Scotticised (and perhaps non-standard or 'bad') *English*, rather than as being part of a distinct and separate Scottish linguistic culture – the forgiveness of exoticism rather than non-standard as it were. In more densely *Scots* contexts, the formality or appropriacy pressures from *English* are less strong, and cognate lexis functions in relation to other *Scots* linguistic items; therefore its similarities to *English* are less noticeable and less important. It is perceived to be more 'truly' Scottish because it is set alongside other Scottish linguistic features. When put alongside *English* lexis, the similarities it bears to *English* are foregrounded. Cognate lexis may therefore have proportionately more contexts towards the *Scots* end of the continuum, that is, more dense contexts, because here the overall context is more Scottish and therefore there are fewer stylistic and register problems. Though both non-cognate and cognate lexis can be used to construct and maintain Scottishness, it is easier to integrate non-cognate than cognate lexis into thinner contexts.

5.6.2 Non-cognate/cognate and open vs closed class lexis

The analysis can be taken one stage further by considering the correlation between open/closed class lexis and cognate/non-cognate lexis. As shown by Figure 5.6, across the corpus (that is 1995 and 2005) the most frequently occurring lexical items (tokens) were non-cognate open class at 49 per cent – that is nouns, adjectives, verbs and adverbs that have no phonological/ orthographic *English* cognates (for example *Sassenach*). The next most commonly occurring were cognate open class words (24 per cent) – that is nouns, adjectives, verbs and adverbs with phonological/orthographic

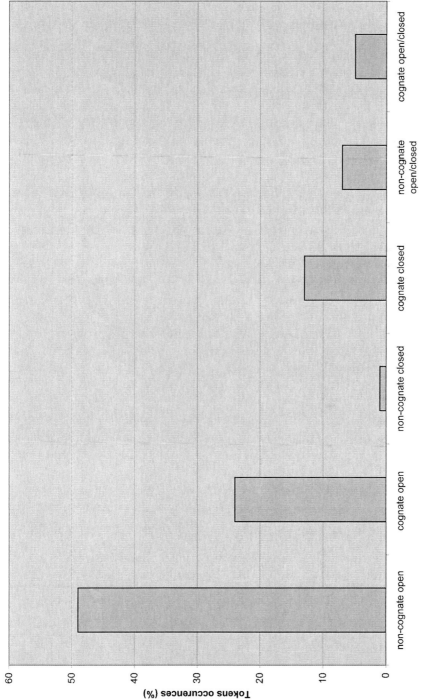

Figure 5.6 Tokens: cognate/non-cognate vs open/closed

English cognates (for example *tak* (take)). Cognate closed class words (for example *ah* (I)) accounted for 13 per cent. Cognate open/closed class words accounted for 7 per cent and non-cognate open/closed class words accounted for 5 per cent. Non-cognate closed class words (for example *gin* (if)) were the least likely to occur (1 per cent).

Section 7.6 gives the breakdown into individual time periods (1995 vs 2005). Building on the discussion of open vs closed class lexis above, it can be argued that open class lexical items, particularly those that are non-cognate with *English*, make more effective and acceptable stylistic overt Scotticisms than closed class *Scots* lexical items (with the proviso that many *Scots* formulaic expressions used as overt signals of Scottishness will of course include closed class *Scots* lexis) (see discussion on formulaic expressions at section 6.2ff). Open class non-cognate items have the advantage of being readily identifiable as *Scots* words, as they are quite markedly differentiated from *English*, and avoid any negative associations of being regarded as 'slovenly' or 'Scotticised' *English* rather than *Scots*. They are therefore the language display lexis of choice in thin contexts. This is borne out by analysis of the correlation with density patterns (see Fig. 5.7). When open/vs closed class and cognate/non-cognate lexis are compared against overall density (calculated at the word level), as expected, non-cognate open class lexis is found in the least dense contexts and cognate closed class lexis was found in comparatively the densest contexts.

5.7 A Language More Fitted for Speech?

As noted in section 3.3, *Scots* operates on two different, though not entirely separate, levels. It operates in both the written and the spoken modes, and although there are links between spoken and written *Scots* language, the two are not necessarily the same thing or as closely related as might be assumed. They are usually rather different types of *Scots*, often exhibiting quite different linguistic characteristics and usage patterns. People will not necessarily use the same amount or type of *Scots* in writing as they do in speech or have the same abilities in both modes, and it is generally accepted that nowadays more *Scots* is spoken than is written. The newspapers are in the written mode but it is worth considering whether direct speech, as a written representation of spoken *Scots*, carries more or less *Scots* lexis than straightforward narrative. Of course, the 'speech' has been mediated by the writer (and indeed editors) and cannot therefore be entirely 'naturalistic'. However, it was considered likely that in the newspapers a potentially significant amount of *Scots* lexis would be found in direct speech (DS) contexts.

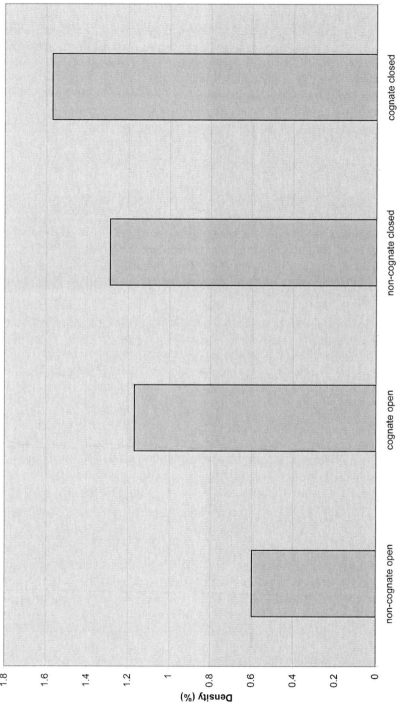

Figure 5.7 Densities: cognate/non-cognate vs open/closed tokens

Thus the corpus was examined to discover whether items of *Scots* lexis were more likely to occur in DS contexts, or in narrative contexts. As discussed in the next section, these two alternatives arguably have implications for the perceived level of commitment to, or distance from, the use of *Scots*, and the potential of *Scots* language for signalling ingroup and outgroup membership. It was also considered possible that certain types of *Scots* lexical items (open/closed class) may be more commonly used in DS contexts (as a representation of the spoken mode in written texts) than in straightforward narrative contexts within the newspapers and this is also investigated in the discussion of DS and open/closed class lexis in the next section.

5.7.1 Methods for research into direct speech contexts

Direct speech was searched for by identifying content contained within quotation marks. There were a few problems with this approach, such as an inability to distinguish direct speech from, for example, literary quotations, as both often used the same conventions. However, arguably the use of *Scots* lexis in literary quotations operates in a similar manner to the use of *Scots* in direct speech. Both show increased distancing compared to the use of *Scots* lexis in narrative. Therefore this 'problem' was not considered to invalidate the analysis. Stretches of first person narration, though likely to show similar patterns to those of direct speech, would have been much more time-consuming to search for, and therefore this avenue of analysis was not pursued.

Overall percentages of direct speech contexts were as follows. In the corpus, the majority of *Scots* lexical items (tokens) (74 per cent) occurred outside quotation marks (that is not DS or quotation). Those that were found within DS/quotation contexts amounted to 26 per cent. Although the majority of contexts were not DS/quotations, a 26 per cent occurrence rate is not an insignificant proportion, especially if one considers that in the newspapers as a whole, the proportion of direct speech/quotation to narrative is likely to be considerably lower than this. Although this was impossible to ascertain definitively (the newspaper resources did not facilitate this type of search), it can be suggested that the use of *Scots* lexis does have some affinity with DS/quotation contexts. A comparison of the average percentages of direct speech contexts at the level of the individual newspapers and years, as discussed in section 7.7, throws up some further interesting points.

It was also suggested in the above, that the actual type of *Scots* lexis (that is open/closed class lexis) might have a bearing on usage inside and outwith DS/quotation contexts vs narrative contexts. Figure 5.8 shows token frequencies in DS and non-DS/quotation contexts categorised by open vs closed class lexis.

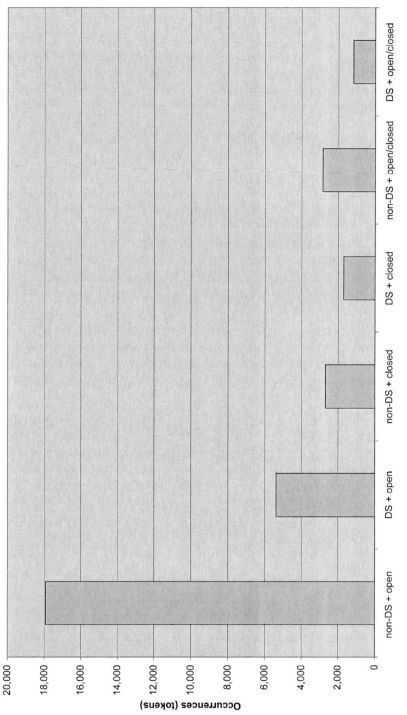

Figure 5.8 DS/non-DS contexts and open/closed class tokens

If we consider the relative proportions of open to closed class lexis in DS and non-DS/quotation contexts, the following patterns emerge. In non-DS contexts, 76 per cent of the tokens were open class, 11 per cent were closed class and 13 per cent could be either open or closed class items. In DS/quotation contexts, 65 per cent of the tokens were open class, 21 per cent were closed class and 14 per cent could be either open or closed class items. Thus there is more of an association of closed class lexis with DS/quotation contexts and for open class lexis with non-DS contexts, and indeed, this is what might have been expected for the following reasons.

One explanation is that some of these closed class lexical items are more generally associated with spoken *Scots* rather than the written mode. Thus, for example, the comparatively high proportions of pronouns such as *ah* and *ye* in DS/quotation contexts are explicable, as these variants are often used to represent unstressed phonological variants (of 'I' and 'you' respectively), and are both listed as such in the *CSD*. These forms are associated with a fairly informal register, and written language is generally more formal than spoken language. Thus it is not surprising that such forms be found in direct speech contexts.

A second explanation for the affinity of closed class lexis for direct speech contexts may be given by the characteristic proportions of open and closed class lexis in written and spoken texts. Although direct speech in the newspapers is evidently in the written mode, it is a representation of the spoken mode, and as such, it may have some characteristics generally associated with speech. The written and spoken modes characteristically have different proportions of open to closed class lexical items. Halliday (1989: 61, 64) argues that written language contains proportionately more lexical content words (that is open class lexis) than grammatical words; and spoken language contains proportionately more grammatical words than lexical content words. Thus it seems reasonable to suggest that straightforward narrative texts may contain comparatively more *Scots* lexical content words than would their spoken counterparts. Conversely, spoken texts, or those in the written mode which represent spoken texts (that is direct speech or first person narrative) may contain a higher proportion of *Scots* closed class/grammatical items than straightforward written narrative prose.

5.7.2 The individual rather than the institutional voice

The patterns noted in this section can be explained by the difference between the individual and the institutional voice. They can also be indicative of the newspapers' degree of commitment to the use of *Scots*.

As suggested above in section 5.7, the use of *Scots* lexis in narrative, rather than through the distancing medium of direct speech, can be perceived as being much more attributable to the journalist or newspaper itself. The use of *Scots* (particularly dense *Scots*) in narrative can be a comparatively risky strategy as there is a reasonably strong implicit suggestion that the journalist and reader share the same variety, that is, that they are being constructed as members of the same discourse community. If, on the other hand, *Scots* is used in direct speech, it need not have that implication and the newspaper, and journalist, is to some extent dissociated from the usage. *Scots* lexis which appears in direct speech can be 'explained' as being the words of an individual. Therefore including *Scots* lexis in direct speech contexts may be 'safer' than using it in straightforward prose as the *Scots* becomes the responsibility of the 'speaker' not the newspaper, with its correct institutional image to maintain.

The situation can again be explained by linguistic appropriacy (see section 4.6). If the speech of individuals, whether in direct or reported speech format, includes some *Scots*, as readers we have the option of adopting an external viewpoint insofar as we can 'explain' their usage in terms of an individual's language choices. This is much easier for a readership to rationalise than the use of *Scots* (especially if it is dense) in extended passages of narrative which appear to belong to the institutional voice of the newspaper. It is reasonably appropriate for real Scottish people to speak, and thus be quoted as speaking, in *Scots*. It is much less appropriate for an institutional voice to do so in narrative. This accords with the observations made earlier in section 5.5.1 that most articles featuring densely *Scots* narrative are not written by journalists.

5.8 Newspapers as a Force for Standardisation?

If the Scottish press, like other newspapers, are engaged in 'verbal hygiene' (defined by Cameron (1995: viii) as 'the urge to meddle in matters of language'), and are therefore concerned to uphold standard language, it is important to consider just what standard form they are seeking to uphold. Due to the prevailing hegemony of *Standard Written English* in Scotland, as everywhere else in the *English*-using world, they are likely to uphold *Standard Written English* or possibly *Scottish Standard English* in formal contexts; but do they or could they also uphold a standard form for *Scots*, at least as far as spelling is concerned? As already discussed in Chapter 3, present-day *Scots* is not a fixed variety and no universally agreed standard *Scots* currently exists. So in the written mode, *Scots* exhibits a fair amount of orthographic variation – a brief look at any of the larger *Scots* dictionaries confirms this. *Scots* orthography has been a hot topic over the years with various recommendations and points of view put forward by language activists, educationalists and academics, but could the newspapers, by adhering to common orthographic preferences, play a role in the development of an agreed standard? This section investigates the variation in orthographic forms used by the newspapers, both within and between newspapers. It was hoped that this would illustrate (1) the level of focus/standardisation associated with the use of *Scots* generally and (2) the emphasis placed on standardised/preferred forms by individual newspapers.

The newspaper data yielded 127 *Scots* lexical items with alternative orthographic forms. The advantage of the expanding word-list methodology was that it found orthographic forms that might not have been anticipated with a fixed word-list of predetermined forms. It should be noted that, in some cases, alternative orthographic forms have different semantic distributions, that is, they do not necessarily have the same meaning in all contexts, and therefore context may determine the preferred form. For example, although there was some overlap between *aye* (843) and *ay* (32), generally each form had a preferred semantic area, with *aye* being used more commonly for 'yes' and *ay* being used more commonly for 'always'.

Across the newspaper corpus, the picture is rather confused. In many cases the frequencies of occurrence were too low to allow any conclusions to be reached. Some items appeared to have only one acceptable variant across all the newspapers, for example *pawky* (48) not *pawkie* (dry sense of humour – there were also 2 occurrences of *pawkily* and 2 occurrences of *pawkiness*), *sonsie* (16) not *sonsy* (plump, cheerful, attractive woman or child), *loon* (68) vs *loun* (1) (boy, lad), but in many other cases significant variation was observed between newspapers. For some fairly common *Scots* items such as *bonnie* (156 occurrences) and *bonny* (115), there seemed to be quite a lot of variation tolerated within each newspaper. Also *fae* (65) vs *frae* (61) (from); *baldie* (21) vs *baldy* (61) (bald-headed person); *stooshie* (30) vs *stushie* (56) (uproar); *scoosh* (18) vs *skoosh* (19) (squirt; easy); *swallie* (11) vs *swally* (23) (drink of alcohol; swallow); *canna* (27) vs *cannae* (109) (cannot); *aa* (15) vs *aw* (122) (all).

On balance, the conclusion must be drawn that at present the newspapers are not actively promoting standardised orthography for *Scots* lexis. Such levels of orthographic variation suggest that standardising *Scots* forms is not seen as a priority. Cameron's (1995) observations on the role of the press in maintaining standards suggest that the Scottish press could have a powerful role to play in the development of a standard *Scots*. However, on the evidence presented here, this looks unlikely to be achieved unless deeply ingrained attitudes to *Scots* in society generally are changed. Developing the argument made in sections 4.4 and 5.4 that newspapers try to use their version of the language of their readers, it can be suggested that a standard *Scots* is probably not important to readers either. Again the discussion returns to the overwhelming hegemony and high status of *Standard Written English* in Scotland today. Even 'good *Scots*' is likely to be viewed as 'bad *English*' if there are no established and agreed models of good *Scots* from which to claim authority. These models do not really exist for *Scots* prose, and therefore it would be very difficult for the Scottish press both to forge and maintain *Scots* standards in the face of the opposition from *Standard Written English*. It is also very doubtful that they would wish to eschew *Standard Written English* or *Scottish Standard English* in favour of a standard *Scots*. The much higher status of *Scottish Standard English* seems likely to discourage the development of a standard *Scots* in the press, as this variety maintains its Scottish identity without compromising, too much, the expected rules of grammar and so on. Problematic status and restricted domains of usage for *Scots* in the newspapers, as demonstrated earlier in this chapter, suggest that, unless there is pressure for the standardisation of *Scots* from other powerful institutions, rather than simply from Scots language activists, *Scots* in the press, and in the public domain generally, is likely to remain unstandardised and crippled by considerations of appropriacy (see discussion in Chapter 8).

5.9 The Industry Perspective

The evidence clearly suggests that the use of *Scots* lexis by the newspapers operates within quite tightly constraining norms which tend to limit its frequency, density and distribution. Language display in the newspapers favours non-cognate and open class *Scots* lexis. There is a frequent association of *Scots* lexis with humour, an interesting affinity of *Scots* lexis for direct speech and/or quotation contexts, but little evidence that the newspapers are worried about normalising orthographic forms for the *Scots* lexis they use. But where do the newspapers stand on all of this? Are they aware of these tendencies in their usage, and/or do they seek to curtail or promote the use of *Scots* lexis? Each of the newspapers studied was contacted in June 2008 and asked the following questions:

1. What are the key means by which your newspaper appeals to its Scottish audience?
2. Is the use of identifiably *Scots* words/phrases something you see as important for a Scottish newspaper/edition to include? If so, why? If not, why not?

3. Does the newspaper have a specific policy as regards the use of *Scots* words/phrases and/or do you provide guidance to your journalists on their use/spelling, for example, in a style guide? To your knowledge, has this policy/guidance changed over time?

Derek Stewart-Brown, managing editor of the *Daily Record*, gave a helpful response (email communication) outlining his views on the use of *Scots* in the press. He explains that, whilst the *Record* is 'a newspaper for Scotland, with Scottish stories and opinion', it also covers UK and international news. It is perceived to be a newspaper that stands up for Scotland, a role it fulfils 'without putting a kilt on everything'. He notes that there is often little cause to use *Scots* lexis in the course of straight news reporting; notable exceptions would be Scots legal stories (because of the distinctive *Scots* terminology) or stories with a particularly Scottish emphasis. In the case of the latter, the journalist might 'use some descriptive Scots. It could be words like *haar*, *dreich*, or expressions commonly used'. He also comments on the much more frequent use of *Scots* words and phrases by columnists, often for humour. His response clearly confirms what has been noted in the foregoing analysis in this chapter, and the *Daily Record* seems typical of the newspapers studied in this respect. *Scots* lexis is certainly not proscribed, but its use does tend to be limited and confined to certain contexts. Stewart-Brown's words aptly sum up the complex relationship between *Scots* lexis and considerations of appropriacy that clearly operates in the newspapers: 'It's probably important that we do use our native language, *where the occasion is befitting*' (my emphasis).

FURTHER READING

1. Electronic versions of most newspapers are now available online via the web. These, and database resources such as *LexisNexis* allow reasonably easy access to a broad range of newspapers and article types. However, it is worth noting that these resources are generally designed for people doing keyword searches to find particular stories or writers, and are not always maximally useful for those wanting to use them for linguistic analysis.

6

A Multifaceted and Formulaic Identity

In Chapter 2, it was suggested that there is no one Scottish identity but
rather that it is a shifting, dynamic and multifaceted phenomenon and that
national identity is likely to be mediated by local and class identities. This
chapter investigates whether this hypothesis is supported by the data by
looking for evidence of regional/local (Edinburgh/Glasgow) and class
(tabloid/broadsheet) identities in the newspaper corpus. Chapter 2 also
underlined the significance of the symbolic as well as the communicative
function of language and argued that language could function as a cultural
totem or signifier. For totems to be effective, they must be visible and
recognisable as such. Thus they depend on the familiar: shared knowledge
and cultural mores, the formulaic and the stereotypical. Discussion in
Chapter 2 suggested that historicity and heritage were important facets in
national identities, and stressed the vertical (historical) as well as horizontal
(contemporaneous) axis. The present chapter investigates the extent to
which this vertical axis can be identified in the newspapers' use of formulaic
features. Formulaic language and Scottish stereotypes offer familiar and
reliable ways of invoking a sense of Scottishness and so this chapter also
deals with the quotations, allusions, proverbs and sayings, idioms and other
fixed expressions and recurring collocations that were noted in the newspaper texts. It considers the potential sources for these and asks what their
significance is in the newspapers' construction and maintenance of a
Scottish identity. This chapter also considers whether particular *Scots* words
and phrases trigger associations with the three well-known Scottish stereotypes outlined in section 2.4.5: Tartanry, Kailyard and Clydesidism, and
investigates whether the appeal to these stereotypes varies between newspapers.

6.1 A Mediated Scottish Identity

This section investigates whether there is any evidence of class-based
and local/regional-based identities in the newspaper data. Class-based

differences were assessed by comparing broadsheet and tabloid data both quantitatively and qualitatively, focusing in particular on usage/non-usage of specific lexical items, lexical frequencies, differences in register of lexical items and usage/non-usage of literary and/or archaic vocabulary. Local/regional differences were assessed by looking for lexis with a localised provenance.

6.1.1 Scottish identity mediated by class identity

Tabloid and broadsheet newspapers are generally perceived to have different readerships, primarily distinguished by class. Although this is a large generalisation, it seems generally to hold true and is borne out by data such as the National Readership Survey where clear correlations can be seen between ABC1 social class groups and broadsheet readerships, and C2DE groups and tabloid readerships. Newspapers also differ widely in their content with tabloids tending to concentrate more on light news, entertainment, celebrity and human-interest stories rather than the in-depth serious news reports that tend to dominate in the broadsheets (see discussion of article types in the *Daily Record* in section 5.2.2). Note, however, that recent years have seen increasing claims of a process of tabloidisation going on in the quality press.

Tabloid and broadsheet newspapers also use different types of language. Again generalisations abound; for example, that the broadsheets tend to write using longer sentences, longer words, using a different type and register of vocabulary from the tabloids, and that the tabloids tend to make more use of word play and other poetic features of language. These differences in language between the newspapers can be viewed as correlating with the differences in their perceived readerships. (C.f. discussion in section 4.4.5.4 surrounding Hall's (1978: 61) assertion that the language newspapers use will be 'the newspaper's own version of the language of the public to whom it is principally addressed' – that is it will be their version of the readers' vernacular. It is a language which is negotiated with the reader, and with which the readership is comfortable.)

The social class divide in readerships is of particular interest in the context of Scottish newspapers, given the broad correlation between social class and linguistic choice posited by the *Scottish-English* continuum. It has frequently been argued that in Scotland, as elsewhere, lexical choice can be indicative of social class. It should of course be remembered that these are tendencies not absolutes, and therefore individuals may on certain occasions, or for certain words, display lexical usage which would not have been expected on the basis of their social class. As discussed in section 3.2.2, working-class and middle-class Scots may have differing degrees of access to and knowledge of the available varieties along the *Scottish-English* continuum, and, of course, in the written mode the situation is considerably complicated by overwhelming hegemonic pressures to write using *Standard Written English*.

Bearing these factors in mind, the Scottish newspapers were investigated to see whether, on a lexical level, any differences could be discerned between the tabloid and broadsheet newspapers. Because data are incomplete for *The Sun* (1995), this comparison has been mainly based on observable differences between the two Scottish broadsheets, *The Herald* and *The Scotsman*, and the tabloid *Daily Record*. Where data for *The Sun* 2005 were available, this has been included for comparison. Unless specified, all data referred to are drawn from both the 1995 and 2005 parts of the corpus. Before looking in detail at the data, it is necessary to note that the perceived differences between use of lexical items in the tabloid and broadsheet newspapers should not be overstated. Many more lexical items in this study appear in all three of the main Scottish newspapers, than have distinctive distributions in the tabloid and broadsheet newspapers. For this part of the study no distinction has been drawn between different orthographic forms of the same word.

As discussed in section 3.10, it was considered likely that the newspapers would use current rather than archaic *Scots* lexis. The original search list deliberately included a few items of archaic lexis to test this hypothesis. As the study progressed it became evident that, especially in the broadsheet *Herald* and *Scotsman*, poetry was quite frequently quoted, and of course, this poetry might in itself contain archaic or essentially literary forms. However, outwith such specialised contexts, it was anticipated that archaic and literary forms were less likely to be used.

Scots items that were found in *The Herald* and *The Scotsman*, but were entirely absent from the *Record* which seem to indicate social class differences or avoidance of archaic and/or literary vocabulary are as follows: *agley* (askew), *airt(s)* (point(s) of the compass), *flyte* (scold, altercate; often used of an abusive contest between poets), *kenspeckle* (familiar), *Lallans* (literary/ Lowland Scots), *makar* (poet), *pawky* (dry sense of humour) and *unco* (very, extremely). These items often occurred as excerpts from well-known literary phrases (for example *a' the airts, the best laid plans o' mice and men gang aft agley, unco guid*). Alternatively, they describe processes, varieties or people associated with literature (*flyte, Lallans, makar*), or are lexical items seldom found outside literary contexts (*kenspeckle*). *Pawky* seems to be another term especially favoured by the broadsheets but avoided by the tabloid *Record*. It is possible it also has literary overtones from a character called Provost

Pawkie in Galt's *The Provost*. The data suggest that Burns has a fairly substantial influence in the lexical choices of the broadsheets ('*A' the Airts*' is a love song by Burns; *agley* occurs as part of a well-known phrase from his poem 'To a Mouse'; 'Address to the Unco Guid' is another of his poems). Further discussion of Burns' influence in the newspapers is given in section 6.9.2.3. The situation was much less persuasive when considered from the opposite point of view, that is which lexical items appeared in the tabloid *Record* but were not found in the broadsheet *Herald* and *Scotsman*, and no clear patterns could be discerned.

The second phase of tabloid/broadsheet analysis was to investigate the relative frequencies with which items appeared in the newspapers. Here again differences were observed between the broadsheet *Herald* and *Scotsman*, and the tabloid *Record*. However, before progressing to the analysis itself, it is important to note that when considering the relative frequencies of certain lexical items, it is necessary also to take into consideration the newspaper's general degree of use of *Scots* lexis (see Table 5.2), that is, is this item proportionately over- or under-represented based on what we know of the newspaper's use of *Scots* lexis generally?

Instances where the *Record* contained higher than expected occurrences of a given lexical item are worth further investigation and are illustrated by Table 6.1. Sometimes *The Sun* (2005) exhibited similar patterns, and therefore the data seem to indicate a tabloid/quality split.

Lexical item	Herald (1995/2005)	Scotsman (1995/2005)	Record (1995/2005)	Sun (2005 only)
Barras	46	31	85	9
bevvy	40	12	112	35
eejit	5	3	21	26
gub	17	15	72	24
ming	2	8	30	36
ned	92	59	357	217
numpty	20	9	51	20
yin	41	52	78	23
wee	1,953	796	3,098	1,141

Table 6.1 Tokens occurring more frequently in the *Daily Record* than expected

Why should these items in particular be especially frequent in the *Daily Record* (and *The Sun*)? The *Barras* is a well-known bargain market near Glasgow Green. *Bevvying* (drinking alcohol) figured significantly in the *Record* and *The Sun* (possibly as related to the Clydeside stereotype – see discussion in section 6.10.3), and the *Record* was the only newspaper to use the colloquial phrase *bevvy merchant* (drunkard). *Eejit* (idiot) is a potentially socially marked item and is not listed in *DSL*; hence slang/colloquial. *Gub* (beat heavily in a contest) is a term most frequently associated with football, which might explain why the *Record* had higher than expected incidences given its well-known strengths in football coverage. *Ming* (to smell strongly and unpleasantly) and its derivatives seems to be a term that has gained wider currency (that is, both within and furth of (*beyond*) Scotland) in recent years. *Ned* (young hooligan) had very high frequencies in the *Record* and *The Sun* (2005). This is interesting as it is a derogatory term most often applied to working-class rather than middle-class hooligans, and hence these newspapers might be expected to avoid it. *Numpty* (stupid person) seems to be another term which is widening in currency. Sixty of the *Record*'s occurrences of *yin* (one) were references to Billy Connolly (the Big Yin), often seen as a working-class icon, compared to 11 occurrences in *The Herald* and 8 in *The Scotsman*, perhaps reflecting the *Record*'s typical tabloid emphasis on entertainment and celebrity 'news'. *Wee* was the most surprising item both in terms of being on the list and also in terms of the very high frequencies found in the *Record* compared to the other newspapers. *Wee* is, of course, a very frequently occurring *Scots* word that does seem to enjoy fairly widespread currency furth of Scotland. As will be discussed in section 6.8, it also has frequent common collocations such as *wee + name* or *wee small hours*.

Some of these differences noted in lexical choice and frequencies between the tabloids and broadsheets may be due to perceived differences in the education and knowledge of Scottish literature of their target readerships. Significantly the *Daily Record* contained few examples of literary lexis. Miller (1998: 55) argues that familiarity with Scottish literature (and hence for some, familiarity with its 'classic' *Scots* lexis/phrases) is usually the preserve of well-educated (usually middle-class) Scots who generally lack *Scots* syntax, whereas younger working-class Scots preserve the *Scots* syntax but have little of the classic vocabulary/phrases. Macaulay (1991), in his socio-linguistic study of variation in speech in the *Ayr* dialect across social classes, notes that 'there are patterns of social class variation in the lexicon' (1991: 117) but cautions that these may not show up in a small corpus and may, to some extent, be mediated by topic (1991: 107). So there do seem to be some differences, but obviously the results of the analysis need to be treated with caution.

Tabloid/broadsheet differences were also noted as regards functional Scotticisms (see section 3.3 and/or Glossary for definition). It is noticeable for *leet* (list of candidates for a job), *retiral* (retirement) and *outwith* (outside, beyond) that the proportion of occurrences in the broadsheets, and *The Herald* especially, are higher compared to the tabloid *Record* than would have been expected, see Table 6.2.

Lexical item	Herald (1995/2005)	Scotsman (1995/2005)	Record (1995/2005)
leet	89	21	8
outwith	637	365	205
retiral	102	25	25

Table 6.2 Functional Scotticisms indicating
a tabloid/broadsheet split

As discussed previously, the broadsheets have different subject matter, and this may be responsible in some part for the differences in figures. They are also generally more formal in tenor which might explain their higher usage of these formal functional Scotticisms. The use of such lexical items in serious formal articles by the broadsheets demonstrates their perceived appropriacy in a very formal text type. That these functional *Scots* lexical items are less often found in the *Record* may also point to deeper issues such as the purposes to which *Scots* lexical items are put in the newspapers, and the linguistic split which seems to exist between the tabloid and broadsheet press. Both the tabloids and broadsheets use some elements of Scottish language, but arguably the language they use shows fundamental differences both in its purpose and realisation. Once again these differences can be related to differences in the Scottish identity (or identities) constructed and maintained by different Scottish newspapers. The broadsheets evidently have a very formal register of *Scottish Standard English* (these functional Scotticisms do not occur with non-standard grammatical features) which is considered suitable for a wide variety of purposes, and is substantially removed from the more usual register associations of *Scots* lexis with informal and humorous contexts.

Aitken's (1984c: 107ff) uber-Scotticisms were also examined (see section 3.9 and/or Glossary for definition). Three of his examples, *to keep a calm sough*, *darg*, and *thrang* were not found in the corpus. Of the remainder, there were only 4 occurrences of *it's back to the auld claes and parritch . . . tomorrow* all in *The Herald* and *The Scotsman*, 25 occurrences of *kenspeckle* all in *The Herald* and *The Scotsman* and *The Times*, and 63 occurrences of *stravaig* – 22 in *The Herald*, 19 in *The Scotsman*, 13 in the *Record*, 8 in *The Times*, 1 in *The Sun*. Aitken suggests that these are primarily used by middle-class Scots and hence might be expected to be more frequent in the broadsheets. However, a clear pattern could not be discerned, so perhaps this is more complicated in the written mode.

So – in summary, although there are many occasions where a particular lexical item is found in all three of the main Scottish newspapers, there were sufficient differences between the tabloid *Record* and the broadsheets to substantiate the hypothesis that they differ to some extent in their use of *Scots* lexis and that these differences broadly correlate with social class divisions in their target readerships.

6.1.2 Scottish identity mediated by local identity

This section investigates whether there was any evidence of an Edinburgh (East)/Glasgow (West) split in the Scottish newspapers. As *The Herald* and the *Daily Record* are produced in Glasgow, and *The Scotsman* is produced in Edinburgh, the corpus was examined to see whether differences could be discerned between the newspapers, as this might indicate local identity is having an impact on Scottish national identity. This assumes that a newspaper's physical location will be reflected in its use of language and, of course, this is not necessarily the case. Smith (1994: 170–1) gives National Readership Survey figures for January–December 1993 (some of which have been excerpted into Table 6.3) which clearly indicate an East/West split. Even though significantly more people reside in Strathclyde than in other parts of Scotland, figures for *The Herald* and the *Record* show proportionately stronger readerships there than elsewhere. Unfortunately detailed 1995 and 2005 breakdown NRS figures were unobtainable, but there is no reason to think these proportions have altered significantly in the intervening years, though undoubtedly actual readership numbers have changed (see section 8.3). There are discernible differences between *The Scotsman* and *The Herald* in terms of content, with *The Scotsman* giving more details on events, advertising and so on based in Edinburgh than in Glasgow, and *The Herald* having a similar Glasgow emphasis. However, that said, *The Herald*, *The Scotsman* and the *Daily Record* all cover a broad range of Scottish stories; therefore they are uncontroversially Scottish national newspapers.

Newspaper	Strathclyde	Lothian	Borders & Dumfries	Fife	Tayside	Grampian	Scotland
Herald	319,500 (82.2%)	10,700 (2.7%)	3,800 (1%)	5,500 (1.4%)	5,500 (1.4%)	6,300 (1.6%)	388,600
Scotsman	23,900 (8.8%)	128,400 (47.6%)	21,000 (7.8%)	23,900 (8.8%)	17,300 (6.4%)	16,700 (6.2%)	269,600
Daily Record	1,113,700 (59.4%)	123,300 (6.4%)	74,300 (4.0%)	128,300 (6.8%)	73,100 (3.9%)	88,000 (4.7%)	1,874,900

Table 6.3 National Readership Survey figures for Jan.–Dec. 1993 showing East/West split (Source: Smith 1994: 170–1)

In order to analyse whether a similar East/West (Edinburgh/Glasgow) split was discernible in the newspaper data, the approach adopted was firstly to see whether there were items which appeared in *The Herald* and *Record* (Glasgow) but not *The Scotsman* (Edinburgh) and vice-versa. Then the relative frequencies of lexical items were investigated to see whether any differences could be detected. *The Herald* and *Record* had a few examples which were not found in *The Scotsman*, such as *bahookie* (backside) (*Glas.*); *gutties* (plimsolls) (*West Central*); *lumber* (a date) (*Glas.*). As can be seen, these lexical items found in both *The Herald* and the *Record* were predominantly drawn from the urban variety Glaswegian, and most are of comparatively recent origin.

On the whole, *The Scotsman* had relatively few words which did not appear in one of the other Scottish nationals and comparatively few of these forms indicated significant differences in provenance. *The Scotsman* was exclusive in having the lexical items *chauve* (struggle, strive) a *north-east* form, and *crannie* (another *north-east* form) which would be contrasted with the lexical item *pinkie* (little finger) elsewhere in Scotland (found in *The Herald*, the *Record* and *The Scotsman*) but the frequencies were much too low to draw any firm conclusions. Many *north-eastern* forms from the original search list were not found in any of the newspapers, for example *barkit* (very dirty), *blaud* (to spoil, damage), *contermacious* (obstinate), *knype on* (to slog), *nabbler* (fast, skilful worker), *peenge* (to moan), *vratch* (despicable, pitiable person). However, *gadgie* (man, lad) (*Herald, Scotsman*), *mannie* (man) (*Herald* and *Scotsman*), *loon* (boy, lad) (*Herald, Scotsman* and *Record*), *quine* (girl) (*Herald, Scotsman* and *Record*), *sharger* (puny person or animal) (*Herald*) and *warsle* (struggle) (*Herald*) are *north-eastern* forms which were found in newspapers from both Edinburgh and Glasgow.

The final strand of analysis for a regional split was based on an investigation of differences in word frequencies. Table 6.4 summarises the interesting points noted, which seem to indicate an Edinburgh/Glasgow divide.

Lexical item	Glasgow (West)		Edinburgh (East)
	Herald	Record	Scotsman
bairn	71	49	29
doon	45	19	28
doon the watter	44	9	8
haar	9	2	41
hen	44	22	6
wean	169	139	29

Table 6.4 Lexical items indicating East/West split

The phrase *doon the watter* (literally 'down the water') is traditionally associated with holidays taken on the Clyde coast, *hen* (a term of endearment, usually applied to women and analogous with 'love', 'duck' and so on elsewhere), is usually thought of as a Glasgow expression, and *wean*, as opposed to *bairn* (child), is generally a West of Scotland usage, and the data bore this out. *Haar* (mist) is traditionally associated with the East coast (although its usage is not restricted to Scotland) and this too was borne out by the data.

The analysis shows that there were some limited lexical differences between the Glasgow-based *Herald* and *Record*, and the Edinburgh-based *Scotsman*; thus to some extent Scottish national identity is being mediated by local identity. (It is interesting to note that in conjunction with the *Daily Record's* 'Real Scots read the Record' campaign, there were also popular bumper stickers saying 'I'm a real Scot from . . .', where the blank was filled by the name of a local Scottish town, for example Airdrie, Dunfermline and so on, thus emphasising local identity.) The term 'limited' is crucial, as an appeal to national identity seems to override local considerations, and highly localised forms are generally avoided or seldom used. It is likely that these newspapers, as they are unwilling to be seen as parochial or regional newspapers and are instead aiming to be Scottish national newspapers, would find it counter-productive to have a high frequency of very localised vocabulary which would be unlikely to be readily understood by readers from other parts of Scotland. As discussed in Chapter 4, it is important that newspapers do not alienate their readers, and a high proportion of localised *Scots* lexical forms would be likely to do this to large sections of the readership. (There seemed to be a particular avoidance of *north-eastern Scots* forms by the newspapers under study, and it would have been interesting to compare results from the *Press and Journal* as it has a very strong following in that part of the country. Presumably for the newspapers based in Central Scotland the use of such forms which are probably alien to their largest readership in the Central Belt, would signal outgroup rather than ingroup membership, and would therefore be avoided.) It can therefore be argued from the data that for these Scottish national newspapers, national Scottish identity outweighs more localised identities. Thus they are unlikely to raise linguistic tariffs which would exclude large proportions of their target readerships from the discourse community. Smith (1996: 73–4) comments on the exclusion of colourful local dialectalisms and the adoption of a '"colourless" dialectal mixture', that is, using forms which 'show no special dialectal distinctiveness' during the evolution of a standard form for *English*. Although as was argued in section 5.8, the newspapers do not seem to be developing or upholding a standard *Scots* in terms of orthography, they do appear to avoid some local dialectalisms and Smith's comment might suggest that perhaps, in some small way, they have made very initial tentative steps on the road towards standardisation.

6.2 IMPORTANCE OF STEREOTYPES AND THE FORMULAIC

In this and the following sections, consideration turns to the analysis of formulaic elements in the language of the newspapers. This takes the discussion of *Scots* lexis in the newspapers one stage further by suggesting that there may be fairly fixed collocational patterns or different types of fixed expressions associated with certain items of *Scots* lexis, and examining what those expressions and lexical items are. 'Fixed expression' is the term used by Carter (1987) and Moon (1998) as a catch-all term for what Fernando (1996: 31) terms 'conventionalised multiword expressions'; so it acts as a blanket term for proverbs, allusions, similes, idioms and so on. The analysis includes examination of quotations, allusions, proverbs, popular wisdom and sayings (including discussion of attribution/non-attribution/labelling) and of idiomatic expressions, other types of fixed expression, and common collocational clusters in the corpus data. Fixed expressions were analysed for variation and productivity as well as frequency.

It can be argued that formulaic language use has as much, if not more, to do with language display and the symbolic function of language, as it has to do with communicative import. Thus it is interesting to consider to what extent the construction/maintenance of Scottish identity by the newspapers depends on well-worn formulaic content (see Wray (2002: 88–9) for discussion of the role of formulaic sequences in helping to assert group identity). Fixed expressions and preferred/restricted collocations were identified using the database's concordance sorting facility. In section 2.4.5, it was suggested that Scottish stereotypes and icons or 'totems', although well-known and mostly clichéd, were still highly salient for Scottish identity. Therefore this analysis of the formulaic elements in Scottish newspaper discourse also includes an examination of the significance or otherwise of the key Scottish stereotypes.

Scots lexis which is used as part of a fixed expression has a rather different significance from *Scots* lexis which stands on its own. Choosing to use *Scots* lexis at all in a text such as a newspaper article is often a largely stylistic decision. There are, however, slightly different stylistic implications between using some items of *Scots* lexis on their own, and using them as part of a longer fixed expression. Choosing to use items of *Scots* lexis in a fixed expression rather than using them as unrestricted lexical options in the language system seems to imply less personal responsibility. Because such expressions are formulaic, their content is predetermined and individual lexical items within the expression cannot be attributed to personal linguistic choices. Their formulaic nature also allows them to be viewed as linguistic totems and icons, as a symbolic act of language display that is sufficiently distanced to be acceptable. Some items of *Scots* lexis may only ever occur as part a fixed expression, that is they are frozen, and therefore have very restricted and predictable contexts. Other items of lexis will occur both as part of a fixed expression, and as stand-alone lexical items.

6.3 Quotations and Allusions

The analysis focused on both straightforward quotations (attributed/un-attributed; with/without quotation marks) and on allusions (expressions which have been ultimately derived from well-known quotations, but the original quotation has been modified in some way and is therefore not in its exact original form (Carter 1987)). In this analysis, as in Carter's, quotations and allusions have been considered together, as quite often both the original quotation and modified versions of it were used by the newspapers, and it is useful to compare both side by side. It is potentially significant whether or not quotations and allusions are attributed and/or placed within quotation marks, as a lack of attribution and/or demarcation from the rest of the text suggests the readership has shared knowledge. This assumption of shared knowledge is highly salient in the construction/maintenance of a common Scottish identity.

The majority of the expressions classed as quotations were straightforward reproductions of the original, generally enclosed within quotation marks. Quotations were especially common from *Scots* poems, and could be in quotation marks and/or attributed. Examples of this type would be *Facts are chiels that winna ding* (Burns: 'Dream IV'), *the best laid plans of mice and men gang aft agley* and *wee, sleekit, cowrin timorous beastie, thou need na start awa sae hasty* (Burns: 'To a Mouse'), *awa wi the excise man* (Burns: 'The Diel's Awa wi the Excise Man'), *sic a wife as Wullie had, I widnae gie a button for her* (Burns: 'Wille Wastle'), *gie's a hand o thine* (Burns: Auld Lang Syne), [God's] *braw birling earth* (Murray: 'Gin I were God'). Whether or not the reader is given any assistance with the attribution of the quotation seems to vary, and probably no strong conclusions can be drawn from the patterns observed. If quotation marks are included, they overtly signal that the enclosed text is a quotation. If attributions are not given, it is presumably assumed that the reader is familiar with the expression, that is, that they have shared knowledge. Some of the attributions, such as 'to paraphrase

Rabbie himself' or 'and this is adapted from another poet, Rabbie What-sisname', overtly suggest familiarity with Burns. 'Ayrshire's bardic dictum' is a more formal example of attribution. Some quotations were neither attributed nor in quotation marks and these are significant as the reader needs a fair amount of knowledge to recognise them as quotations. As will be discussed further in section 6.9.2.3, clearly Burns is the source of many of the quotations.

Allusions, like quotations, could also be attributed or unattributed. Many of the allusions 'worked' by playing around with the original wording to create interesting effects or word play. Thus for example, *the best laid plans o' mice, men and homebuyers go desperately agley* (discussed further in section 6.7). It was noticeable that the majority of quotations and allusions were to be found in the broadsheets rather than in the tabloids. So the prediction that a familiarity with Scottish literature is more likely to be presumed of broadsheet readers seems to be sustained.

6.4 Proverbs, Popular Wisdom and Sayings

According to Carter (1987: 59), proverbs 'convey some kind of aphoristic truth, are usually in the simple present tense and are normally neither syntactically divisible nor substitutable (though this is not to say that creative mutation or distortions are not possible)'. Examples from the newspapers would be: *a close mouth catches nae flees* (a closed mouth catches no flies); *mony a mickle maks a muckle* (many little things make a big thing); *ne'er cast a cloot til May is oot* (don't cast a cloth until May is out); *a fat soo's erse is aye well greased* (a fat sow's behind is always well greased); *a gaun fit's aye getting* (lit. a going foot is always getting there); *a fair maid tocherless will get mair wooers than husbands* (a pretty girl without a dowry will get more wooers then husbands); *we maun dree our weird* (we must endure our fate); *a bairn maun creep afore it gangs* (lit. a child must crawl before it can walk). Popular wisdom and sayings are fairly closely related to proverbs. However, although these are popular 'sayings', they do not contain the 'aphoristic truth' element which sets proverbs apart. Thus, for example, *hauf past ten and no' an erse skelpt* (half past ten and not a behind smacked) in *The Herald* would fall into this category.

The data illustrated several interesting points concerning *Scots* proverbs and sayings. Firstly, a large proportion of these expressions were explicitly labelled as 'proverbs' or 'popular wisdom' by the newspapers. These were often identified in the newspapers as being something along the lines of 'the old saying' or 'the Scots proverb'. This marks the expression as formulaic, and as an overt act of language display. It acts in a similar way to attribution in terms of drawing attention to the source of the expression, and overtly signalling an act of language display. The use of phrases such as 'old Scots saying' highlights the appeal to shared knowledge which constructs readers as part of the same Scottish national culture as the newspaper. These glosses also claim historicity, especially with the frequent inclusion of the word 'old'. This can be seen as an attempt to kindle cultural nostalgia, and as was noted in section 2.1, a sense of historicity (that is the vertical dimension) is very important in constructing national identity. Many of these proverbial expressions were contained within inverted commas. This marks them off from the rest of the text and explicitly draws readers' attention to the fact that the saying is formulaic. It also distances the saying from the surrounding narrative.

One factor that was surprising was how many of these proverbial expressions were contained within lists of proverbs and sayings, presumably there for display purposes, that is, for their own sake, rather than to communicate any informational or attitudinal content. Many of these lists suggested that there was an ongoing dialogue between the readers and the journalist about what these sayings actually meant, whether or not they were significant, and who could collect and display the largest number, a sort of proverbial trophy hunt with many of the proverbs provided by readers 'writing in', often to *The Herald* or *The Scotsman* 'Diary'. The corpus suggests it is overwhelmingly the broadsheets that go in for such proverb displays. Proverbs were found in the tabloids, but not usually as part of a proverb collection. Interestingly Donaldson (1986: 29), in his study of the Victorian press, notes of the *People's Journal* (a newspaper aimed at the working classes) that there were frequently articles on *Scots* proverbs and songs, so the phenomenon is not a new one, though its target audience may have shifted.

It can be argued that this dialogic exchange of proverbs is significant for two reasons. Firstly, it helps to maintain the reader/writer/newspaper relationship by encouraging readers to get involved in the discussion. Thus, this ongoing exchange of proverbial wisdom can be considered to be a feedback mechanism within the discourse communities which serve to strengthen it (c.f. Bex 1996). Secondly, this process is, in itself, a sort of language display. These expressions are not included in the newspaper to fulfil any communicative purpose; they are simply there in a symbolic capacity, as part of a common linguistic heritage. Knowing the proverb is a sign of group membership. Comments made by journalists such as 'impenetrable thought for the week' and 'translations provided on request' suggest that comprehension is less important for these expressions than visibility and obvious Scottishness. The latter comment might also suggest that readers, as part of the discourse community, do not need translations, as they will already be familiar with these expressions, and this is also suggested by the comment in *The Scotsman* that the reader who supplied the proverb has provided the unnecessary translation of *tocher* as 'dowry'. The assumption is that Scottish readers, as part of the discourse community, will have shared knowledge and understand and be familiar with the proverb and the lexis it contains. Whether or not this presumed knowledge has any basis in reality is, of course, open to debate. I am not at all sure that most readers would know what *tocher* actually means, but as noted in section 2.3.1, language display is most successful in contexts where it is unlikely to be challenged. However, whether accurate in its assumptions or not, the process emphasises shared knowledge of Scottish proverbs, hence strengthening and reaffirming the notion of the wider Scottish community. The use of proverbs and popular wisdom by the newspapers seems to presuppose a common Scottish culture with a common Scottish heritage, and knowledge of the proverbial expression is the linguistic tariff, simultaneously constructing 'knowledgeable' readers as part of the Scottish culture, and excluding others who do not share the same knowledge. Moon (1998: 257) asserts that 'metaphors and proverbs, informational and evaluative FEIs [fixed expressions and idioms], appeal to shared knowledge and to shared values . . . FEIs represent institutionalised sociocultural values.' The assumption that readers will have shared knowledge, the appeal to historicity, the overt language display and the feedback mechanisms for contributing examples of Scottish proverbs to the newspaper all serve to construct the readership as part of a shared Scottish culture, and contribute to the construction/maintenance of Scottish identity.

6.5 IDIOMATIC EXPRESSIONS

'Pure idioms' (Fernando 1996) or 'full idioms' (Carter 1987) are defined as being semantically opaque; that is to say the semantic sum of their constituent parts does not 'add up' to give their idiomatic meaning. They do not mean what they literally say. An example of an 'idiom' from the newspaper data would be *to put one's gas at a peep* (to take the wind from one's sails), versions of which are found in all three Scottish newspapers. Other idioms found in the newspaper data include: *to get one's jotters* (to get the sack); *jacket on a shoogly nail/peg* (one's job being insecure); *cauld kale het up* (an old story retold); *birling in his grave* (turning in his grave). These were found across the newspaper types. All three of the Scottish newspapers used *Scots* idioms to some extent.

6.6 OTHER FIXED EXPRESSIONS

Other types of fixed expression (Carter 1987) or 'conventionalised multi-word expressions' (Fernando 1996: 31) noted in the data were:

1. similes, for example *as obvious as clabber on a coo's erse* (as obvious as muck on a cow's behind) (*Herald*)
2. what I have termed colloquial imperatives (expressions which are colloquial in register, and imperative in mood) for example *bile yer heid* (boil your head) (*Herald* and *Record*) and *haud yer wheesht* (be quiet) (*Herald* and *Record*)
3. common colloquialisms (formulaic 'turns of phrase' which are fairly fixed in form, well-known and hence institutionalised, and colloquial in register) for example *Help ma boab* in *The Record*, a well-known phrase from *The Broons* and *Oor Wullie*.

Similes were more frequent in the broadsheets; colloquial imperatives and common colloquialisms were found in both tabloid and broadsheet newspapers.

6.6.1 Language variety of contexts for idioms and fixed expressions

Even a cursory glance shows that fixed expressions and idioms are mainly found in thin *Scottish-English* contexts, but very seldom in broad *Scots* contexts. Why should this be the case? The answer may well be found in a consideration of the functions of idioms and fixed expressions in language as a whole, and the function of Scottish language elements in the language of Scottish newspapers. The use of a *Scots* fixed expression in a passage of thin *Scottish-English* can be viewed as a shorthand and safe way of evoking Scottishness, and an overt act of symbolic language display. Where there are self-contained *Scots* fixed expressions or idioms, the digression into *Scots* can be easily compartmentalised by the reader as being a *Scots* saying, and not directly attributable to the habitual language use of the individual or the newspaper. They can be accepted as 'merely turns of phrase' and the fact that many of them are glossed in the text as being (old) sayings, probably reinforces this view. Thus language display is achieved without the usual compromise in register that would attend extended passages of dense *Scots*, which would be more likely to require mental engagement by the reader, and could be interpreted as showing much more commitment to the use of *Scots* language varieties. Interestingly Backus (1999) argues that code-switching transitions occur 'at the boundaries of formulaic sequences' (cited in

Wray 2002: 41), so people are often switching from thin contexts when using these *Scots* formulaic phrases.

Some of these expressions seemed to contain words that are unlikely to appear using their literal meaning elsewhere, unless perhaps in a sample of dense *Scots*. Lexical items such as *pairt(s)* from *airt(s) and pairt(s)* and *lad o' pairts* fall into this category. The concordances for *pairt* show that, other than in these formulaic contexts, it is only ever used in passages of dense *Scots*. Hence this word, if not in dense *Scots* contexts, seems to be restricted to use in these formulaic expressions and does not seem to be available in the newspapers for thin *Scottish-English* contexts.

6.7 Variation and Productivity

Fixed expressions work and are used by very virtue of their familiarity. They start from a conventional and agreed basis, and then either reiterate the construction, or modify it in some way. Analysing the data, it became evident that some fixed expressions were more productive (that is could be modified, played around with) than others. The data were analysed to discern the extent to which variation was allowable and types of productivity found in fixed expressions. Variation within idioms and fixed expressions can be syntagmatic and paradigmatic; that is to say there can be variation at the level of the actual grammatical word slots, that is, different noun choices, verb choices and so on, or there can be variation in terms of the overall syntactic structure of the expression or idiom. Obviously there are some places where it is more likely that variation will occur than others. For example, it is presumably quite common for different parts of the verb, 1st person, 3rd person, plural forms and tenses, to be used to make the expression fit better with that to which it refers. The situation can therefore be considered as having a cline of variation vs fixity, with some expressions allowing considerably more variation than others. Certain categories of fixed expression seem more tolerant of variation than others. The general areas where expressions can be modified were observed to be as follows.

Firstly there can be variation between singular and plural forms: for example *chiels* or *chiel* in versions derived from the base form *facts are chiels that winna ding* (*Herald, Scotsman* and *Record*), such as *it's a chiel that winna ding*. This is very superficial variation.

Secondly, there can be variation in form: either between different Scottish spellings – for example *laldie* and *laldy* in *Gie it laldy* (do it with vigour) (*Herald, Scotsman* and *Record*) that is orthographic variation; or between Scottish or English versions of the same lexical item – for example *jaiket/jaikit* vs *jacket* in *jaiket on a shooglie nail* (*Herald, Scotsman* and *Record*). Idioms with alternative forms included: *There's* **no** place like **home** vs *there's* **nae** *place like* **hame**; **turning** *in his grave* vs **birling** *in his grave*; *going* **down** *the* **drain** vs *going down/***doon** *the* **stank**; *to get your* **books** vs *to get your* **jotters**. Anglicisation seems to explain *the best laid plans o' mice and men* **gang** *aft agley* becoming . . . **go** *agley*; **mony** *a mickle* becoming **many** *a mickle*; *a fat* **soo's** *erse is aye* **weel** *greased* becoming *a fat* **sow's** *erse is aye* **well** *greased*; **maun** *sit on the blister* becoming **must** *sit on the blister*; *auld* **claes** *and* **parritch** *varying with auld claes and* **porridge**; *doon the* **watter** in one instance becoming *doon the* **water**; **bile** *yer/yir heid* can become **boil** . . . *heid*; **Whaur's yer** . . . *noo?* varying with **where's your** . . . *noo?*. It is interesting to note that in most cases of Anglicisation, an item of cognate *Scots* lexis has been replaced with its *English* cognate form. Presumably cognate lexis is easier to replace with an *English* item precisely because they are already closely related cognates. These are more or less direct lexical substitutions. The substitution does not appear to be entirely random, as some permutations would appear to be disallowed. For example *bile yer head* would be very unlikely, although *boil yer heid* is allowed; as would *old clothes and parritch* as opposed to *auld claes and porridge* which would be acceptable. As Aitken (1979: 86) notes, '[T]here is a general tendency to associate Scots expressions with other Scots expressions and English expressions with other English expressions and some juxtapositions of items across the system are probably disallowed.' There were also examples of straightforward lexical substitution of one synonym for another without a change in linguistic variety: to return to the example above, *coats* or *jackets* (c.f. *jaikets/jaikits* discussed above) can be used, as can *nails* or *pegs. Also God's braw birling earth/world* (*Herald* and *Scotsman*). In such cases neither the semantic nor the stylistic import is greatly affected.

Thirdly, there can be minor lexical substitutions for person, tense and so on: for example (*will be*) *birling in his/their grave(s)*. Again, these do not have much effect on the semantic import of the expression; they merely make it more relevant to the situation being described. More significant lexical substitutions which seek to tie the expression more closely to the subject under discussion can also be seen. This may also involve word play, for example, *Scots wham* **Malcolm** *Bruce has aften led* in the *Record*, instead of *Scots wham Bruce has aften led*; *Whaur's your* **Torremolinus** *noo?* in *The Times*, instead of *Whaur's yer Wullie Shakespeare noo?*; *ya wee sleekit, timrous, cowerin'* **bassstart** in *The Herald*, instead of *wee sleekit, cowerin, timorous beastie* (the last being another quotation from Burns).

There are examples of syntactic variation where the syntactic form of the derived version is significantly different from the original: for example *like all the best plans, this one went agley* (Herald); *Where, come to that, are all those cloots actually cast when May is 'oot'?* (Herald). This may include the reversal of the usual order in a paired construction, for example *auld claes and parritch* (Herald) or *back to parritch and auld claes, as my grandmother used to declare* (Scotsman).

Some expressions are shortened, for example *a gaun fit's aye getting* in The Scotsman. Note that quite often the abbreviated version comes to be better known than the full version.

Finally there are instances of semantic productivity (c.f. Glucksberg 1993: 15–16) where the alterations result in a change to the meaning of the expression: for example *cauld kail followed by mince* in the *Record*, instead of *cauld kail het again*. This example is interesting as it actually modifies the meaning of the expression. It also defamiliarises it, as in the original the *cauld kail* is purely figurative. When put alongside mince, which in addition to being a synonym for 'rubbish' is also a foodstuff, it seems to concretise the 'kail' and remove the figurative aspect. In *lang may your lum no reik peat* in *The Scotsman*, a modified version of *lang may your lum reek* which wishes long life and prosperity on the recipient, a similar change is being made. Peat gives a very smoky fire, and thus although the overall meaning has not been changed, the figurative meaning of the expression has in a sense been concretised. *Jock Tamson's enfants* in *The Herald* is a variation on the well-known expression *we're all Jock Tamson's bairns*, which means we are all part of a common humanity. The substitution of the *French* word *enfants* for *bairns*, which makes it more relevant to the French content of the story, the Auld Alliance anecdote competition, seems to comically undermine the expression; *enfants* although meaning much the same, presumably being much more pretentious (also language display!) than *bairns*. Semantic productivity is likely to be quite important in newspaper texts and especially headlines, as these texts often 'play' with language through puns and so on. Versions of *the best laid schemes o' mice and men* seemed to be the most productive of the expressions considered, that is, it allowed the greatest amount of variation. This may be because it is very well-known. It is, of course, also from Burns.

Based on the results obtained it is not possible to say definitively that the broadsheets use more idiomatic and fixed expressions than the tabloids, or vice versa. However, as suggested above, there may be a case for attempting to distinguish in register between the expressions found in the tabloids and the broadsheets, a split which has been investigated throughout this study. Again, this is not an exact science, and there are colloquial expressions which are found in the broadsheets, and more 'learned' ones which are found in the tabloid *Record*. For example, *dinnae rax yer cackie* is found only in *The Scotsman*, but the *Record* does include a variation of *facts are chiels that winna ding*. That proviso aside, there were some expressions that were exclusively found in the broadsheets which tend to be associated with middle-class Scots speakers. Certain examples of these fixed expressions do seem to signal membership of the middle-class Scottish club. Expressions such as *lad o' pairts* and *frae/from a' the airts* fall into this category, and are more frequently found in *The Herald* and *Scotsman*, that is, Scottish broadsheet newspapers. Others which were exclusive to the broadsheets included some of the literary quotations, for example *best laid plans . . .*, *wee sleekit, cowerin, timorous beastie, sic a wife as Wullie had . . .* which are all Burns quotations and only appear in *The Herald* and *Scotsman*, not in the *Record*. As was argued in Chapter 5, this may be attributable to perceived differences in the literary knowledge of the majority of the newspaper's readership.

The argument is more difficult to apply in the opposite direction, with many colloquial expressions being included in the broadsheets; however, a few fixed expressions which are found only in the *Record* and seem to be quite colloquial in register are *on the bevvy* (also found in *The Sun* 2005); *to go one's dinger* (to lose one's temper or do something enthusiastically) which Aitken (1979: 109) cites as a predominantly working-class expression, *gies a break, tak a dram wi' a trusty fiere* (slogan for Grant's whisky advertising campaign). Thus once again, the data illustrate differences between the *Scots* expressions used by the tabloid and broadsheet newspapers. The contrast in the use of literary quotations, in particular, suggests that these differences can again be related to the social stratification of the target readerships.

6.8 Common Collocational Clusters

Common collocational clusters are characterised by being generally shorter, behaving differently from, and usually being less restrictive than fixed expressions. In this study collocations were simply considered to be words which occurred next to each other, that is co-occurrence. The research focused primarily on immediate collocations, that is, words which occurred right next to, or very near to each other. The maximum horizons on either side of the node word for collocations in this study (meaning the central word in the concordance display, that is, the initial word searched for) were three words to either side of the node word. There is no magical significance attached to this number. It simply made the data collection manageable.

Any word occurring next to any other word can be considered to be a collocate of that word, but in this part of the study the focus is on collocations which are repeated or seem to be significant in some way. Within the syntagmatic constraints of the sentence or phrase unit, there are vast numbers of words that can fill the noun, verb, adjective slots and so on. What is interesting is where these choices seem to be preferred or restricted in some way. It can be argued that, as is the case with idioms and fixed expressions, clichéd/dead collocations can be used either as a shorthand way of signalling Scottishness, in terms of subject matter, point of view and so on, or in a rather tongue-in-cheek self-conscious manner. Using a corpus with a reasonable amount of data, it is possible to see collocational patterns that might have been previously unsuspected. Sometimes this can give quite a lot of extra information about the connotative meanings associated with particular words.

The most commonly occurring phrase in the newspaper data was * *wee bit* with 1,113 occurrences. As the most commonly occurring lexical item in the corpus and in each of the newspapers, *wee* had other characteristic collocations such as proper names, *wee Andrew* and so on, for siblings *wee brother/sister*, people *wee boy/girl/lad/laddie/ lassie/man/wumman*, but also, for example *wee small hours*, *wee ones* and so on and applied to both animate and inanimate objects. Quite often lexical items or node words tend to have collocates that have similar semantic import. Some lexical items seem to have even tighter semantic restrictions on the collocates they can have. For example *gey* (very, exceptionally) generally seems to be associated with negative concepts – *gey auld*, *gey difficult*, *gey few*, *gey hacket*, *gey hard*, *gey queer*, *gey scarce*, *gey sinister*, *gey strange*, *gey weird*. This is not something that is discernible from the *DSL* dictionary definition. Possibly it is characteristic of the use of this lexical item in newspaper texts, but *gey bonnie* and so on seems fairly unlikely and is not attested here. *Bonnie/bonny* is predictable with *baby*, *lad*, *lassie* but much less so with *man/woman*. This suggests that Sinclair's (1991: 110–12) argument that 'the idiom principle' places restrictions on the way lexis is used is correct. Sometimes only a sizeable corpus can reveal such patterns. Some predictable collocations become so firmly entrenched that they become clichéd or dead collocations and are therefore unavailable for regular descriptive use – for example *bonnie Scotland*.

6.9 Sources of the Formulaic

The following sections discuss the sources and influences behind many of these fixed expressions and restricted/clichéd collocations.

6.9.1 Importance of kinship, ancestral wisdom and nostalgia

Two of Scotland's prominent cultural stereotypes, Kailyardism and Tartanry, look backwards to 'better times'. As discussed in Chapter 2,

Anderson (1991) stresses the importance of historicity in the construction of national identity. *Scots* sayings and proverbs have symbolic significance because they are at least ostensibly old. Whether or not they would be used frequently in present-day Scotland is not the issue. What matters is that they are a link with the past. This is of course not restricted to *Scots* proverbs. Most proverbs and old sayings are imbued with a sense of wisdom because they are perceived to be old. What is significant with respect to the *Scots* ones, however, is the way in which they preserve, in that very restricted context, *Scots* words which are not now generally part of the Scottish repertoire. For example, lexical items such as *tocherless* ('without a dowry' – now chiefly literary), *gryce* (a young pig – now a localised term), *weird*, meaning 'fate' (now chiefly literary) (all as cited in *CSD*) are not now in general use but are preserved or fossilised in fixed expressions. There can be persistence of symbolic function even if communicative function has now largely been lost.

It is not surprising that 'age', in terms of 'historicity', is often cited to claim authenticity and importance for some of these expressions. As discussed earlier, many of the proverbs are glossed by the newspapers themselves as being 'old sayings/maxims' and so on. A strong link in the maintenance of a nation's culture has always been the family. Sayings and stories are passed down through the generations from father to son, mother to daughter. In two of the newspapers' glosses to these expressions, this idea is explicitly referred to. The *back to parritch and auld claes, my grandmother used to declare*, and the reference to 'a saying of my [the writer's] father's' with reference to *a fat soo's erse is aye weel greased*, both invoke the authority of ancestral wisdom and a feeling of cultural nostalgia.

6.9.2 Interaction with other facets of Scottish culture

There are other aspects of Scottish culture that appear to be important. Many of the expressions seem to tap into resonances from various facets of Scottish life and culture, such as music-hall routines, popular Scottish songs, the importance of national rugby and football in creating a national focus, and references to well-known Scottish literature, particularly the works of Burns. These aspects of Scottish culture are discussed in the following.

6.9.2.1 The music hall

As already suggested, there appears to be an attempt made to invoke a nostalgic sense of Scottishness. One such resource is the Scottish music-hall culture of the Stanley Baxter, Harry Lauder and 'Francie and Josie' stable.

Aitken (1979: 109) describes *crivvens! jings! help ma boab!* (found in *The Herald*, *Scotsman*, *Record* and *The Sun* 2005) as a 'stock music-hall stereotype'. The expression is also familiar to readers of *The Broons* and *Oor Wullie* (comic strip characters in *The Sunday Post*, annual collections also published). *C'moan get aff* (found in *The Herald* and *Record*) is derived from the music-hall stereotype of a *clippie* (bus conductor) (see Marshalsay (1992) for discussion of these influences).

6.9.2.2 Sport

As seen in the preceding chapter, sports reports account for a substantial part of the overall usage of *Scots* lexical items. There is also a connection between sport and certain *Scots* fixed expressions. It may be useful to consider whether the well-known syncretism of national sport (especially football and rugby) and nationalism in the minds of many Scottish people is having an influence. The quotation from 'Flower of Scotland', about being *sent hamewards tae think again* seems mostly to be reserved for reports on national football or rugby events, especially where there is a contest against the English; thus the conceptual metaphor about sport being war is being applied very specifically to conflicts between the English and the Scots. Of course, 'Flower of Scotland' is also used as an anthem at such events, and therefore has a close association with national matches.

6.9.2.3 Burns: the national bard

Burns seems to play a very significant role in newspapers' attempts to constitute a sense of Scottish culture. Many of the quotations identified by the study were quotations from Burns. This is perhaps not surprising given his popularity and his works being relatively well-known to a large part of the population, more so than those of say Gavin Douglas or William Dunbar. To use or refer to a quotation from Burns seems to be a reliable way of evoking a Scottish atmosphere, but perhaps one which has become a little hackneyed. Burns is considered to be Scotland's national bard, and it can be argued that the recognition of quotations from his works, or allusions made to them, is an integral part of being Scottish. Thus again, a linguistic tariff (or in this case a literary tariff) is being raised, which must be met if one is to be truly considered Scottish. Drakakis (1997: 153) suggests that the Shakespeare canon can be used 'as a resource for what Dr Johnson called "practical axioms and domestick wisdom" and as a repository for universal truths'; that is Shakespearean quotations being used as out of context 'sound-bites' to comment on current events, thus either legitimising events or obscuring their reality. Corbett (1998: 79–82) suggests that for Scots, Burns as a national bard may be an equally potent figure, and may be invoked in much the same way. Thus knowledge of the works of Burns helps construct readers as Scots. Burns was salient for the tabloid *Record* as well as for the broadsheets, although proportionately fewer Burnsian expressions were found in the *Record*. His appeal as Scotland's national bard appears to transcend class boundaries; to some extent this may be due to his image as a working-class hero.

6.10 Words which Trigger Scottish Stereotypes

This section considers whether certain lexical items trigger certain stereotypes, and whether this can in turn be related to the differences in social class reflected in linguistic choice discussed earlier. As discussed in section 2.4.5, Scottish newspapers may make use of or refer to particular Scottish stereotypes. The main consideration there was the key features of these stereotypes and why they might be used by the newspapers. Here consideration moves to whether certain lexical items trigger Scottish stereotypes, and therefore whether certain stereotypes can be associated with certain newspapers. With such a large volume of data, it would have been extremely time consuming to read every article and assess whether or not it exploited or made reference to any of these Scottish stereotypes. More importantly, as the main focus of this study was on the use of *Scots* lexis by the Scottish newspapers as an essential part of the Scottish construct, it was more useful to begin with the lexis and then search for the stereotypes. The hypothesis was that individual items of *Scots* lexis can act as 'triggers' for Scottish stereotypes. For example, mention *heather* and a whole series of associations may be made. The clichéd collocation *bonnie purple heather* springs to mind, or a mental picture of the Scottish countryside, complete with its stereotypical associations of ruggedness, the Highlands and Tartanry, and so on. Just as a cartoon of a Scotsman in a kilt can trigger a whole set of associations, so too can certain items of *Scots* lexis. The stereotypes themselves can act as 'shorthand' for Scottishness; and similarly certain lexical items can act as shorthand for Scottish stereotypes. This is, of course, an argument with applications beyond this particular study.

Whilst it would have been a mistake to attempt to assign all the *Scots* lexical items under analysis to particular Scottish stereotypes, there were certain ones which did seem to be associated particularly strongly with certain stereotypes. For example, the *lad o' pairts* is essentially a Kailyard concept, and therefore might be expected to be used in essentially Kailyard contexts, or to express essentially Kailyard values.

6.10.1 Tartanry

For the Tartanry stereotype, the very productive lexical item *bonny/bonnie* was investigated. *Bonny/bonnie* is often linked to concepts such as Bonnie Prince Charlie (an icon of Tartanry), the Scottish Tourist Board's use of 'bonnie Scotland' and so on. There were 271 occurrences of *bonnie/bonny* in the corpus. (The proper name collocation *Bonnie/Bonny Prince Charlie* was omitted from the original corpus searches and concordance results.) *Bonnie/bonny* was often associated with Loch Lomond as in the song lines 'bonnie, bonnie banks of Loch Lomond'. This construction could either be given in the original form, or modified in some way; but it is clearly highly formulaic. (There were 47 occurrences of the collocation *bonnie/bonny* [sometimes *bonnie/bonny* was repeated] *banks*.) However, other interesting associations with this lexical item in *The Herald* were concepts such as the description of scenery, golf, cultural events (for example Burns festival), conservation, thistles, pipe bands, the TV programme *Take the High Road*, in addition to the quoting of song titles or lines containing this lexical item. *Bonnie/bonny* may also be used in other formulaic contexts such as *bonnie purple heather*. Other things which are often described as *bonnie/bonny* are flowers, women, babies and children. *The Scotsman* largely followed these sorts of themes, with the addition of Scottish rugby, Highland regiments, haggis and references to *Bonnie Dundee*, sometimes used in its original historical sense (that is as a name) and sometimes modified to discuss the present-day Scottish city. The *Daily Record* generally followed this pattern of using *bonnie/bonny* in traditional or stereotypical Scottish (cultural) contexts, for example, references to Flora MacDonald, films such as *The Bruce*, tartan and tweeds. It is thus fair to say that *bonnie/bonny* was used in the newspapers in fairly restricted contexts which often fit in with concepts associated with Tartanry such as Scotland's scenery, its historic past, the Highlands and haggis.

6.10.2 Kailyard

For the Kailyard stereotype, *lad o'pairts* and *pawky* were investigated. *Lad o' pairts* has already been discussed above (section 6.10), and *pawky*, with its associations of down-to-earthness and humour, fits in with Kailyard notions. It had originally been intended to include *canny* as an item which triggered the Kailyard stereotype, but although this seemed likely, it was abandoned for two reasons: firstly, because *canny* can also be used in *English* (sometimes with a slightly different meaning) therefore it is not unique to *Scots*, and secondly because there were far too many entries to make this practicable. There were only 15 occurrences of *lad o' pairts* in the corpus; its variant, *man o' pairts*, had 3 occurrences. *Lad o' pairts'* meaning of 'poor boy made good' with the aid of that perceived great leveller, the Scottish educational system, is central to the Kailyard stereotype; therefore it was unsurprising to see that these were usually the contexts in which it was mentioned. Thus, for example, *The Herald* contains stories of poor students surviving at university on porridge (albeit tongue-in-cheek), a prominent Glasgow lawyer from humble origins, and the son of a shepherd who was sent to Rome to study for the priesthood and became a scholar. What is potentially much more interesting, however, is that this item was much more likely to be used by *The Herald* and *The Scotsman* than the *Record* which had only one occurrence of this expression, and that as a graphics caption rather than in the body of the text. This might fuel speculation that the *lad o' pairts* stereotype is predominantly a middle-class concept, and is not a rallying point for readers of the (presumably generally more working-class) *Daily Record*. It is very interesting to note that when the *Record* (1995) was speaking of the golfer Sam Torrance, he was associated with the term *bunnet* (head covering for men or boys, including all kinds of caps) and described as 'a local boy made good'. Thus the concept of the *lad o' pairts* was there, but not lexicalised. Instead, he was described as 'the archetypal working class hero'.

A similar example, although not investigated exhaustively here, would be the use of *Jock Tamson's bairns* (thirty-one occurrences in the corpus). McCrone (1992) discusses both the *lad o' pairts* and *Jock Tamson's bairns* and links them with the egalitarian 'myth': the former (*lad o' pairts*) expressing the idea that anyone, no matter if from humble origins, can 'get on in life' if they work hard and apply themselves to their education; and the latter (*Jock Tamson's bairns*) being that rich or poor, we are all part of the same common humanity. The commonly occurring phrase *we're all Jock Tamson's bairns* of course constructs readers as part of a shared community.

Pawky has 48 occurrences in the corpus. In *The Herald*, it often had in its immediate context 'humour' or 'humorous', which is not surprising given its meaning. People are often described as *pawky*, and there seems to be no real restriction on who can be described as *pawky*, although it is often associated with traditionally positive Kailyard attributes such as honesty, canniness, integrity and shrewdness (Galt's Provost Pawkie, however, was shrewd, but also cannily lined his own pockets). Other patterns do suggest themselves, such as the association between writing/writers and something being described as *pawky*. Music seems to be another creative area where *pawky* might, perhaps rather unexpectedly be used. These tendencies were also borne out in *The Scotsman*. As noted in section 6.1.1, the *Record* had no occurrences for *pawky*, and based on the newspaper evidence, this seems to be an essentially middle-class word.

6.10.3 Clydesidism

For the Clydeside stereotype, *blooter* (wild kick of a ball or *blootered* meaning drunk), *bunnet*, *broo/buroo* (from Unemployment Bureau) and *bevvy* were all considered; *blooter* and *bevvy* suggesting the hard drinking often associated with Clydesidism, *broo/buroo* suggesting the unemployment, and *bunnet* being associated with the ubiquitous working man's cloth cap (it should be noted that *blooter* is also often associated with football). Each lexical item under investigation was considered in light of its context in the article, to see whether it was used in the expected stereotypical context.

Blooter has two possible meanings: either drunkenness or a violent blow, especially of kicking a football hard, both of which could be considered semantically to fit quite comfortably into the Clydeside stereotype. With the drunkenness meaning, this lexical item is often found in fairly colloquial contexts and is largely a term of disapprobation. In the *Record* it was associated with concepts such as football, and Glaswegians going to Blackpool on holiday, both of which can be described as traditionally stereotypical working-class pastimes. It was also associated with pubs, over-indulgence and 'boozing', but these examples could be explained simply by its meaning. The others, however, do seem to fit loosely into some sort of Clydeside stereotype. If the other meaning is considered, that of a violent blow, here again the lexical item seemed to fit into Clydeside stereotypical contexts, given that it was often used in association with football, though this may be a throwback to the terms used by certain Scottish football commentators.

Bunnet (128 occurrences overall) splits into two traditions in *The Herald* (46 occurrences): one, the most prevalent, being the Clydeside stereotype; and the other being some sort of Tartanry. Thus *bunnet* is associated with Clydeside contexts such as football, pie suppers, traditionally working-class communities such as Dennistoun and Airdrie; but also with elements of Tartanry such as Highland crofters, the islands, and the Scottish regiments. A similar split was observed in *The Scotsman* and the *Record*. As an interesting aside, in the majority of cases, *bunnets* are worn by men. In the examples given by the Scottish newspapers, only a small minority of the *bunnets* were worn by women. Again this would fit in with the notions of these Scottish stereotypes, as it is always a *man* wearing a kilt for Tartanry, a *lad o' pairts* for Kailyardism, and a *wee hard man* for Clydesidism. McCrone (1992: 190) observes that 'there is no analogous "lass o' pairts"; the image of tartanry is a male-military image (and kilts were not a female form of dress); and the Clydeside icon was a skilled, male worker who was man enough to "care" for his womenfolk.'

Both *broo* and *buroo* are generally associated with Clydeside type contexts, such as poverty, unemployment, Govan, James Kelman. Examples were found in all three of the Scottish newspapers.

Bevvy is semantically associated with pubs, drinking and so on. However, it does seem to be frequently linked to other stereotypical Clydeside or working-class traits, such as football, betting, racing, unemployment, karaoke, Rab C. Nesbitt, manual workers, pub darts and so on. It was often found in colloquial language contexts, but this is not surprising as it is a colloquial term. As noted earlier in section 6.1.1, the *Record* had a very high frequency for this item (112 occurrences, compared with 40 in *The Herald* and 12 in *The Scotsman*; note also 35 in *The Sun* (2005)). It is interesting that the *Record* also had more occurrences for *swally* than either of the broadsheets (15 occurrences in the *Record*, compared to 4 occurrences in both *The Herald* and *Scotsman* respectively). The *Record* was also the only newspaper to use the term *Swallython* – presumably a term for an extended drinking session.

What conclusions can be drawn from these results? Firstly, it should be reiterated that the argument being put forward is not that certain lexical items can only ever be associated with one particular stereotype. However, the above results do show some correlation between certain lexical items and certain stereotypes. There are particular lexical items such as *lad o'pairts* and *pawky* which trigger the Kailyard stereotype and, as discussed in the previous section, are more likely to occur in the Scottish broadsheets. Based on the evidence collected, the *Record* seems less likely to allude to the Kailyard stereotype, perhaps replacing some of its central themes such as poverty and down-to-earthness with similar attributes from the Clydeside stereotype. Analysis of *bonnie/bonny* suggests that the Tartanry stereotype was accessed by both the tabloid and broadsheet newspapers. *Bunnet* is interesting as it can apparently trigger either the Tartanry or the Clydeside stereotypes. This duality was in evidence in all the newspapers. Those lexical items which trigger the Clydeside stereotype seemed to be fairly evenly distributed across the newspapers, although the *Record* featured *bevvy* and *swally* more often than the broadsheets.

Thus again there seems to be some sort of tabloid/broadsheet split that can be correlated with social class. Certainly the data present strong evidence that these lexical items do trigger particular stereotypical schemata, thus validating the argument made in section 2.4.5 that stereotypes provide useful shortcuts which are often exploited by newspapers.

As far as the use of stereotypes in the newspapers is concerned, the stereotypes may be used verbatim, although I suspect this is usually rather tongue-in-cheek; or they may use the stereotypes simply as an easy way of evoking a sense of Scottishness; or they may subvert or challenge the stereotype in some way, perhaps using humour. As was argued in section 2.4.5, it is important to recognise that readers are not simply passive recipients of stereotypes. They too are involved in their development, promulgation or rejection. Fowler (1991: 17), speaking of the use of stereotypes by newspapers, argues that 'our relationship with newspapers makes a major contribution to this process of construction [the construction of the world via stereotypes].' They are not just foisted on us by the newspapers. Fowler (1991: 43) argues, persuasively, that being a reader is an active process. We can choose to accept or reject the ideology of the text. We can be an accepting or a resisting reader. This is a viewpoint again echoed in McCrone (1992: 189).

Given the widespread criticisms of Scottish stereotypes, are the Scottish newspapers constructing a 'realistic' Scotland and an 'authentic' Scottish identity? The answer depends largely on what one considers 'real' Scottishness and the 'real' Scotland to be about; and as I have argued, these may be very individualistic or even indefinable constructs, meaning different things to different people. Certainly the use of Scottish stereotypes might lead us to the conclusion that some of the Scottishness evoked by the newspapers is not particularly 'real'. But it does not really matter whether or not it is the 'real' Scotland that is being evoked, or a true representation of Scottishness that is being constructed. What does matter is that a sense of solidarity is created and that the readers are made to feel part of a wider shared Scottish community. Clichéd representations of Scottishness or even clichéd items of *Scots* lexis are not necessarily a bad thing in this context. At least they are immediately recognisable as in some way representing Scotland, Scottishness and the Scottish culture. What is being aimed for is reader identification with the general idea of Scottishness.

To conclude then, as was argued in previous chapters, the newspapers often seem to be using a variety of easily recognisable Scottish stereotypes as a method of constructing and maintaining a sense of Scottish identity. Furthermore, the use of well-worn formulaic content appears to form an important and highly salient part of the construction and maintenance of a shared Scottish identity by the newspapers. That national Scottish identity, the data suggests, is, to some extent, mediated by class and regional identities; hence it is multifaceted.

Further Reading

1. Carter (1987), Moon (1998) and Fernando (1996) give comprehensive overviews of idioms and fixed expressions more generally, though Carter is the most accessible text.

A Changing Identity?

This chapter makes a comparison between the pre- and post-devolution phases of the corpus, and asks whether there have been any changes in the use of *Scots* lexis by the newspapers. If so, what conclusions can be drawn, and what explanations can be offered?

7.1 WHAT ANALYSIS OF NEWSPAPER LANGUAGE CAN TEACH US ABOUT SCOTTISH IDENTITY

As was argued in section 4.2, newspapers and national identity are crucially linked. As discussed in sections 4.2 and 4.4.5.1, both Anderson (1991) and Billig (1995) considered the media to be central to the development and maintenance of a sense of an imagined national community (for Anderson print media was key). McCrone claims that

> Along with law, the Church, education and banking, *the media can be ranked as a key civil institution in Scotland which reinforces national identity.* After all, the press is often referred to as the 'fourth estate', reflecting its role in social politics in modern societies. (McCrone 2001: 44–5, my emphasis)

As discussed in Chapter 4, newspapers have, for many years, been seen both as barometers of society and as powerful agents in fostering a sense of national identity. Andersen's (2001) study found that 'those who read Scottish newspapers are more likely to have a strong Scottish identity' though failed to reach firm conclusions as to the cause of this correlation. Was it that those who have a stronger sense of Scottish identity were more likely to read Scottish newspapers because they 'cater' for their viewpoint, or alternatively did more frequent reading of Scottish newspapers actually increase a sense of Scottish identity? Is there any evidence to suggest that the reading of Scottish newspapers increases a sense of Scottishness? Bechhofer et al. (2006) claim that, whilst Scottish nationals tend to take a Scottish media and its perspective for granted, English migrants find this is something to which they have to adjust. Further, they claim that those migrants who want to become more Scottish often cite increased consumption of Scottish media products as a key way of becoming Scottish: 'In short, media consumption plays a part in the process of acculturation or assimilation for migrants' (Bechhofer et al. 2006). So national newspapers have the capacity to create, develop, maintain and reinforce national identity. In Scotland, where for historical, political and cultural reasons the concept of 'nation' has been and continues to be a contested and rather problematic issue, the potential for the national press to fulfil this role is significant.

This study has argued that the linguistic construction of Scottishness via the use of *Scots* lexis gives the newspapers a powerful way of negotiating a shared Scottish identity with their readerships. But, as has been noted, language is, like nation, a contested and problematic issue in Scotland, and analysis of the newspapers gives us a useful insight into the status and appropriacy constraints operating on *Scots*. Using the corpus approach, it has been possible to see whether there have been changes in the use of *Scots* lexis by the press, by comparing pre- and post-devolution results. The key findings are summarised in the following.

7.2 Changes in the Frequencies of Scots Lexis Used

The overall number of occurrences (tokens) of *Scots* lexis did not alter markedly between 1995 and 2005. In 1995, the total *Scots* lexical occurrences were 15,517; in 2005 this had risen slightly to 16,229. So a cursory glance might suggest there is nothing much to talk about in this chapter. What is more illuminating than the summative figures, however, is the comparison across years made at the level of the individual newspapers.

As Figure 7.1 shows, the total *Scots* lexical occurrences (tokens) in *The Herald* in 2005 were less than half (41 per cent to be precise) of what they were in 1995. Meanwhile the *Daily Record* has seen its total *Scots* lexical occurrences more than double from 1995 to 2005 (an increase of some 107 per cent). These are significant differences and effectively *The Herald* and the *Daily Record* are moving in opposite directions – the *Record* becoming much more linguistically marked as Scottish, *The Herald* much less so. Figures for *The Scotsman* were more consistent across the time periods with the 2005 *Scots* lexical totals showing a rather more modest drop of 27 per cent from the 1995 figures. But both Scottish broadsheets have decreased the amount of *Scots* lexis they include, whilst the tabloid *Record* has increased its use of *Scots* lexis.

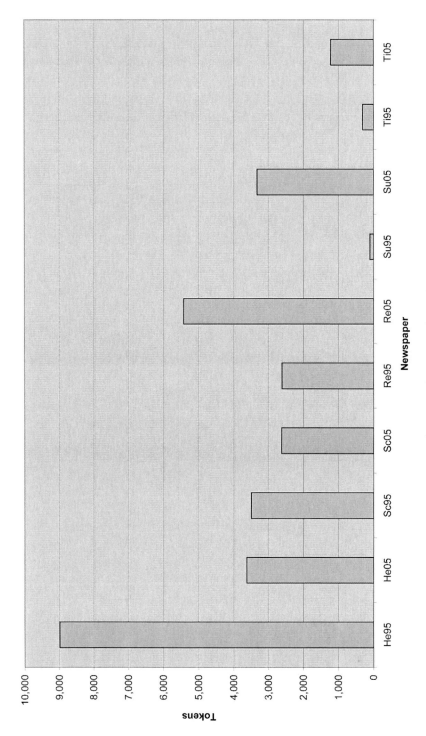

Figure 7.1 Total *Scots* tokens (1995/2005 comparison)

The apparently large increases for *The Sun* when comparing 2005 with 1995 data can, to some extent, be accounted for by the partial nature of the 1995 *Sun* data. However, what is clearly significant is that the 2005 *Sun* data show it contains more occurrences of *Scots* lexis than the *Record* did in 1995, more than *The Scotsman* (2005) and nearly as many as *The Herald* (2005). It begs the question: why are the figures for a Scottish edition of an English newspaper so high compared to the indigenous Scottish newspapers? Is *The Sun* trying to Scotticise linguistically its Scottish edition in a bid for readers? Its News International stablemate, *The Times*, seems to be doing something similar, although to a much lesser extent. In 2005 *The Times* is using nearly four times more *Scots* lexis than it did in 1995 (the increasing Scotticisation of *The Sun* and *The Times* is discussed further in section 8.9).

A cross-newspaper comparison of occurrences of *wee*, the most commonly occurring Scots word in the data, shows similar patterning: *The Herald* (1995) had 1,399 occurrences, *The Herald* (2005) had 554; *The Scotsman* (1995) had 410, *The Scotsman* (2005) had 386; the *Record* (1995) had 980, the *Record* (2005) had 2,118; *The Sun* (1995) had 9, *The Sun* (2005) had 1,141; *The Times* (1995) had 64, *The Times* (2005) had 208 occurrences. Thus over the ten-year period 1995–2005 there has been a clear shift in terms of which newspapers use most *Scots* lexis.

Generally the patterns for individual items of *Scots* lexis followed the overall frequency patterns noted in each newspaper. There were, however, some notable exceptions. *Ned* was one such case. Its frequency was noticeably higher in all the newspapers in the 2005 corpus, but it was in the tabloids especially that the greatest increases could be seen. The frequencies were as follows: *The Herald* 1995 (16), *The Herald* 2005 (76); *The Scotsman* 1995 (12), *The Scotsman* 2005 (47); the *Record* 1995 (44), the *Record* 2005 (313); *The Sun* 1995 (no occurrences, but remember figures are partial), *The Sun* 2005 (217). Why did this happen? Was Scotland suddenly overrun by delinquents? Of course, the answer is an obvious 'No!'. What we are seeing is the newspapers reflecting the more widespread use of this lexical item in the culture generally. *Ned* made it into the *Concise Oxford Dictionary* in 2001, the *Oxford English Dictionary* in 2003, and into the *Collins English Dictionary* in 2005. Rosie Kane (Scottish Socialist Party MSP) famously stood up for *neds* in the Scottish Parliament in June 2003, a year in which *neds* had featured heavily in the Scottish Executive's crackdown on anti-social behaviour (BBC 2005). The BBC Comedy Show *Chewin' the Fat* featured a sketch 'News for Neds'. *Nedworld: A Complete Guide to Ned Life and Living* (Pilrig and McGlinchy 2005), a satire of 'ned culture', and the publication of *The Little Book of Neds* (Bok 2005), *Ned Speak* (Bok 2006) and *Ned Jokes* (Bok 2007) continue the trend (see Law (2006) for further discussion of 'ned humour'). (See also discussion of *ned* in section 6.1.)

7.3 Changes in Number of Stories containing Scots Lexis

Patterns noted for lexical occurrences (tokens) seem to be largely repeated at the stories level (see Fig. 7.2) and the shape of the graph in Figure 7.2 is a fairly close match for that in Figure 7.1, showing the same highs and lows with a few significant exceptions as discussed below.

As can be seen from Figure 7.2, in 2005 the *Daily Record* actually overtook *The Herald*'s 1995 lead in terms of the numbers of stories found containing items of *Scots* lexis. In 2005, *The Sun* overtook *The Herald* and *The Scotsman* in terms of the number of stories returned by the search. *The Times* has also seen a dramatic increase in the number of *Scots* lexis-containing stories, more than trebling from 1995 to 2005, though it is still the least Scottish newspaper.

7.4 Changes in Lexical Density

The average number of *Scots* lexical items (tokens) found in each story follow similar trends to the overall word occurrences and stories patterns, though caution must be exercised due to the low numbers involved. From 1995 to 2005, average occurrences of *Scots* lexis in each article saved from *The Herald* fell from 2.3 to 1.7; in *The Scotsman* they were fairly stable at 1.9 and 1.8 respectively; in the *Daily Record* they rose from 1.5 in 1995 to 1.8 in 2005. So again figures in *The Herald* are falling and figures in the *Record* rising. *The Sun* 1995 had an average of 1.4 *Scots* tokens in each article saved; in *The Sun* 2005 this figure rose to 1.8. *The Times* was consistent across both time periods with an average of 1.8 *Scots* tokens in each article saved. So in 2005, the average occurrence of *Scots* lexis in each of the articles saved has evened out across the newspapers.

More persuasive still is analysis of the most densely *Scots* stories. As noted in section 5.5.1, the top ten most Scottish stories in terms of density of *Scots* lexis were drawn, in the main, from the 1995 corpus, and from *The Herald* (1995) in particular (the notable exception being a story in *The Times* 2005). In 1995, *The Herald* was including more dense *Scots* articles than any other newspaper. By 2005, the situation looked rather different and *The Herald* had been overtaken by other newspapers, with the most densely *Scots* story in *The Herald* in terms of word occurrences (tokens) now coming in at 11.16 per cent (c.f. 26.46 per cent in 1995), and in terms of sentences containing at least one item of *Scots* lexis, the 1995 high of 96.30 per cent dropped to 71.53 per cent in 2005. From consistently topping the bill in terms of having stories containing the most *Scots* lexis in 1995 (656 tokens being the highest noted in one story in *The Herald* 1995), in *The Herald* 2005 this figure

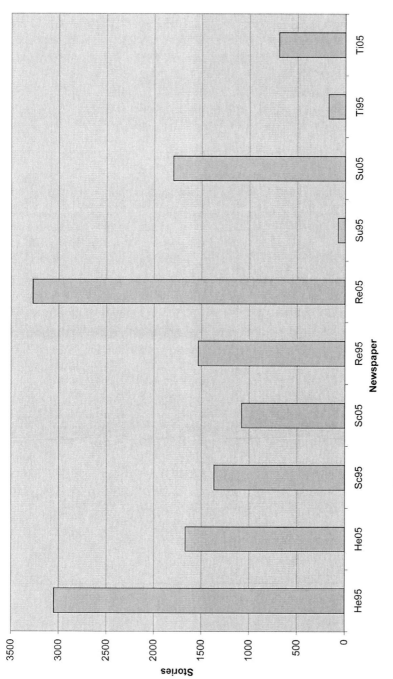

Figure 7.2 Total stories (1995/2005 comparison)

dropped to a new maximum of only 35 items of *Scots* lexis in the one article. In terms of Scotsness ratios for word occurrences and sentences, *The Herald* in 2005 when compared with the other newspapers drops to thirteenth and fourteenth place respectively. It is clear that dense *Scots* does not appear in the latter part of *The Herald* corpus.

Having ascertained that there are some noticeable differences in lexical frequencies, story frequencies and lexical density (certainly at the level of the individual newspapers) between the 1995 and 2005 corpora, it is now useful to consider the language the newspapers used in more detail. In the following section attention moves to proportions of open vs closed class lexis, and cognate vs non-cognate lexis. Also under consideration is the proportion of *Scots* lexis occurring in direct speech/quotation contexts.

7.5 Open Class Lexis: 1995 and 2005 Comparison

(C.f. section 5.5.2.) As can be seen from Figure 7.3, the overall proportions of open class *Scots* lexis used by the newspapers did not alter significantly between 1995 and 2005. However, the figures become slightly more revealing when considered at the level of the individual newspapers. Both *The Herald* and *The Scotsman* remained constant across the 1995 and 2005 corpora. Proportions of open class lexis were noticeably higher in the *Daily Record* than in *The Herald* and *The Scotsman* in both 1995 and 2005. Figures for the other tabloid newspaper, *The Sun*, were also higher than those in the Scottish broadsheets. *The Times* also had higher (though less noticeably so) proportions of *Scots* lexical occurrences in the open class category than either *The Herald* or *The Scotsman*. So both *The Sun* and *The Times* are using higher percentages of open class lexis than either of the indigenous Scottish broadsheets, and the indigenous *Daily Record* uses a higher proportion of open class *Scots* lexis than any other newspaper studied. What can be deduced from these patterns?

Clearly the predominance of open class lexis noted in section 5.5.2 persists across both time periods. It was suggested that open class lexis was more likely to be prevalent due to its salience for language display (especially in thinner contexts) and also because of its diminished threat to notions of correctness. This probably explains why the non-indigenous newspapers are even more likely to prefer using open rather than closed class *Scots* lexis. It is more difficult to explain why the *Daily Record* should exhibit the same pattern, but it clearly coincides with a massive increase in the use of *Scots* lexis generally by this newspaper (see Fig. 7.1).

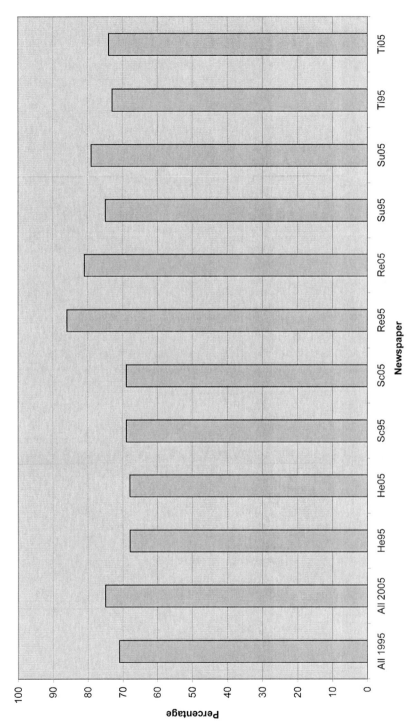

Figure 7.3 Open class tokens (1995/2005 comparison)

7.6 Non-Cognate vs Cognate Lexis: 1995/2005 Comparison

Chapter 5 also examined the proportions of cognate vs non-cognate *Scots* lexis in terms of both lexemes and lexical token frequencies and found that in terms of lexemes, cognate lexis predominated, but when it came to actual lexical frequencies (or tokens) that non-cognate lexis predominated. If *Scots* forms are compared across newspapers and across years it can be seen that, in most cases, cognate lexemes still predominate (the exception being the *Daily Record* which has roughly equivalent figures for non-cognate and cognate lexemes in 1995 and 2005). Comparison of the overall *Scots* lexical frequencies (tokens) in terms of cognate/non-cognate lexis also shows some interesting shifts across the 1995 and 2005 parts of the corpus. Of the total 15,517 1995 *Scots* lexical tokens, 52 per cent were non-cognate, and 48 per cent were cognate. In 2005, of the total 16,229 *Scots* lexical tokens, 63 per cent were non-cognate and 37 per cent were cognate. Thus there is an 11–percentage-point increase in non-cognate tokens between the 1995 and 2005 data and a corresponding drop in cognate items. So there is an increasing trend whereby non-cognate lexis, potentially much less problematic for language display, predominates.

As Figure 7.4 shows, the biggest differentials between usage of non-cognate and cognate lexis occurred in the *Record*, *The Sun* and *The Times*. In each of these newspapers, for both the 1995 and 2005 time periods, non-cognate lexis was significantly more commonly found than cognate lexis, often by proportions of nearly 2:1. So it appears that, though these newspapers are using more *Scots* lexis, they are tending to choose non-cognate rather than cognate items, perhaps because these items are often found in less dense contexts and/or because non-cognate lexical items are potentially less problematic for language display. The preference for non-cognate over cognate *Scots* lexis for the *Daily Record* and *The Sun* is an interesting finding as it seems to run counter to Aitken's (1984a: 521) predictions that this will vary according to social class, as discussed in section 3.6. Aitken is primarily discussing speech, so perhaps this explains the discrepancy. The preference for non-cognate lexis by *The Sun* and *The Times*, as essentially English papers, can perhaps be explained by the smaller risks posed by using 'bona-fide' *Scots* lexis, rather than something that looks like Scotticised *English*. The *Record* also is showing this tendency, so clearly Englishness is not the whole explanation. Perhaps it is a combination of Englishness and/or tabloidness. Certainly there is something interesting going on which marks these newspapers out as using rather different types of *Scots* lexis from the Scottish broadsheets.

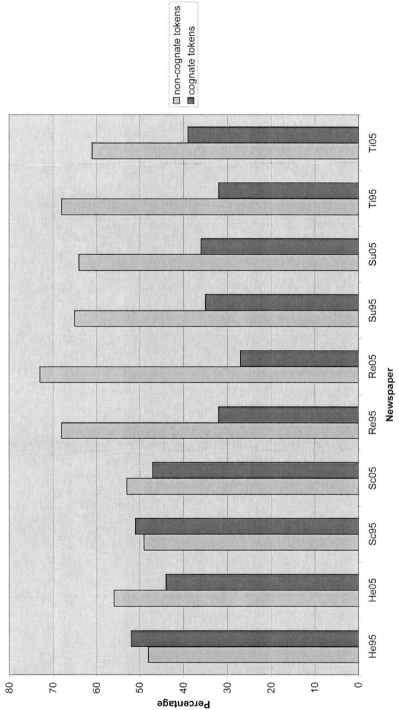

Figure 7.4 Cognate vs non-cognate tokens (1995/2005 comparison)

If the analysis is taken one stage further, by considering the correlation between open/closed class status and cognate/non-cognate lexis (see section 5.6.2) it can be seen that the patterns do vary somewhat between the 1995 and 2005 parts of the corpus (see Fig. 7.5). In the corpus as a whole (that is 1995 and 2005), the most frequently occurring class of *Scots* token (at 49 per cent) was non-cognate open class lexis, followed by cognate open class lexis at 24 per cent, cognate closed class lexis at 13 per cent. Cognate open/closed class words accounted for 7 per cent, non-cognate open/closed class words accounted for 5 per cent, and finally non-cognate closed class lexis accounted for only 1 per cent. (See section 5.6.2.)

Non-cognate open class lexis has become ten percentage points more frequent in the 2005 corpus. This, coupled with the analysis in the previous two sections, suggests that the newspapers are increasingly favouring open class and non-cognate lexis. Both seem less problematic for language display and less encumbered by concerns about correctness, appropriacy or even 'bad Englishness'. There may also be implications for the perceived level of commitment to *Scots*. This is something that is considered further in the next section where the proportions of *Scots* lexical occurrences found in DS/quotation contexts are examined.

7.7 Direct Speech/Quotation Contexts: 1995/2005 Comparison

Overall proportions of *Scots* lexis occurring in DS/quotation contexts did not alter between 1995 and 2005. In both time periods, 26 per cent of items occurred in DS/quotation contexts whereas 74 per cent did not. Once again, consideration of the situation at the level of the individual newspapers yields more interesting results (see Fig. 7.6).

As can be seen, all the newspapers follow the overall trend of higher non-DS/quotation contexts, but some are more likely to have higher non-DS/quotation contexts than others, perhaps indicating differences in their attitudes to and degree of commitment towards *Scots*. Although the overall frequencies of *Scots* tokens have more than halved in *The Herald* from 1995 to 2005, the proportion of *Scots* lexis occurring in DS/quotation contexts actually increased quite significantly in 2005 – perhaps suggesting that *The Herald* was increasingly limiting the use of *Scots* to such contexts. It could also be seen as evidence that this newspaper is increasingly distancing itself from *Scots* lexis and reducing its degree of commitment to *Scots*. By contrast, the *Daily Record* figures have gone the other way, with significant increases in terms of *Scots* lexical tokens being noted in 2005 compared with 1995, and a corresponding marked decrease in the proportion of *Scots* lexis restricted to DS/quotation contexts from 1995 to 2005. Thus once again the *Record*

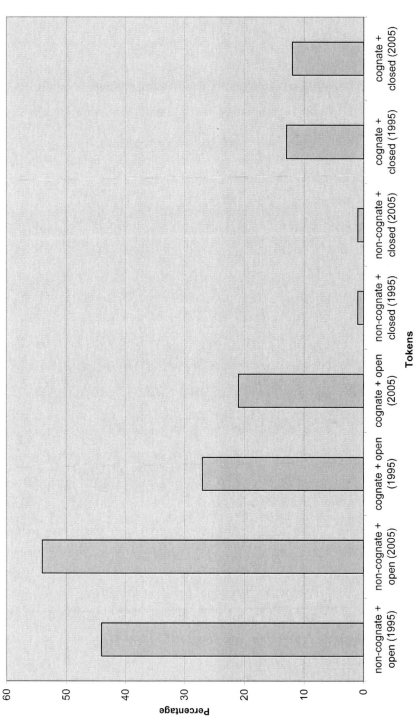

Figure 7.5 Cognate/non-cognate vs open/closed class tokens (1995/2005 comparison)

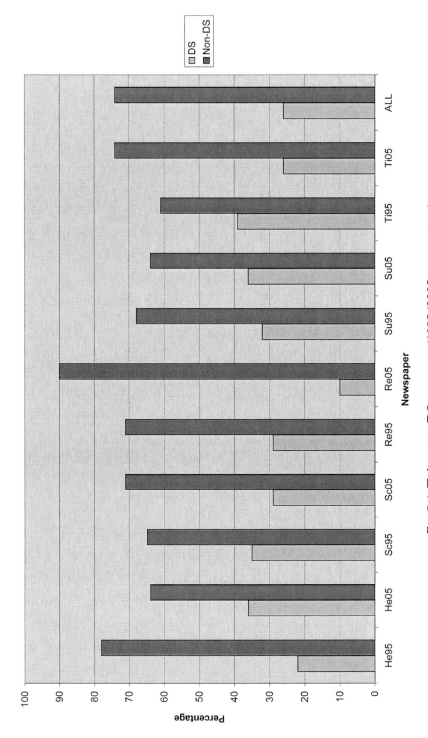

Fig 7.6 Tokens in DS contexts (1995/2005 comparison)

and *Herald* appear to be behaving in opposite fashions. On the basis of the data collected here, it can be suggested that in 1995 *The Herald* relied less on 'filtered' direct speech *Scots* contexts than the other Scottish newspapers, and hence could in a sense be seen as much more 'committed' to the use of *Scots* lexis than it was in 2005. The *Record* has gone the other way in 2005, becoming more committed to the use of *Scots* lexis outside DS/quotation contexts. This ties in with the observations made earlier in section 7.2, which suggest that *The Herald* has become less Scottish over time whilst the *Record* has become more Scottish over time. As Figure 7.6 shows, lexis in DS contexts fell modestly over the period in *The Scotsman* and more markedly in *The Times*. With 36 per cent of lexical occurrences happening in DS/quotation contexts, *The Sun* 2005 figures are once again comparable with those for the Scottish broadsheet – *The Herald* (2005).

7.8 Overall Findings of the Study

What, then, does analysis of the newspapers' use of *Scots* lexis across the time periods tell us? One of the first things that can be said is that, as is often the case with symbols of identity, the newspapers seem to use *Scots* lexis in a fairly tokenist and unthreatening fashion in both periods. Thin *Scottish Standard English* rather than dense *Scots* contexts are the preferred norm. The occasional item of *Scots* lexis is more effective for Scottish identity in the newspapers than extended passages of dense *Scots* prose. The latter might well prove a 'turn-off' for most readers. Open class and non-cognate lexis predominate. Clearly they are much more acceptable for language display than are closed class and cognate lexis. *Scots* lexis is to be found in the newspapers, but it is generally constrained within the boundaries of 'acceptable' parts of the newspaper such as features and sports articles. There are linguistic tariffs to be met if one wants to be a fully-functioning member of the discourse community and get all of the jokes/puns in 'The Diary' columns. What there is on the whole in the newspapers is inoffensive and fairly innocuous linguistic flag-waving.

The newspaper evidence also stresses the importance of the formulaic, in terms of well-worn constructions like idioms, proverbs and *weel-kent* quotations. Scottish identity as constructed/maintained by the Scottish press also often buys into recognised Scottish stereotypes. As already considered in section 4.1, newspapers traditionally tend to appeal to particular social class groups, and, as Andersen (2001: 15) claims, '[T]here is a strong positive relationship between national identity and the newspapers people read.' Section 6.1.1 found some evidence of a class divide in the newspapers, so perhaps the tabloid and broadsheet newspapers are using rather different types of *Scots* lexis on occasion, precisely because they are trying to appeal to rather different types of readership, such as in the avoidance of literary terms and densely *Scots* articles by the tabloid *Daily Record*. Considered in the context of Andersen's (2001) study which claims that feelings of national Scottish identity and attitudes to independence in particular are often related to social class, this becomes a more interesting finding. So to some extent, national Scottish identity is being mediated by class identity.

There is also only limited evidence of a Glasgow/Edinburgh split in terms of the *Scots* lexis they use. So mediation of Scottish national identity by local or East/West identity in the Scottish newspapers is much less obvious. This might have significance for the rumours of a future merger of *The Herald* and *The Scotsman*, discussed later, in section 8.8, in terms of future lexical choices. As these newspapers shared far more lexis than they had lexical differences, certainly on this front the obstacles do not seem insurmountable.

As illustrated by section 5.8, there is little evidence that the newspapers are actively seeking to standardise *Scots*, or indeed their spelling of isolated *Scots* lexical items, something which could, some might argue, usefully raise their and the language variety's profile. This potential is discussed further in sections 8.2.4 and 8.2.5.

Finally some very telling differences between the 1995 and 2005 corpora, particularly as regards the behaviour of individual newspapers, have been noted. *The Herald* has become much less Scottish in 2005 (it was the front-runner in 1995), and the *Daily Record* has become much more so. These newspapers seem to have swapped places. Both *The Sun* and *The Times* are linguistically much more Scottish in 2005 than they were in 1995, and in the case of *The Sun*, sometimes more so than the indigenous Scottish newspapers. This is a very significant development, and was not envisaged at the outset of the research. We will return to discussion of this rather surprising finding in Chapter 8.

7.9 How Can the 1995/2005 Differences be Explained?

Various suggestions can be put forward to explain the differences noted between the 1995 and 2005 parts of the corpus and can be summarised as internal and external forces. This chapter concludes by discussing the possible internal forces. Discussion of external forces and how they relate to the newspaper market more generally is reserved for Chapter 8.

Possible internal forces are changes in editor and/or editorial policy and/or changes in key personnel. As might be expected, in the space of a decade, each of the newspapers had changed editor. *The Scotsman*, in particular, had numerous editors over the period, with some only lasting a short while (see Reid 2006 for details). Some editors moved between newspapers, for example Bruce Waddell edited the Scottish edition of *The Sun* from 1998 to 2003 and during that time greatly boosted sales, before taking up the post of editor at the *Daily Record*. Editors of the newspapers under study have been a mixture of Scots and non-Scots, and no clear patterns could be discerned linking one or other group with more or less Scots language usage. As noted in Chapter 5, there have been some other notable changes in personnel over the period, with some of the very prolific users of *Scots* lexis, such as *The Scotsman*'s diarist Fordyce Maxwell, ceasing to write their noticeably Scottish columns. Maxwell did, however, continue to be a fairly frequent user of *Scots* lexis, though still in feature-type articles. Personnel changes at the newspapers can be largely offset by expectations centring on the part of the newspaper someone writes and the sort of language it habitually uses and which is accepted as appropriate in that context. For example, when the reins of *The Scotsman* 'Diary' were handed over to Simon Pia, the 'Diary' continued to be marked by fairly frequent use of *Scots* lexis. So there are ongoing and inherited expectations associated with the article types themselves.

An explanation which focused solely on personnel changes, whether at journalist or editorial level would be rather simplistic anyway. As writing professionals, we would expect journalists to have a range of written styles at their disposal and to be able to employ them in different contexts or different newspapers at will. Whilst it is less likely that a non-Scot would be using significant quantities of *Scots* lexis, it is naïve to suggest that the way journalists write is necessarily dictated by their background (hence use of the term 'rootedness' in section 4.4.3). It would be quite possible, in the written mode, for non-Scots to employ items of *Scots* lexis as a way of trying to negotiate acceptance by the Scottish discourse community. That is to say some linguistic choices can be motivated and deliberate.

Stewart-Brown's comments (see section 5.9) suggest differences noted in the *Daily Record* data are unlikely to be as a result of deliberate editorial policy, and it is likely that the position of the other indigenous newspapers towards the use of *Scots* lexis is similar. It cannot be going entirely unnoticed, considering the issues around using *Scots* lexis in the written mode, the strictures of copy-editing and the inevitable use of *English* spell-checkers. The non-random distribution of *Scots* lexis across article types suggests there is an acceptance and maintenance of appropriacy constraints by the newspapers, so there are loose controls, or at least norms operating. But given the powerful relationship that exists between identity and language and the potential for *Scots* lexis to evoke a sense of shared Scottishness, one cannot help wondering if some of the indigenous news-papers are rather missing a trick by not being more deliberate in their exploitation of such a useful emblem of Scottish identity.

Further Reading

1. ABC (Audit Bureau of Circulation) and ABCe (Audit Bureau of Circulation electronic circulations) summary statistics on newspaper circulations are available on the web. However, backdated figures and statistics on individual newspapers are a subscription-only service. NRS (National Readership Survey) average issue readership (AIR) figures have similar availability and drawbacks for the casual browser.

8

Conclusion

This final chapter considers the possible external explanations for the differences noted in the pre- and post-devolution corpora and so it begins by examining whether devolution has had tangible effects on Scottish identity. It then assesses the evidence for post-devolution changes in the use of *Scots* language, and asks whether prevailing linguistic hegemonic and appropraicy norms are being challenged, before looking to the future for *Scots*. Finally this chapter investigates post-devolution changes in the press. It considers the shifting Scottish newspaper market, drawing comparisons between indigenous and non-indigenous newspapers fighting for readers. It also examines the growth of the so-called 'tartan' editions, before questioning the impact of the digital era, the growth in free dailies and devolution itself on the press. The chapter concludes by considering what the future holds for newspapers in Scotland and asking whether this study into the use of *Scots* lexis suggests that a salutary lesson could be learned by newspapers competing in the Scottish market.

8.1 Is Scottish Identity Changing?

Chapter 2 considered the links between nation status, identity and language. Since devolution, Scotland may no longer be a stateless nation, but neither is it an independent one. The situation is one of quasi-autonomy or as McCrone (2001: 6) puts it, Scotland is 'an imagined community with considerable institutional autonomy, and, at least as yet, no sovereign parliament'. So what, if any, have been the effects of devolution on Scottish identity? Bond and Rosie (2006: 141) ask whether devolution has heightened a sense of Scottish identity 'or alternatively whether its political expression will in fact mean that people feel less need to emphasise their Scottishness' (Paterson et al. 2001). Studies have consistently shown that whilst there is for many Scots a sense of British identity, there is also generally a strong, perhaps even stronger, sense of Scottish identity. McCrone (1992: 24) notes that, in a 1991 opinion poll carried out

— 143 —

for *The Scotsman*, '40 per cent of Scots considered themselves to be Scottish not British, and a further 29 per cent more Scottish than British' (21 per cent considered themselves to be equally Scottish and British). McCrone et al.'s fairly small study of National Trust for Scotland members' attitudes (1995) suggested that Scots have a stronger affiliation for Scottish rather than British identity. Scottish identity is important to the Scots, and surveys have consistently shown that 'Scottish' rather than 'British' has been their preferred identity for the last twenty-five years (Bond and Rosie 2002; McCrone 2001). Note that some individuals are clearly operating with a dual identity of Britishness and Scottishness, whereas for others it is a question of 'otherness'. Bond and Rosie (2002: 2) go further and, based on the Scottish Election Surveys (1974, 1979, 1992 and 1997), the Scottish Parliamentary Election Survey (1999) and the Scottish Social Attitudes Surveys (2001 and 2002), present figures which suggest that 'over the last quarter of a century Scottishness has been the most popular form of national identity in Scotland, and has increased significantly since the late 1970s apparently at the expense of Britishness' (although they do sound a note of caution based on the precise wording of the survey questions and on the grounds that many Scots profess to hold dual Scottish and British identity). Devine and Logue (2002: xi), again drawing on the 2002 Social Attitudes Survey, report findings that suggest 'Scottishness seems to have soared to unprecedented levels', with 75 per cent of respondents classifying themselves as 'more Scottish than British', and an increase in denial of British identity by Scots rising from 20 per cent to 40 per cent. They also cite evidence that 'people rank the importance of being Scottish second only to being a mother and father and ahead of issues of employment and class.' Clearly Scottishness is alive and well. Recent years have also seen an upsurge in English national identity (see discussion in Kumar 2003). These trends have significant implications for the perceived fragmentation that is alleged to be affecting the media post-devolution (see section 8.7 for further details).

But, of course, one obvious question to ask in the face of all this evidence is whether people's sense of Scottish identity has altered in any way as a material result of the reinstatement of the Scottish Parliament – something which might have been expected to validate and promote a stronger consciousness of Scottishness. McCrone (2002) argues that his evidence gleaned from a series of surveys on national identity in Scotland shows that the reinstatement of the Scottish Parliament 'has not made people feel any more, or indeed, any less Scottish, although both the referendum and the first Scottish parliamentary election saw a firming up of "Scottish only" identity'. Bond and Rosie's (2002) article is an interesting deconstruction of identity surveys, and they suggest that rather than concluding that devolution has initiated a further disassociation between national identity, party identification and favoured constitutional option, a more robust conclusion would be that the relationship between these factors remains as complex in the wake of Scottish devolution as it was before the re-establishment of the Scottish Parliament. (Bond and Rosie 2002: 8)

Their analysis of the results of the 2003 Social Attitudes Survey in Bond and Rosie (2006) reaches similar conclusions, with 2003 responses to the so-called 'Moreno question' very close to those of 1999 – devolution year. Bond and Rosie (2006: 156) observe that the latest Social Attitudes Survey shows 'the extent to which people in Scotland continue to emphasise their Scottish national identity in the wake of devolution' and that 'this is an identity which, for around half of all respondents, is very important to their sense of self.' However, they also conclude that 'we certainly cannot say that the re-establishment of the Scottish Parliament has increased the saliency of Scottish national sentiment and eroded Scotland's sense of Britishness' (Bond and Rosie 2006: 145), and, in fact, go further in suggesting that devolution may actually have helped stabilise levels of perceived Britishness in Scots.

So it seems it cannot really be argued that allegiance to Scottish identity has materially altered in the wake of devolution. Studies (Bond and Rosie 2002, 2006; McCrone 2002) have shown Scottish identity to be as complex a phenomenon after devolution as it was before, and it is clear that there is no simple cause and effect relationship between increased political power and a heightened sense of identity. Indeed, it might be argued that a sense of being the underdog and a minority stateless nation is so central to the Scottish psyche that enhanced political autonomy could damage as well as sustain and build up notions of Scottishness.

The Scottish Nationalist Party has promised a referendum on independence for Scotland in 2010, and the Scottish Government has launched the 'National Conversation' which examines the constitutional options (Scottish Government 2007a). But just what steps towards or the achievement of full independence for Scotland might mean for Scottish identity is anyone's guess. If devolution has had no marked effect in increasing a sense of Scottish identity, would a step further to independence for Scotland do so either? As was argued in section 2.4.1, identity is often as much about otherness as it is about sameness. So it is debatable whether a split from its larger English neighbour (against which Scotland has arguably often constructed its identity) and the rest of the UK would strengthen or weaken Scottish identity. The status of Scotland as an independent nation in the European context is likely to complicate matters further. It is therefore difficult to predict how Scottish identity might alter or develop in the future.

8.2 The Changing Role of Scots Language in Post-Devolution Scotland

What then is the role of *Scots* language in post-devolution Scotland and has the reinstatement of the Parliament had any discernible linguistic effects? Post-devolution, with political power now on a firmer footing, two possible scenarios might be envisaged. Increased political power may have the knock-on effect of increasing linguistic confidence and hence the use of *Scots* language might be expected to increase and extend into new domains. Alternatively, now that some level of political autonomy has been achieved, arguably there is a less pressing need for language to function as a key cultural identifier of Scottishness and so the use of *Scots* might diminish.

As discussed in previous chapters, *Scots* has no standard variety, problematic status and restricted registers, and these factors mean that its use is heavily limited by appropriacy constraints, especially in written, formal and public discourse such as that of the newspapers. Fairclough (1995: 243) objects to the appropriacy argument on the grounds that it gives 'an image of *clearly distinguished language varieties* being used in *clearly distinguished contexts*, according to *clear-cut conventions*, which hold for *all members* of what is *assumed* to be a *homogeneous speech community*' (my emphasis). Given the discussion of the complexities and difficulties of definition associated with the *Scottish-English* linguistic situation (not clearly distinguishable language varieties, blurred conventions, and certainly not a homogeneous speech community that holds true for all members), perhaps the appropriacy constraints operating on *Scots* are not the immovable and monolithic presence that they might be imagined to be. Fairclough complains that notions of appropriacy are presented as unchallengeable and static truths, which are somehow inherent in the language itself, and argues that notions of appropriateness arise from social forces that can, and perhaps should, be challenged. Thus for Fairclough, appropriacy is dynamic not static, and can change over time as a result of different pressures on the language. Fairclough (1995: 94–5) argues that discourse is often used as a tool both to further and to struggle against hegemonic practice; but also that discourse itself is a hegemonic battleground where certain discourse practices are dominant within the language community. Hence, in the following we examine whether there is any evidence of the hegemonic norms for *Scots* being challenged, by looking at post-devolution political developments affecting *Scots* language and charting the use of *Scots* across a range of discourse types.

8.2.1 Political arena

In the political arena, the evidence is somewhat mixed, but arguably the new Parliament has meant that requests to discuss and address the state of the language have become more visible and have had to be heard. A cross-parliamentary group for the Scots Language was established in January 2001 to further the cause of *Scots* and lobby for it in the Scottish Parliament. Since then, there has been a breakthrough in the development and use of an official public *Scots* (Corbett and Douglas 2003) as evidenced in documents such as the 'Education, Culture and Sport Committee Report' (McGugan 2003), a *Scots* version of the 'Making Your Voice Heard in the Scottish Parliament' document (Public Information Service 2003), Donati et al.'s (2003) 'Scots: A Statement of Principles' and a *Scots* version of the Parliament's Language Policy (Scottish Parliamentary Corporate Body (SPCB) 2004). There are also a few information pages on the Scottish Parliament website in *Scots*, as there are in other 'minority' languages (Scottish Parliament n.d.), and several MSPs have sworn their oath of allegiance in *Scots* and/or *Gaelic* as well as in *English*. In 2004, James Robertson (co-founder of Itchy-Coo and author of several best-selling books written in *Scots*, including the non-fiction *A Scots Parliament* (Robertson 2002)) became the Scottish Parliament's first writer-in-residence. Scots language activists have continued to petition the Parliament on behalf of *Scots* as evidenced by periodic Parliamentary Motions and Questions on *Scots* and the National Language Strategy. (An online listing is maintained by the Scots Language Centre.) *Scots* has also been lobbied for at European level, but although it gained recognition as a 'minority language' from the European Bureau for Lesser Used Languages (EBLUL 2003) and at the time there were hopes that this would improve perceptions of and attitudes towards *Scots* at UK Government level, some would argue that little seems to have come of it. Under the *European Charter for Minority or Regional Languages*, ratified by the UK Government in 2001, the Scottish Government is committed to a number of undertakings to promote and develop the use of the *Scots* language; interestingly one of these commitments is to the use of *Scots* in the media.

The Cultural Commission's (2005) online report made various recommendations as regards *Scots*, one of which was that 'a representative body for the indigenous languages of Scotland [which it defines as *Gaelic*, *Scots* and *English* – their ordering] should be created' and that it should have responsibility for 'a national indigenous language strategy'. This is a development that grows out of proposals (1999 onwards) from the academic community and other language agencies for an 'Institute for the Languages of Scotland (ILS)' (an institute which, at the time of writing, had not been established). More recently, February 2007 saw the publication of the Scottish Executive's online draft consultation paper 'A Strategy for Scotland's Languages' (Scottish Government 2007b) published in *English* and *Gaelic*, though, interestingly, not in *Scots*. The Executive's strategy document had a less than enthusiastic response in some quarters and was criticised by some for its perceived inaccuracies and failure to do anything significant for the *Scots* language. (Responses can be viewed online at the Scottish Government website.) Many of the respondents argue the strategy does not go far enough and in their response to the consultation document (see SLD website), Scottish Language Dictionaries renewed calls for an Institute for the Languages of Scotland to work in partnership with Bòrd na Gàidhlig. However, the fact that the Executive strategy document exists at all does show that *Scots* and *Gaelic* were still on the political agenda. The 'National Conversation' document (Scottish Government 2007a), published in the autumn of 2007, was belatedly translated into *Scots*, after criticisms were received that it was the only indigenous language into which the document had not been translated (the document was also published in various of Scotland's community languages).

Early in 2008, the Scottish Government announced that it would be carrying out an audit of current *Scots* language provision in Scotland, linking it with pre-election manifesto commitments to promote an increased awareness of *Scots* and its literature, to introduce a question on *Scots* in the Census (see section 1.2), to ensure that European obligations to develop the language are honoured, and actively to encourage the use of *Scots* in education, broadcasting and the arts. Research tenders were invited from interested parties, with the project, addressing the main points below, running from April to September 2008, and being used to inform ministerial policy.

1. A review of the main providers of Scots language provision and the types of provision available in Scotland focusing on, but not limited to that provided by, local authorities and other public bodies, or organisations in receipt of funding from these bodies for this purpose;
2. An assessment of the availability of current provision in terms of the requirements of the Council of Europe's *European Charter for Minority or Regional Languages* (1992)
3. An appraisal of the gaps in current provision and a consideration of potential areas where provision could be developed further. (Scottish Government n.d.)

A description of the audit is available on the Scottish Government website. One of their main interests is the 'current extent of Scots language provision in schools'. At the political level, although there seem to have been some significant developments and there is certainly increased visibility for *Scots* language questions, it remains unclear what the tangible effects will be.

8.2.2 Academe

In academe, there have been some notable developments furthering *Scots*. A well-respected series of conferences on the languages of Scotland (both *Scots* and *Gaelic*), Northern Ireland (*Ulster Scots*) and the Republic of Ireland (*Irish*) held at Queen's University Belfast have led to a series of volumes (*Belfast Studies in Language, Culture and Politics*) containing papers published in each of these languages (Kirk and Ó Baoill, 2000, 2001, 2002, 2003). *The Scottish Corpus of Texts and Speech* (SCOTS), a significant new tool for research into *Scottish-English*, in all its varieties, (see Douglas 2003) was launched in January 2001. At May 2007, it contained over 1,100 written and spoken texts, totalling over 4 million words of running text, 80 per cent of the total being made up of written texts and 20 per cent being spoken texts. Although the active phase of *SCOTS* is now completed, the team hopes to have the resources to continue to add any newly contributed material to the online *SCOTS* corpus. (The *SCOTS* team is now working on a new Corpus of Modern Scottish Writing (*SCOTS* website).) In 2002, The Scottish Arts Council announced its intention to provide substantial funding for the Scottish Language Dictionaries organisation, and remains SLD's core funder. In education more broadly, there have been continuing calls for *Scots* to be more deeply embedded in the curriculum. On 18 January 2006, a petition was presented to the Public Petitions Committee of the Scottish Parliament, calling for greater provision for the teaching of Scottish literature, culture (which includes language) and history in schools. As we have seen, the provision of *Scots* language in schools is one of the topics addressed by the Scottish Government's 2008 audit, so perhaps these concerns are being heard.

8.2.3 Publishing

In publishing, *Scots* continues to come to the fore. The ItchyCoo imprint, a publisher of mainly children's books written in *Scots*, continues to enjoy significant success. At April 2008, it had produced twenty-eight titles, as well as a series of teachers' notes, audio and Braille materials – no small achievement in the six years since it was launched. April 2008 also saw the publication of a series of four small paperbacks by members of the Scottish Language Dictionaries team, concentrating on *Scots* lexis from different semantic areas: *Say it in Scots: Scottish Placenames* (Scott 2008); *Say it in Scots: Scottish Weather* (Robinson and Finlayson 2008); *Say it in Scots: Scottish Wildlife* (Robinson 2008); *Say it in Scots: Wha's Like Us?* (Robinson 2008). Significant as such publications are, it is noticeable that they are very much restricted to the traditionally 'appropriate' domains for *Scots* language.

8.2.4 Press

How do these developments sit with the language of the press? As outlined in section 4.5, newspapers embody a type of institutional discourse. The language they use has to be negotiated with their readers, tends to conform to prevailing societal norms, and is much more likely to uphold and promulgate hegemonic norms than to subvert them. The study of the amount, location and nature of *Scots* lexis contained within the newspapers as discussed in the preceding data chapters therefore gives a good indication of society's views on the status of *Scots* and *Scottish Standard English*. As this book shows, *Scots* language (or at least *Scots* lexis) has a presence, though crucially still a limited one, in the press. Recent years have seen the establishment of two regular short *Scots* language (or to be more accurate – word) slots – Maggie Scott writes 'Scots Word of the Week' in *The Herald* (2005 onwards), and Chris Robinson contributes a 'Scots Word of the Week' to *The Sunday Times* (personal communication). Significantly both columns are written in *English*, and interestingly both focus on *Scots* lexis. So clearly writing about *Scots* lexis, albeit describing it as though it is some sort of cultural artefact, continues to be acceptable. Hegemonic principles can be challenged, though as we have seen, currently such challenges to the prevailing hegemony in the newspapers are the exception and not the rule. There are only occasional bouts of dense *Scots*, usually limited to discussions of essentially Scottish topics, and the evidence from *The Herald* (1995/2005) suggests that such bouts are actually diminishing. There is also little or no evidence that the newspapers are likely to be a force for standardisation of *Scots* any time soon. The position of *Scots* in the newspapers, though enough to maintain a sense of Scottishness, seems, at present, unlikely to challenge linguistic hegemonic norms and break through appropriacy constraints. *Scots* language continues to be a visible, though often contested and mutable, influence in Scotland today. But of course, the goalposts can shift.

8.2.5 The future for Scots language

As Fairclough (1995: 76) reminds us, hegemony is 'never achieved more than partially and temporarily'; rather it is in an 'unstable equilibrium'. Following this argument to its logical conclusion, it is not impossible, though from the present status quo unlikely, that *Scots* could one day successfully extend its registers into more formal types of mainstream prose; just as it can be argued that historically *Scots* was used for a much wider variety of purposes and registers of texts which were presumably considered perfectly appropriate at the time. The position of linguistic varieties can alter and appropriacy norms can be challenged. As discussed above there is some evidence that this has already started to happen for *Scots* with it starting to be used, though in a limited capacity and by a small, dedicated group of people, mainly language activists, in hitherto unexplored domains. Just how far these developments will actually reach and affect the language of the ordinary person in the street, that is, the majority of the estimated 1.5 million *Scots* speakers, is, however, a moot point. Scots language activists, publishers and academe can exert their best efforts to revive the use and acceptance of *Scots* in a broader range of discourse types and contexts, but until the general populace (and arguably the media) joins them, their efforts may well prove fruitless. Certainly the newspaper evidence suggests that this process has some way to go.

8.3 INDIGENOUS VS INTERLOPER NEWSPAPERS – THE SHIFTING SCOTTISH MARKET

The newspaper industry in Scotland, as elsewhere in the UK, is facing a crisis. Readership figures are declining and the market is becoming increasingly competitive. The following snapshots using ABC (Audit Bureau of Circulation) circulation figures and NRS (National Readership Survey) average issue readership (AIR) data provide an indication of how the Scottish readership market has behaved over the last decade or so. They are given here with the proviso that readership figures are always subject to fluctuations, and are out-of-date almost as soon as they are published. Up-to-date figures can be found on the ABC and NRS websites. It should be noted that readership figures are usually estimated at three times higher than circulation figures as it is thought that one newspaper purchased is likely to be read by an average of three people. Individuals may also, of course, read more than one newspaper.

NRS (National Readership Survey) average issue readership (AIR) figures for the three Scottish newspapers studied in this book indicate some fluctuations as shown in Table 8.1.

Average issue readerships	Herald	Scotsman	Daily Record
March 2003–4	274,000	193,000	1,424,000
Apr 2005–Mar 2006	281,000	206,000	1,234,000

Table 8.1 NRS average issue readership (AIR) figures

Chapter 4 noted the distinction made by Law (2001) between 'indigenous' newspapers such as *The Herald*, the *Daily Record* and *The Scotsman*; 'interloper' newspapers such as *The Scottish Sun*; and what he terms 'Anglocentric' newspapers such as *The Times*. Traditionally the indigenous Scottish newspapers have done much better in the Scottish market than their UK rivals. The tabloid *Record* enjoyed many years as Scotland's best-selling newspaper. Although the indigenous quality press, as represented by *The Herald* and *The Scotsman*, could not rival the sheer volume of its sales, they traditionally performed much better than UK broadsheet sales of, for example, *The Times* and *The Telegraph* which had fairly token presences in the Scottish market. Based on the November 1998 ICM poll, McCrone (1999: 40) noted that one in three Scots read the *Daily Record* (traditionally Scotland's most popular tabloid and most popular newspaper) compared with one in five reading *The Scottish Sun*, the best-selling UK tabloid north of the border. Clearly in 1998 *The Scottish Sun* had a long way to go to rival the popularity of the home-grown *Record*, and in 2002, *The Scottish Sun* was selling 386,236 copies compared to the *Daily Record*'s 497,754 (ABC). Four years later, in 2006, however, sales of *The Scottish Sun* overtook those of the *Daily Record*. This reversal in fortunes of the two newspapers, after a nearly twenty-year battle, was seen as so unusual and noteworthy that it was commented on widely, for example *The Sunday Herald* (Vass 2006a), the *Press Gazette* (2 June 2006), *The Scotsman* (Sheppard 2006). Interestingly the ongoing battle for readers has been very heavily reported on by an English newspaper, *The Guardian*. *The Scottish Sun*'s success has been largely attributed to the outcome of an aggressive price war. According to *The Sunday Herald* (Vass 2006a), sales of the *Daily Record* in 2006 were almost half the 1994 figure. Although the *Record* responded by launching new PM editions on 4 September 2006, these were thought to be detracting from sales of the main paper and contributing only a small increase in overall sales figures (*The Sunday Herald*, 10 September 2006). Scotland's two main broadsheets, *The Herald* and *The Scotsman*, whilst never able to rival sales of the *Daily Record*, experienced an overall drop in circulation figures from 2000 onwards. This downward trend in sales is something that can be seen across the board, though interestingly, the *Press and Journal* has not seen the huge drop in circulation experienced by Scotland's other newspapers. Note, however, that ABC classifies it, as many would, as a regional rather than a national newspaper, so perhaps it is competing for a rather different market. The balance of evidence suggests that, on the whole, Scotland's indigenous newspaper industry is waning whilst the 'interloper' UK titles gain ground.

May 2008 figures show *The Scottish Sun* selling 399,321 papers against the *Record*'s 363,411, *The Herald* selling 65,286, *The Scotsman* selling 50,790 and the *Scottish Daily Mail* (traditionally not a strong paper in Scotland) selling 126,542 (McGurk 2008). McGurk says that 'industry figures show that over past 20 years, the Record has fallen by 48.6 per cent. The Herald has dropped 46.4 per cent while The Scotsman's sale is down 41.5 per cent. The Courier in Dundee has lost 41.1 per cent while the Press and Journal remains the best performing Scottish quality daily with a drop of 26.5 per cent.' A month later in June 2008, the *Record*, though still sustaining losses, had started to recover some ground in its ongoing battle for readers with *The Scottish Sun*. *Daily Record* sales fell by 9,637 to 355,123; *The Scottish Sun* sustained losses of 16,194 and sales dropped to 384,709 (Fitzsimmons 2008). Evidently there are some fluctuations and localised successes, but on the whole the indigenous Scottish newspapers are in crisis, with readership figures declining sharply.

8.4 TARTAN EDITIONS

It appears the UK newspaper titles are increasingly realising that, in order to appeal to a Scottish readership, they have to market themselves as Scottish. As discussed in section 4.4.1, interlopers routinely self-brand as Scottish and also exploit archetypal Scottish iconography in, for example, mast-heads. But the Scotticisation process for many of these newspapers goes further than marketing and labelling. By the late nineties, the Scottish editions of UK newspapers were increasingly challenging indigenous titles by putting out 'tartan' editions (McCrone 2001: 45). These tartan editions arose in a climate where the domination of the print unions has ended and Rupert Murdoch's era at Wapping meant that it had become increasingly easier and cheaper to produce extra sections or special regionalised (or Scotticised) editions. Having identifiably Scottish content is an important factor, and certainly the growth in supplements and regional/national editions attendant upon changes to the printing process in recent years has made this not only possible, but also easy and affordable. McNair, quoted in

The Scotsman (29 Sept. 2000) (McGinty 2000), talks about the UK papers *'beef[ing]* up their Scottish editions in an attempt to give them an *authentic Scottish identity'* (my emphasis). This 'beefing up' ranges from the introduction of Scottish supplementary material, such as *The Sunday Times* 'Écosse' to more refined alterations to copy made possible by recent technological advances and changing methods of newspaper production. Rosie et al. (2006c) note from their interviews with journalists that 'considerable care is taken to tailor some Fleet Street titles to their Scottish audiences by flagging 'Scottish' stories'. They note that Fleet Street journalists denied that they were merely 'putting a kilt' on stories and thus tartanising them for a Scottish audience. However, they did concede that there was considerable salience in catering to a more localised audience – that is news about Scotland for readers in Scotland.

So increasingly the superficial nod to their Scottish audience which relied mainly on branding has been replaced with much more actual Scottish content. Arguably this Scotticisation of copy has been a crucial factor in the growing success of the UK titles in the Scottish market in recent years. Nowadays, examples of very fine tuning of articles to a Scottish audience can be found – see case study analyses of editorial changes to newspaper articles across editions by Rosie et al. (2004) which indicate small but nevertheless significant changes at a lexical level. It is interesting that Rosie et al., sociologists, have also focused on changes at lexical level. In short, words matter!

Rosie et al. (2004: 442) identify some London-based newspapers (*The Times, The Telegraph, The Guardian, The Independent*, the *Scottish Mirror*, the *Daily Star of Scotland*) as having 'minimal editorial changes' in their Scottish editions, whilst contending that others (*The Scottish Sun*, the *Scottish Daily Mail* and the *Scottish Daily Express*) 'contain a substantial amount of specifically Scottish copy, as well as Scotticised versions of stories published in English editions of the same paper'. Their 'comparisons of different editions suggested that some newspaper editors go to great lengths to tailor their products to different national markets, and that the amount of this effort is broadly related to circulation patterns' (Rosie et al. 2004: 450). Rosie et al. (2006a: 331) attribute *The Sun*'s success in Scotland to a 'thoroughgoing process of Scotticisation'. It is clear that many commentators see this increased Scotticisation of content as directly linked to increased interloper sales in the Scottish market. But there are other factors that should be considered.

Commercial factors are also significant. Certain UK titles have realised that the Scottish market, with its higher than average appetite for newspaper consumption (see section 4.1), was ripe for exploitation. With seventeen daily titles now in circulation in Scotland, even though news-paper circulations have experienced a serious decline in recent years (as in the industry generally), Scotland is still seen as a potentially lucrative market. One way of carving out a niche in this increasingly competitive marketplace is through aggressive price wars, and this is a tactic that has been particularly successful for *The Scottish Sun* in its struggle for supremacy over the *Daily Record*. Tryhorn (2008a; 2008b) draws attention to the highly subsidised sales of *The Scottish Sun* in Scotland (only 22 per cent being sold at full price in January 2008, dropping to 17 per cent in April 2008) and compares this with the *Record* which sells 99.5 per cent of its copies at full cover price. The indigenous Scottish newspapers cannot afford to compete in such aggressive price wars with larger and more deeply-pocketed UK titles, nor can they easily afford to offer incentives such as free CDs or DVDs.

Increasingly UK titles seeking a place in the Scottish market are seeing the value of having journalists on the ground in Scotland rather than working out of London offices. *The Times* has launched a proper Scottish edition (with an editor based in Scotland) and moved its printing operation from Merseyside to Eurocentral (just outside Glasgow) in April 2007 (Vass 2006c; Reid 2006: 179). It has appointed the experienced journalist and one-time editor of *The Scotsman*, Magnus Linklater, as its editor. In section 4.4.2, it was argued that having a visible presence in Scotland was an important factor in creating and maintaining a Scottish identity for a newspaper and certainly *The Scottish Sun* (based at Kinning Park in Glasgow), *The Times* and now *The Telegraph* (both at Eurocentral) have all now set up satellite operations in Scotland (coincidentally all in the West). Law's (2003) study of deictic centres (see section 4.4.5.1) suggested that *The Scottish Sun*, as an interloper title trying to claim authentic Scottishness, had at that time adopted a deictic centre which was proximal to those of the indigenous Scottish newspapers – that is it had adopted/manufactured a Scottish viewpoint, whilst *The Times*, he claimed, retained an Anglo-centric deictic viewpoint. Of course, deictic centres for such publications need not correlate with the physical geography of their operations, but perhaps now having bases in Scotland and potentially more Scottish journalists on the payroll, it is inevitable that their deictic centres will shift to be more closely aligned with a Scottish point of view.

Other commercial factors negatively impacting on the indigenous news-papers' ability to fight back in the wake of increased competition include claims that, because most Scottish titles are run by PLCs rather than single proprietors, they are less able to compete due to the need to pay attention to shareholders' returns and falling advertising revenue. As of May 2008, it has been announced that most public sector jobs will cease to be advertised in the Scottish national press. Local authorities will use in-house recruitment websites instead and the Scottish Government plans to follow suit with an estimated loss of £47 million per annum for the newspapers concerned. The Scottish newspapers look set to continue to struggle financially.

8.5 Newspapers in the Digital Age

The ongoing threat from online news sources is having a huge impact on the newspaper market. In an increasingly web-based culture, people are no longer relying on newspapers as their primary source of news information. Readership of print newspapers is declining, both in Scotland and elsewhere in the UK, and with it comes a serious decline in advertising revenue, traditionally the most lucrative source of funding for newspapers. Advertising revenue from online newspapers is not enough to compensate for the loss of revenue from print editions, and many advertisers are less fond of online advertising because it cannot guarantee targeted audience management in the same way as is possible with print editions.

This trend towards web presence has had a huge impact on the newspaper industry and in order to survive, most titles now provide online editions. Many newspapers are responding with enhanced website content featuring video and audio material, as well as podcast downloads. In February 2006, *Scotsman.com* became 'the first UK newspaper site to produce a vodcast . . . (a video podcast)' (Kirkpatrick 2006). *The Herald* announced that it would be launching a new 24/7 online service in 2008, combining the forces of *The Herald* and *The Sunday Herald* to provide a whole range of enhanced digital content such as podcasts, video interview, blogs and so on. Many online newspapers are also including increased interactive capabilities offering blogging and discussion groups. So how does this affect readership figures? Vass (2006b) argues that readership figures are no longer reliable indicators of the state of play. Pointing to quarterly NRS figures (available at Sept. 2006), he notes 'a long-term trend of sales and readership decline' for many newspapers' print editions and bewails the fact that figures for e-readers are not routinely collected and counted. (At September 2006, of the Scottish titles, only *The Scotsman* had a listing with ABCe. Although an ABC news release (4 July 2006) states that, in future, combined print and digital edition information will be available, this depends on individual publishers auditing their digital editions take-up.) Vass notes large increases in online readerships in recent years:

> Telegraph.co.uk, for instance, has seen the number of monthly unique users 'eyeballing' its pages rise from 3.5 million in April 2003 to 5.9

million in April 2006. Scotsman.com's user figures have grown from 748,000 to 2.8 million over a similar period, while the unaudited Herald and Times sites now have about one million users. (Vass 2006b)

Exactly what these new e-figures mean can be difficult to discern. Rather confusingly, *theherald.co.uk* claims an online readership of 558,524 ('unique readers') for August 2006, with 3.78 million 'page views'. Online readerships increase the likelihood of people outside the target readership area accessing the newspaper (for example as a Scot in Yorkshire I find it difficult to get paper copies of Scottish newspapers but online access is instantaneous), and so offer the possibility of expansion. However, they also make it more difficult (if not impossible) to track where readerships are based and probably damage print sales. ABCe measurements have come in for some criticism (for example Kiss 2008) though they are becoming increasingly important, especially for advertisers trying to gauge online activity in target publications.

8.6 IMPACT OF FREE DAILIES

The situation is further complicated by the growth in free daily newspapers such as the *Metro*. *Metro* was launched in London in 1999 and in 2006, was available in thirteen cities nationally, including Glasgow and Edinburgh. It claims to be the world's largest free newspaper and the fourth largest UK newspaper (*Metro* 2006). Recent ABC average circulation figures for the Scottish edition of the *Metro* (31 July–27 Aug. 2006) gave a figure of 117,491 – a significant share of the available market and ahead of all the Scottish broadsheets. The free newspaper market is also seen as still having potential for expansion. *The Sunday Herald* (2006) reported that Scottish versions of the News International new free title 'the londonpaper' could soon be launched in Glasgow and Edinburgh following the purchase of the domain names 'the glasgowpaper' and 'the edinburghpaper'. If it goes ahead, it would mean more competition in an already overcrowded market.

8.7 DEVOLUTION AND THE SCOTTISH PRESS

What has been the impact of devolution on the fortunes of the Scottish press? As has been shown, the newspaper evidence shows no significant alteration in the overall frequency of usage of *Scots* lexis by the press between the 1995 and 2005 parts of the corpus. However, there are, as have been noted in this and previous chapters, some noticeable differences in the behaviour of individual newspapers pre- and post-devolution. But is it possible or even sensible to argue that devolution is responsible for these differences? Unfortunately we have no clear method of establishing precisely the level of influence of post-devolution developments on the language of the newspapers, or how this might interact with other internal or external factors. However, we can comment more generally on the effects of devolution on the press.

Reid (2006: 56) notes that 'the delivery of devolution was expected, among many other things, to be to the benefit of the indigenous Scottish press.' However, as demonstrated by the figures above, clearly this has not happened. McGinty (2000) also argues that the creation of the Scottish Parliament has not reversed the fortunes of the Scottish press as had been previously anticipated. As Colin McClatchie (Rupert Murdoch's senior manager in Scotland) observes, '[T]he irony is that, in post-devolution Scotland, exactly the opposite has taken place, and the indigenous players have performed worse' than the non-indigenous Scottish editions of UK newspapers (quoted in Reid 2006: 56–7). So why has this happened? Reid (2006) argues that in part this might be blamed on the Scottish press' criticism of the new Parliament and its building. He also suggests, '[I]t could be argued that, now that they have gained devolution, Scots are more confident and secure about their place and role within the UK, and therefore feel less need to assert their Scottishness through buying indigenous Scottish newspapers' (Reid 2006: 58). This line of reasoning has similarities with the discussion in section 8.2 where it was suggested that post-devolution, Scots might feel less reliant on Scottish language as a marker of their Scottish identity. Luckhurst, writing in *The Independent* on 22 July 2007 comments that

> A nation that anticipated media excellence to emerge naturally from the creation of the Scottish parliament has been disappointed. . . . Recent investment at The Scotsman cannot disguise a circulation half that of the Scottish edition of the Daily Mail.
>
> While political power has been repatriated to Edinburgh, media power is heading in the opposite direction, leaving Scotland short of the indigenous newspaper and broadcast culture required to scrutinise its infant political institutions. (Luckhurst 2007)

In a similar vein, Andrew Neil claims that the health of Scottish democracy is undermined if it loses its own press (*Morning Extra* 2008). Scotland now has its own parliament, and is considering independence, but meanwhile its national press is described by some as being in free-fall decline. The newspapers themselves are keen to counter claims that they are in crisis, but it is clear that the reinstatement of the Scottish Parliament has not revived the fortunes of an ailing Scottish press.

It also seems that devolution has not helped coverage of Scottish affairs furth of Scotland. Rosie et al. (2006b) found evidence of increased parochialisation in the press south of the border following devolution: '[T]he amount of reporting of Scottish (or Welsh, or Northern Irish) affairs within papers sold in England has declined after constitutional change. This, though, is hard to measure since we are describing an apparent shift from very little to even less.' Fraser (2008) makes the same point and draws an interesting contrast between the increasing provision of Scottish editions by some UK titles, whilst at the same time they are 'taking the opportunity to strip out almost all their Scottish coverage from editions sold in England'. Perhaps more alarmingly, Fraser, political editor for *The Herald*, points to occasions when English editions of these same newspapers have run articles clearly not intended to be seen by a Scottish readership, such as the comment by Ann Leslie, writing in the *Daily Mail* in March 2000, that 'Scotland was on course to become "some tiny, relatively unimportant nation, on a par with Finland", its identity defined by shortbread tins and tartan souvenirs and that the "auld enemy, England, was, in fact, their saviour, and – but for the chattering-class posturing, could still be so now" (quoted in *The Sunday Herald* 2000)'. Even allowing for the relative freedom afforded to the columnist, such views would clearly not have gone down well with a Scottish audience. So there is a negative side to the opportunities afforded by audience-tailored editions.

Fraser (2008) asks whether, post-devolution, 'nation [is still] speaking unto nation'. He argues that the problem is not restricted to the newspapers, and his discussion also looks at the effects on broadcast media. On 11 June 2008, the BBC Trust published an in-depth report looking at whether the Corporation was effectively meeting the needs of all its UK viewers post-devolution (BBC 2008). Concerns had been raised that licence payers in different parts of the country were having an unequal experience from a London-dominated BBC. In light of this ongoing discussion on the post-devolution parochialisation of the media, it has to be asked whether the Scottish Nationalist Party's bid in July 2007, dubbed 'devolution max', to increase the Scottish Parliament's powers, which included discussion on responsibility for broadcasting, would address or alternatively exacerbate this fragmentation of media coverage.

8.8 THE FUTURE FOR SCOTTISH NEWSPAPERS

Scotland's national press continues to face an increasingly bleak picture. Journalists at *The Herald* staged a series of strikes in July 2007. Official reports suggest the cause of dispute was compulsory redundancies, but media commentators have speculated that the real reason has more to do with the future of quality journalism in Scotland. A BBC Radio Scotland *Morning Extra* (16 May 2008) broadcast by John McGurk (previously editor of *The Scotsman*) announced that the Scottish newspaper industry is in serious decline. In the same broadcast, Andrew Neil (again, a previous editor of *The Scotsman*), claimed that the indigenous Scottish newspapers are facing the same fate as that experienced by the Scottish shipbuilding industry. Even more worryingly, Philip Meyer (an eminent journalism professor) (cited in McGurk 2008) predicts that at the current rate of decline, the Scottish newspapers will survive for only another ten years.

So in the face of such gloomy forecasts and depressing readership and circulation statistics, what can be done to address the problems of the indigenous Scottish press? Job cuts and claims of under-investment have done nothing to increase confidence, so significant investment might help stem the tide. The launch of new compact editions, in line with developments elsewhere in the industry, for *The Scotsman* (Saturday edition March 2004; weekday editions August 2004), and also *The Sunday Herald* do not seem to have reversed the downward spiral. As the newspapers themselves are keen to point out, the situation is not all doom and gloom. There are monthly fluctuations in the figures, and they are starting to fight back with an enhanced online presence. But perhaps more aggressive and drastic measures are necessary, particularly if Scotland's broadsheet press is to be saved.

For quite a few years now, there have been rumours of a merger of *The Herald* and *The Scotsman*, fuelled at different times by things such as the sale of *The Herald* by Scottish Media Group (SMG) in 2003 (Reid 2006: 79). Andrew Neil (*Morning Extra* 2008) argues that the merger was stopped by the Scottish political establishment. Reid (2006: 184) also talks about 'at least one proprietor who fairly recently prepared very detailed feasibility plans for a proposed merger'. The BBC (*Morning Extra* 2008) report on 'Scotland's newspapers' crisis' again raises the possibility of merger as one solution to Scotland's beleaguered broadsheets. Whilst at one time the different perspectives and regional audiences of *The Scotsman* and *The Herald* were strengths, now, it is claimed, they simply dilute the overall available readership. Opinions differ as to whether this would be a desirable or even sustaining move by the newspapers concerned. Meyer (*Morning Extra* 2008) argues that it does not matter if titles merge as long as the newspapers are edited with the local community in mind. Given his doomsday scenario predictions, perhaps this would, reluctantly, be a price worth paying.

8.9 A Salutary Lesson for Newspapers in Scotland?

To draw the study to a close, we need to ask whether analysis of the newspaper data suggests there is a salutary lesson to be learned by newspapers operating in Scotland and seeking to gain a larger share of the Scottish market. Does increased use of *Scots* lexis translate to increased newspaper sales?

In the indigenous press, the picture is confusing. Substantial increases in the use of *Scots* lexis by the *Record* between the 1995 and 2005 corpora have not yielded increases in readership figures. Without this increased lexical Scotticisation, would its readership figures have slid further? It is hard to say. *The Herald's* use of *Scots* lexis has more then halved from 1995 to 2005 and its circulation figures have tumbled by some 30,000 over the same period. *The Scotsman's* use of *Scots* lexis across the time periods has decreased, and it has seen frequent fluctuations and ultimately decreases in circulation figures. But it is unlikely that the misfortunes of the indigenous newspapers can be explained solely by their linguistic practice. Price wars, tartan editions, free dailies and the web have all taken their toll on Scotland's indigenous press.

What then of the 'tartan' editions? A detailed comparison of three hard copy editions of *The* (English) *Sun* and *The Scottish Sun* (11, 12 and 14 March 1996 – that is pre-devolution) found very limited differences between the two editions. Many pages had exactly the same content in both the English and Scottish editions, or in many cases, any differences noted were marginal such as a change of address for readers' comments, some formatting differences, or a slightly longer or shorter version of the same story being used. In some cases the substitution was quite obvious and unsophisticated, as with the insertion of one column of Scottish 'Dear Deirdrie' letters on 11 March 1996. The sports section however, as might be expected, did vary more between editions. The 11 and 12 March issues of *The Scottish Sun* exploited very little *Scots* lexis; but 13 March 1996 was the day of the Dunblane massacre, when a lone gunman went on the rampage in a Scottish school, killing sixteen children and their teacher. Obviously it was a story that got huge coverage in the media generally, but particularly in the Scottish media. Interestingly, although the quantity of *Scots* lexis in *The Scottish Sun* was still very low, it did increase markedly on 14 March with coverage of the Dunblane story, with the use of *wee fella, wee children* and *wee boy* in direct speech and *wee bairns* in quotation marks (see discussion of the use of *Scots* lexis to discuss tragedy in section 5.2.2). As has been demonstrated, things have clearly moved on at *The Sun* since then and the process of Scotticising copy is much more advanced today. *The Sun* is now a much more frequent and consistent user of *Scots* lexis.

Those non-indigenous newspapers which have gone furthest down the road of Scotticising their Scottish editions, particularly *The Sun*, are those which are currently enjoying the greatest success in the Scottish market in terms of circulation. So it clearly pays to be maximally Scottish (Rosie et al. 2006b; 2006c). Increases in circulation figures for *The Times* and especially *The Scottish Sun* coincide with significant increases in the use of *Scots* lexis by each of these newspapers. In 2005, *The Sun* was outstripping *The Scotsman*'s use of *Scots* lexis (both in 1995 and 2005) and coming very close to the greatly reduced 2005 *Herald* frequencies. When looking at the number of individual stories returned by the search list, again *The Times* and *The Sun* have made significant increases, with *The Sun* in 2005 outstripping both *The Herald* and *The Scotsman*. Of the 2005 newspapers, *The Sun* contained the highest proportions of identifiably *Scots* to non-*Scots* lexis (see Fig. 5.1). So in many respects *The Scottish Sun* is behaving as more linguistically Scottish than some of Scotland's indigenous newspapers. It is self-evident that these trends must be down to its increasingly Scotticised Scottish edition.

For a non-indigenous newspaper such as *The Scottish Sun*, these are very significant inroads. Is this coincidence or does the use of *Scots* lexis give those non-indigenous newspapers looking to optimise sales in the Scottish market and seeking to appeal to a Scottish readership and make themselves more Scottish yet another, and more covert but nevertheless highly effective way of doing so? *The Scottish Sun* and the *Daily Record* have, for some time now, been engaged in a battle for readers. Rosie et al. (2006b) talk about Scottish tabloids being 'engaged in a commercial dispute over "authentic" Scottishness'. Part of that 'authentic Scottishness' may well be generated by using the language of their Scottish readers. It is unlikely, though further research would be worthwhile, that readers of these inter-loper newspapers are aware of or are overtly persuaded by an increased use of *Scots* lexis in the newspaper copy. However, I suspect they may be covertly or sub-consciously persuaded and/or flattered by it. As was argued in section 4.4.5.4, if newspapers are written in the vernacular of their readers (c.f. Hall 1978: 61 and Fowler 1991: 48), then using identifiably Scottish language is a very powerful way of making those Scottish readers feel more at home and validating the 'authentic Scottishness' of the newspaper. So do 'Real Scots *still* read the *Record*' or are many of them now reading *The Scottish Sun* instead, convinced by its Scottishness?

The evidence suggests that 'interloper' newspapers are making very determined efforts to gain Scottish readers for their tartan editions by slashing prices, starting to employ Scottish editors and journalists, moving to bases in Scotland, and increasing their coverage of Scottish stories. Most significantly for this study, there is clear evidence that they have gone as far as adopting the one thing that previously made the indigenous Scottish press stand out, *Scots* lexis, the language of its readers. It seems likely that this increased use of *Scots* lexis is linked to and an integral part of the overall Scotticisation of these non-indigenous newspapers in terms of their content, rootedness and profile. Both the physical locations and the deictic centres of these newspapers have altered over the period, and they have shifted from speaking *English* from London to the Scots, to speaking to them from Glasgow in an 'authentic' Scottish voice. Such changes are largely pragmatic, and designed to capitalise on a traditionally avid newspaper-reading Scottish public. These are changes driven by commerce rather than idealism. If these newspapers can successfully develop tartanised editions that appeal sufficiently to Scottish tastes and help their titles succeed in the competitive Scottish market, clearly they will do so. And if *Scots* lexis sells, they will use it! To that end, it seems that non-indigenous newspapers such as *The Sun* are increasingly getting their sales pitch right.

The substantial increases and visibility in the use of *Scots* lexis by these tartan editions, in some cases outstripping that of the indigenous newspapers, are doubly significant when considering the code-switching that must be taking place. It is to be expected that Scottish indigenous newspapers will use *Scots* lexis and will choose linguistic options from along the *Scottish-English* continuum, because they are intrinsically Scottish. It is much more noteworthy when non-indigenous newspapers, that one would expect to be using linguistic options from outside the *Scottish-English* continuum, start doing the same. This really is language display as Eastman and Stein (1993) originally defined the term. As noted in section 4.4.3, in the spoken mode it is not usually possible convincingly to adopt another's language, but, of course, in the written mode, this is much more feasible. And the evidence suggests that the 'interlopers' are engaging in deliberate linguistic Scotticisation, and doing it very successfully. Preston provocatively argues that

> Scottish papers, produced by Scots for Scotland, have seldom, if ever, had it so bad. . . . Can you see why Scots are buying more English papers while the papers that traditionally fight their corner are on the skids? It's a fascinating dislocation and one oddly echoed around our isles. . . . *London's press may don a green dress (or a kilt), but it's coming to get you out there on the Celtic fringe, coming to bury the very sense of nationhood that, otherwise, seems on an upswing. . . . Watch the most intense media arena in Britain fracture and lose its native voice then.* (Preston 2006, my emphasis)

As Preston suggests, the consequences for the indigenous Scottish press are potentially very serious indeed. One has to ask then, whether the indigenous newspapers should be making more of their own and essentially Scottish linguistic resources, and challenging rather than accepting the hegemonic constraints of *Standard English*. Perhaps as Preston (2006) suggests, they really are in danger of 'losing [their] native voice', and allowing those from outside the discourse community to speak for them. Therein lies a salutary, though rather painful, lesson for Scotland's indigenous press.

As we have seen (section 4.2), Anderson (1991: 35–6) emphasises the significance of national newspapers in 'raising national consciousness' and sustaining a sense of nation. Given the evidence presented earlier in the chapter of the link between a sense of Scottish identity and the reading of a Scottish newspaper, the importance of maintaining this indigenous fourth estate for Scotland cannot be overstated. The consequences of a devolved or even independent Scotland without its own national press to speak for it and scrutinise it are unthinkable. Meyer (cited in McGurk 2008) has given the Scottish press ten years. The clock is ticking . . .

Glossary of Terms

accent The pronunciation of a particular language variety.

Anglian dialects The Northumbrian and Mercian dialects of *Old English*.

anglicisation The process whereby *Scots* is influenced by *English*.

appropriacy The way in which certain language varieties are generally considered more or less appropriate for use in certain contexts.

ausbau An ausbau language is one which has been accepted and adapted for a wide range of uses. The term was coined by Kloss (1967). *Scots*, unlike *English*, has not achieved ausbau status.

Celtic Languages belonging to the Celtic branch of the Indo-European language family, including *Scottish Gaelic*, *Welsh* and *Irish*.

closed class Closed class or grammatical lexis includes auxiliaries, conjunctions, determiners, interjections, prepositions and pronouns. It is difficult to add new words to this class. Contrasts with **open class**.

Clydesidism A Scottish stereotype, which, as the name suggests, is associated with the Clyde shipbuilding yards. Key attributes are socialism, alcoholism, oppression and the working class.

code-switching Switching between one or more languages, dialects or linguistic varieties.

cognate Cognate languages share a common ancestor. Evidence can often be seen in their lexis, for example, *Scots* 'hame' is cognate with *English* 'home', and both are derived from *Old English* 'hām'.

common-core Lexis, grammar and phonology that is shared by *Scots* and *English* due to their common ancestry.

concordance A type of display generated by text analysis software such as *Wordsmith Tools* which allows words to be viewed in their original context and sorted on the basis of one word to the left or right and so on. Examples of the search word (the **node**) are usually arranged vertically for ease of comparison. A sample concordance (sorted one word to the right and one word to the left) follows:

He	had	a		wee brother
She	was	only	a	wee girl
They danced until the			wee small	hours
			The wee woman	quickly sat down

connotative meaning The denotative meaning of a word is its core dictionary meaning – for example *spinster* (unmarried woman). The connotative meanings of a word are its associated extra meanings, so in this case, perhaps an old woman, who nobody wanted and who keeps cats.

constructivist viewpoint This viewpoint states that individuals do not merely reflect what they are, but rather that they play an active part in the representation, negotiation, construction or maintenance of those identities to which they have an allegiance.

corpus (pl. corpora) A large (nowadays usually electronic) collection of texts which are selected and organised in such a way as to be useful for linguistic analysis. Ideally a corpus should be balanced in terms of the types and quantities of texts, genres and so on it contains, and it should be representative of the overall population, of which it can only ever be a sample.

corpus linguistics A branch of linguistics that uses corpora as the key tool for analysis.

cultural Scotticisms Scottish expressions that are enshrined in the Scottish culture such as *kirk*.

deixis (deictic) Deictic elements in language are personal, spatial or temporal locators, for example *you, I, over there, here, yesterday, in the summer*. They can usefully be analysed to see how speakers/writers situate themselves, and also how listeners/readers are being situated, with respect to the discourse. A **deictic centre** is the deictic reference point indicated by deictic elements.

dense A text that is densely *Scots* will have significant quantities of *Scots* lexis, contain orthographic forms that betray *Scots* pronunciation or etymology, and have *Scots* grammar and idiom. (Contrast with **thin**.)

diachronic Analysis across time periods. (Contrasts with **synchronic**.)

dialect A linguistic variety that is distinguished by particular features of lexis and grammar. Dialects are commonly thought to be contained within languages, though there is little linguistic justification for this point of view. *Dialect*, as used in this book, does not include the study of **accent**.

direct speech The representation, in writing, of what someone actually said, for example *'Have you finished reading that book yet?', she said.*

discourse Structured sequences of text (or speech) that are longer than the sentence. Often used synonymously with 'text'.

discourse community Term used by Bex (1996) to denote a group of individuals who share spoken or written discourse practices, and mastery of which is necessary for group membership.

etymology The study of a word's origins and history.

feedback mechanism A **discourse community** has participatory feedback mechanisms which allow members to comment on the discourse community and its practices, for example the letters pages in newspapers function as a feedback mechanism.

fixed expression These are formulaic multiword expressions such as proverbs, allusions, similes and idioms.

functional Scotticisms Defined in this study as peculiarly Scottish expressions that are found in very formal institutional discourse such as *uplift*.

Germanic Germanic languages such as *English* and *Scots* belong to the *Germanic* branch of the *Indo-European* language family, as do *Old Norse*, *Dutch*, *German* and so on.

grammar Grammar = **syntax** + **morphology**.

heteroglossic A situation whereby slightly different versions of the same national language are used in different contexts. Contrasts with **polyglossic**: a situation whereby two or more different national languages are interacting within the same cultural system. (C.f. Bakhtin 1981.)

ideal reader Texts are written with an ideal audience in mind, the ideal reader, who is anticipated to agree with the central ideology and viewpoint of the text.

idiolect An individual's linguistic system. It will differ in some respects from that of other speakers of the same dialect or language.

idiom Idioms are fixed expressions whose full meaning cannot be discerned from the literal sum of their parts, for example *kick the bucket*.

inflexions A change in the form of a word (usually by adding a suffix morpheme) to indicate a change in its grammatical function, for example the –ed suffix in *walk***ed** to indicate past tense.

ingroup Those belonging to the social group. (Contrasted with **outgroup**.)

isogloss The geographical boundary of a particular linguistic feature, for example, vocabulary or pronunciation. Often plotted on maps.

Kailyard Literally meaning 'cabbage-patch', this refers to a Scottish stereotype associated with a literary movement celebrating Scottish rural quaintness with key attributes such as domesticity, rusticity, modesty, decency and poverty.

KWIC Key Word in Context. The type of output display commonly seen in a concordancing program which allows occurrences of a search word to be viewed as they occur in context. (See **concordance**.)

Lallans Plastic or synthetic literary *Scots* which uses both archaic items of *Scots* lexis and lexis from different dialects. (Can also be used to refer to *Lowland Scots*.)

language display A term coined by Eastman and Stein (1993) to refer to a special type of borrowing or code-switching whereby individuals use foreign languages as a way of associating themselves with the attributes of social groups beyond their own.

lexis (pl.), **lexical item** (sg.) The vocabulary of a language. This book concentrates specifically on the use of *Scots* lexis (that is words and phrases that have Scottish provenance and are not generally shared with *English*. The term lexeme is used where it is necessary to indicate that what is meant is a group of possible lexical items rather than individual lexical types.

lingua franca A common language used by those with different native languages to allow them to communicate with each other.

linguistic continuum A range of linguistic varieties which may be regionally and/or socially defined and along which individuals can move in either direction.

linguistic hegemony The social forces whereby certain language varieties (usually those associated with powerful social groups) become dominant in society, not through force, but by general consensus.

morphology The study of meaning in individual units of language. Morphology is concerned with the structure of words, for example the morphemes walk + –ed form *walked*.

narrative Used in this book to refer to straightforward prose and contrasted with **direct speech**.

node See **concordance**.

Old English Applied to those historical varieties of *English* used between AD 450 and 1100.

open class Open class (content) lexis is comprised of nouns, verbs, adjectives and adverbs. New items can readily be added. Contrasts with **closed class**.

orthography The study of a language's spelling system and how it relates to its phonology.

outgroup Those outside/excluded from the social group. (Contrasted with **ingroup**.)

phonology Phonology is the study of pronunciation features. See **accent**.

productivity In this book applied to the ability of fixed expressions to be altered or extended in some way, for example by substitution or word play.

reflectivist viewpoint This viewpoint says that the way people use language and so on is determined by who they are. This view underlies some, but not all, sociolinguistic accounts of language variation. (Contrast with **constructivist viewpoint.**)

register The variation in language features according to context and situation. Key variables are mode (that is written or spoken), tenor (level of formality) and domain (the subject matter).

schema (sg.), **schemata** (pl.) Systems of knowledge whereby concepts are linked together in ways that help us make sense of the world.

Scots A range of linguistic varieties generally held to include localised Scottish vernaculars known variously as *broad Scots* or *dialect Scots*, for example, rural or more traditional varieties such as the *Ayrshire* dialect or the *Doric* of north-eastern Scotland. The regional dialects of *Scots* are conventionally grouped into the following broad geographic areas: *Insular Scots, Northern Scots* (+ *North-East Scots*), *Central Scots* (*East, West* and *South-West*), *Southern Scots, Ulster Scots* (*SND*). The term can also be applied to **Lallans**. *Scots* is at the dense extreme of the *Scottish-English* linguistic continuum.

Scotticisms Expressions peculiar to Scots, of which they may be aware, **overt**, or unaware, **covert**. Overt Scotticisms may be used deliberately to badge the speaker/writer as Scottish. See also **cultural, functional** and **uber-Scotticisms.**

Scottish-English Umbrella term for native varieties in Scotland which are ultimately descended from *Old English*; thus including everything from broad *Scots* dialect at one extreme to *Scottish Standard English* at the other.

Scottish Standard English Prestigious form of *Scottish-English* most often used in formal situations and at the extreme thin end of the linguistic continuum.

standard language A prestigious, usually written, language variety that is used in institutional discourse (for example education, the mass-media, government), that is often codified in dictionaries and grammars. It is concerned with matters of agreed grammatical, orthographic and to a lesser extent lexical practice. It has nothing to do with pronunciation.

style-drifting Drifting between one or more languages, dialects or linguistic varieties in a rather unpredictable and fluctuating manner. Usually contrasted with **code-switching** which is often more deliberate and predictable.

synchronic Analysis at one point in time. (Contrasts with **diachronic**.)

syntax The structure of the sentence, for example clauses, noun phrases and so on.

Tartanry A Scottish stereotype which concentrates on elements such as Highland ancestry, tartan, the bagpipes. It forms the source for many Scottish tourist souvenirs.

thin A thin text contains few *Scots* words and other *Scots* features. (Contrast with **dense**.) The limiting case of thin *Scottish-English* is *Scottish Standard English*.

token The total number of tokens in a text is the total number of (running) words. Tokens are usually contrasted with **types**. The number of tokens is usually significantly higher than the number of types, as some words in a text are likely to be repeated.

type The number of types in a text is the total number of different words that occur. Types are usually contrasted with **tokens**.

uber-Scotticism Marked or overt Scottish expressions generally only ever used for overt stylistic purposes, not part of the normal Scottish repertoire for most Scots, and with a tendency to be found in the company of *English* rather than *Scots* lexis.

vernacular The local or native language of a place or social group.

XML Extensible **M**arkup **L**anguage. A computer language used to mark up significant features in a text using tags. Often used in web documents.

Bibliography

Adolphs, S. (2006), *Introducing Electronic Text Analysis*, London: Routledge.

Ager, D. (2003), *Ideology and Image: Britain and Language*, Clevedon: Multilingual Matters.

Aitken, A. J. (1979), 'Scottish Speech: A Historical View with Special Reference to the Standard English of Scotland', in A. J. Aitken and T. McArthur (eds), *Languages of Scotland*, Edinburgh: Chambers, pp. 85–118.

Aitken, A. J. (1981a), 'The Good Old Scots Tongue: Does Scots have an Identity?', in E. Haugen, J. D. McClure, D. Thomson, A. J. Aitken (eds), *Minority Languages Today*, Edinburgh: Edinburgh University Press, pp. 72–90.

Aitken, A. J. (1981b), 'The Scottish Vowel Length Rule', in M. Benskin and M. L. Samuels (eds), *So Meny People Longages and Tonges, Philological Essays in Scots Mediaeval English*, Edinburgh: Published by editors, pp. 131–57.

Aitken, A. J. (1982), 'Bad Scots: Some Superstitions about Scots Speech', *Scottish Language* 1: 30–44.

Aitken, A. J. (1984a), 'Scots and English in Scotland', in P. Trudgill (ed.), *Language in the British Isles*, Cambridge: Cambridge University Press, pp. 517–32.

Aitken, A. J. (1984b), 'What's so Special about Scots?', *Northern Ireland Speech and Language Forum Journal* 10: 27–44.

Aitken, A. J. (1984c), 'Scottish Accents and Dialects', in P. Trudgill (ed.), *Language in the British Isles*, Cambridge: Cambridge University Press, pp. 94–114.

Andersen, R. (2001), 'National Identity and Independence Attitudes: Minority Nationalism in Scotland and Wales', Centre for Research Into Elections and Social Trends (Working Paper No. 86). ‹www.crest.ox.ac.uk/papers/p86.pdf› [accessed Nov. 2008].

Anderson, B. [1983] (1991), *Imagined Communities: Reflections on the Origin and Spread of Nationalism*, London: Verso.

Audit Bureau of Circulation (n.d.), *ABC*, ‹www.abc.org.uk› [accessed May 2008].

Audit Bureau of Circulation (n.d.), *ABCe*, ‹www.abce.org.uk› [accessed May 2008].

Bakhtin, M. (1981), *The Dialogic Imagination: Four Essays*, ed. M. Holguist, trans. C. Emerson, Austin: University of Texas Press.

BBC (2005), 'Neds make it into the dictionary', *BBC News Online*, 9 June 2005, ‹www.bbc.co.uk› [accessed July 2005].

BBC (2008), 'The BBC trust impartiality report: BBC network news and current affairs coverage of the four UK nations', ‹www.bbc.co.uk/bbctrust/research/impartiality.html› [accessed June 2008].

Bechhofer, F., R. Kiely and D. McCrone (2006), 'Reading Between the Lines: National Identity and Attitudes to the Media in Scotland', *Identity Briefings* 18, University of Edinburgh: Institute of Governance, ‹www.institute-of-governance.org/forum/Leverhulme/briefing_pdfs/IoG_-Briefing_18.pdf› [accessed June 2008].

Bell, A. (1991), *The Language of News Media*, Oxford: Blackwell.

Benhabib, S. (1996), *Democracy and Difference*, Princeton, NJ: Princeton University Press.

Bex, T. (1996), *Variety in Written English – Texts in Society: Society in Texts*, London: Routledge.

Billig, M. (1995), *Banal Nationalism*, London: Sage.

Bok, L. (2005), *The Little Book of Neds*, Bath: Crombie Jardine Publishing Limited.

Bok. L. (2006), *Ned Speak*, Bath: Crombie Jardine Publishing Limited.

Bok. L. (2007), *Ned Jokes*, Bath: Crombie Jardine Publishing Limited.

Bond, R. (2006), 'Becoming and Belonging: National Identity and Exclusion', *Sociology* 40 (4): 609–26.

Bond, R. and M. Rosie (2002), 'National Identities in Post-Devolution Scotland', *Scottish Affairs* 40: 34–53. Also online at ‹www.institute-of-governance.org/onlinepub/bondrosie›

Bond, R. and M. Rosie (2006), 'Routes into Scottishness', in C. Bromley, J. Curtice, D. McCrone and A. Park (eds), *Has Devolution Delivered?*, Edinburgh: Edinburgh University Press, pp. 141–58.

Bourdieu, P. (1997), 'Forms of Capital', in A. H. Halsey, H. Lauder, P. Brown and A. S. Wells (eds), *Education, Culture, Economy, Society*, Oxford: Oxford University Press, pp. 46–58.

Broun, D., R. J. Finlay and M. Lynch (eds) (1998), *Image and Identity: The Making and Re-Making of Scotland through the Ages*, Edinburgh: John Donald Publishers.

Cameron, D. (1995), *Verbal Hygiene*, London: Routledge.

Carter, R. (1987), *Vocabulary: Applied Linguistic Perspectives*, London: Allen and Unwin.

Cheshire, J. and L. Milroy (1993), 'Syntactic Variation in Non-Standard Dialects', in J. Milroy and L. Milroy (eds), *Real English: The Grammar of English Dialects in the British Isles*, London: Longman, pp. 3–32.

Collins Gem Scots Dictionary (1995), ed. M. Makins, Glasgow: Harper Collins.

Concise Scots Dictionary (1996), ed. M. Robinson, Edinburgh: Edinburgh University Press.

Cooper, R. L. (1989), *Language Planning and Social Change*, Cambridge: Cambridge University Press.

Corbett, J. B. (1997), *Language and Scottish Literature*, Edinburgh: Edinburgh University Press.

Corbett, J. B. (1998), 'The Missionary Positions: David Livingstone as a British Scots in Africa', *Scotlands*, 5 (1): 79–92.

Corbett, J. B. and F. M. Douglas (2003), 'Scots in the Public Sphere', in J. M. Kirk and D. P. Ó Baoill (eds), *Towards our Goals in Broadcasting, the Press, the Performing Arts and the Economy: Minority Languages in Northern Ireland, the Republic of Ireland and Scotland*, Belfast: Queen's University, pp. 198–210.

Corbett, J. B., J. D. McClure and J. Stuart-Smith (eds) (2003), *The Edinburgh Companion to Scots*, Edinburgh: Edinburgh University Press.

Cormack, M. (1995), 'The Use of Gaelic in Scottish Newspapers', *The Journal of Multilingual and Multicultural Development* 16 (4): 269–80.

Crawford, R. (1994), 'Bakhtin and Scotlands', *Scotlands* 1: 55–65.

Cultural Commission (2005), 'Our Next Major Enterprise – Final Report of the Cultural Commission, ‹www.scotland.gov.uk/Resource/Doc/69582/0017085.pdf› [accessed June 2008].

Davidson, D. (2004), 'Paper Chase', ‹mad.co.uk› [accessed June 2008].

Devine, T. and P. Logue (eds) (2002), *Being Scottish: Personal Reflections on Scottish Identity Today*, Edinburgh: Polygon.

Dictionary of the Older Scottish Tongue (1937–2002), ed. Craigie et. al, 12 vols, Oxford: Oxford University Press.

Dictionary of the Scots Language (2004), ed. S. Rennie, ‹www.dsl.ac.uk› [accessed July 2008].

Donaldson, W. (1986), *Popular Literature in Victorian Scotland: Language, Fiction and the Press*, Aberdeen: Aberdeen University Press.

Donaldson, W. (1998), 'Language and Identity: Modern Sources of Written Scots', in J. M. Fladmark (ed.), *In Search of Heritage: As Pilgrim or Tourist, Papers presented at the Robert Gordon University Heritage Convention*, Dorset: Donhead, pp. 193–204.

Donati, C., J. Hendry, J. Robertson and P. H. Scott (2003), *Scots: A Statement of Principles: A Road Forrit for the Scots Language in a Multilingual Scotland*, Edinburgh: The Scots Pairliament Cross-Pairty Group on the Scots Leid, ‹www.scottish.parliament.uk/msp/crossPartyGroups/groups/scots/SoP%20version%202.PDF› [accessed June 2006].

Donnachie, I. and C. Whatley (1992), *The Manufacture of Scottish History*, Edinburgh: Polygon.

Douglas, F. M. (2000), *The Role of Scots Lexis in Scottish Newspapers*, University of Glasgow: Unpublished Ph.D. thesis.

Douglas, F. M. (2002), 'The Role of Scots Lexis in Scottish Newspapers', *Scottish Language* 21: 1–12.

Douglas, F. M. (2003), 'The Scottish Corpus of Texts and Speech: Problems of Corpus Design', *Literary and Linguistic Computing* 18 (1): 23–37.

Douglas, F. M. (2006), 'English in Scotland', in B. Kachru, Y. Kachru and C. Nelson (eds), *The Handbook of World Englishes*, Malden, MA: Blackwell, pp. 41–57.

Drakakis, J. (1997), 'Shakespeare in Quotations', in S. Bassnett (ed.), *Studying British Cultures*, London: Routledge, pp. 152–72.

Eastman, C. M. and R. F. Stein (1993), 'Language Display: Authenticating Claims to Social Identity', *Journal of Multilingual and Multicultural Development* 14: 187–202.

EBLUL (2003), *The UK Committee of the European Bureau for Lesser Used Languages*, ‹www.eblul.org.uk/› [accessed June 2008].

Eckert, P. and S. McConnell-Ginet (1992), 'Think Practically and Look Locally: Language and Gender as Community-Based Practice', *Annual Review of Anthropology* 21: 461–90.

Edwards, J. (1985), *Language, Society and Identity*, Oxford: Blackwell.

Electronic Scots School Dictionary (1998), ed. I. Macleod and P. Cairns, Edinburgh: Scottish National Dictionary Association.

Fairclough, N. (1995), *Critical Discourse Analysis: The Critical Study of Language*, London: Longman.

Ferguson, W. (1998), *Identity of the Scottish Nation: An Historic Quest*, Edinburgh: Edinburgh University Press.

Fernando, C. (1996), *Idioms and Idiomaticity*, Oxford: Oxford University Press.

Fishman, J. A. (1989), *Language and Ethnicity in Minority Sociolinguistic Perspective*, Clevedon: Multilingual Matters.

Fitzsimmons, C. (2008), 'ABCs: Daily Record closes in on Scottish Sun', *The Guardian* (11 July), ‹www.guardian.co.uk› [accessed July 2008].

Fowler, R. (1991), *Language in the News: Discourse and Ideology in the Press*, London: Routledge.

Fraser, D. (2008), 'Nation speaking unto nation: Does the media create cultural distance between England and Scotland?', Institute for Public Policy Research, ‹www.ippr.org/ipprnorth/publicationsandreports› [accessed June 2008].

Galtung, J. and M. Ruge (1973), 'Structuring and Selecting News', in S. Cohen and J. Young (eds), *The Manufacture of News*, London: Constable, pp. 62–73.

Gellner, E. (1983), *Nations and Nationalism*, Ithaca, NY: Cornell University Press.

GRO(S) (2008), *General Register Office for Scotland*, ‹www.gro-scotland.gov.uk› [accessed May 2008].

Glauser, B. (1974), *The Scottish-English Linguistic Border: Lexical Aspects*, Bern: Francke.

Glucksberg, S. (1993), 'Idiom Meanings and Allusional Content', in C. Cacciari and P. Tabossi (eds), *Idioms, Processing, Structure and Interpretation*, New Jersey: Lawrence Erlbaum, pp. 3–26.

Görlach, M. (1990), 'The Development of Standard Englishes', in M. Görlach (ed.), *Studies in the History of the English Language*, Heidelberg: Carl Winter, pp. 9–64.

Gupta, A. F. (2002), 'Privileging Indigeneity' in J. M. Kirk and D. P. Ó Baoill (eds), *Language Planning and Education: Linguistic Issues in Northern Ireland, the Republic of Ireland and Scotland*, Belfast: Queen's University Belfast, pp. 290–9.

Gupta, A. F. (2006), 'Standard English in the World', in R. Hall and M. Saraceni (eds), *English in the World: Global Rules, Global Roles*, London: Continuum, pp. 95–109.

Hall, S. (1978), 'The Social Production of News', in S. Hall, C. Crichter, T. Jefferson, J. Clarke and B. Roberts (eds), *Policing the Crisis: Mugging, the State, and Law and Order*, London: Macmillan, pp. 53–77.

Hall, S. (1992), 'The Question of Cultural Identity', in S. Hall, D. Held and T. McGrew (eds), *Modernity and its Futures*, London: Polity Press, pp. 273–316.

Hall, S. (1996), 'Introduction: Who Needs Identity?', in S. Hall and P. DuGay (eds), *Questions of Cultural Identity*, London: Sage, pp. 1–17.

Halliday, M. A. K. (1989), *Spoken and Written Language*, 2nd edn, Oxford: Oxford University Press.

Higgins, M. (2004), 'Putting the Nation in the News: The Role of Location Formulation in a Selection of Scottish Newspapers', *Discourse and Society*, 15 (5): 633–47.

Institute of Governance (n.d.), 'Institute of Governance Leverhulme Identity Briefings' (Nations and Regions Research Programme), ‹www.institute-of-governance.org› [accessed July 2008].

Jakobson, R. (1960), 'Closing Statement', in T. A. Sebeok (ed.), *Style in Language*, Cambridge, MA: MIT Press, pp. 350–77.

Johnston, P. (1997), 'Regional Variation' in C. Jones (ed.), *The Edinburgh History of the Scots Language*, Edinburgh: Edinburgh University Press, pp. 433–515.

Jones, C. (ed.) (1997), *The Edinburgh History of the Scots Language*, Edinburgh: Edinburgh University Press.

Joseph, J. E. (2004), *Language and Identity: National, Ethnic, Religious*, Houndmills and New York: Palgrave Macmillan.

Kachru, B., Y. Kachru and C. Nelson (eds) (2006), *The Handbook of World Englishes*, Malden, MA: Blackwell.

Kiely, R., F. Bechhofer, R. Stewart and D. McCrone (2001), 'The Markers and Rules of Scottish Identity', *Sociological Review* 49 (1): 33–55.

Kiely, R., D. McCrone and F. Bechhofer (2006), 'Reading between the Lines: National Identity and Attitudes to the Media in Scotland', *Nations and Nationalism* 12 (3): 473–92.

Kirk, J. M. and D. P. Ó Baoill (eds) (2000), *Language and politics: Northern Ireland, the Republic of Ireland, and Scotland* (Belfast Studies in Language, Culture and Politics), Belfast: Queen's University.

Kirk, J. M. and D. P. Ó Baoill (eds) (2001), *Linguistic Politics: Language Policies for Northern Ireland, the Republic of Ireland, and Scotland* (Belfast Studies in Language, Culture and Politics), Belfast: Queen's University.

Kirk, J. M. and D. P. Ó Baoill (eds) (2002), *Language Planning and Education: Linguistic Issues in Northern Ireland, the Republic of Ireland, and Scotland* (Belfast Studies in Language, Culture and Politics), Belfast: Queen's University.

Kirk, J. M. and D. P. Ó Baoill (eds) (2003), *Towards our Goals in Broadcasting, the Press, the Performing Arts and the Economy: Minority Languages in Northern Ireland, the Republic of Ireland and Scotland* (Belfast Studies in Language, Culture and Politics), Belfast: Queen's University.

Kirkpatrick, S. (2006), 'Vod almighty, it's the news of the future', *Edinburgh Evening News* (25 Feb.), ‹www.edinburghnews.scotsman.com› [accessed July 2008].

Kiss, J. (2008), 'ABCe: Web traffic standards to be reviewed', *The Guardian* (22 May), ‹www.guardian.co.uk› [accessed July 2008].

Kloss, H. (1967), 'Abstand languages and Ausbau languages', *Anthropological Linguistics* 9 (7): 29–41.

Kumar, K. (2003), *The Making of English National Identity*, Cambridge: Cambridge University Press.

Law, A. (2001), 'Near and Far: Banal National Identity and the Press in Scotland', *Media, Culture and Society* 23: 299–317.

Law, A. (2003), 'Language and the Press in Scotland', in J. M. Kirk and D. P. Ó Baoill (eds), *Towards our Goals in Broadcasting, the Press, the Performing Arts and the Economy: Minority Languages in Northern Ireland, the Republic of Ireland, and Scotland*, Belfast: Queen's University Belfast, pp. 105–18.

Law, A. (2006), 'Hatred and Respect: The Class Shame of Ned "Humour"', *Variant* 25, ‹www.variant.org.uk› [accessed June 2008].

Learning and Teaching Scotland (LTS) (1991), 'National Guidelines 5–14: ENGLISH LANGUAGE', ‹www.ltscotland.org.uk/curriculumforexcellence› [accessed July 2008].

Learning and Teaching Scotland (LTS) (n.d.), 'Curriculum for Excellence', ‹www.ltscotland.org.uk/curriculumforexcellence› [accessed July 2008].

Le Page, R. B. and A. Tabouret-Keller (1985), *Acts of Identity: Creole-Based Approaches to Language and Ethnicity*, Cambridge: Cambridge University Press.

LexisNexis Group, (2006), *LexisNexis Professional*, ‹www.w3.nexis.com/new/› [accessed July 2008].

Luckhurst, T. (2007), 'Read all about it: the end of quality Scottish papers', *The Independent* (22 July), ‹www.independent.co.uk› [accessed July 2007].

Macafee, C. I. (1983), *Glasgow (Varieties of English around the World)*, Amsterdam: Benjamins.

Macafee, C. I. (1992), *Characteristics of Non-Standard Grammar in Scotland*, ‹www.abdn.ac.uk/enl038/grammar.htm› [accessed Jan 2005].

Macafee, C. I. (1994), *Traditional Dialect in the Modern World: A Glasgow Case Study*, Frankfurt: Peter Lang.

Macafee, C. I. (with A. J. Aitken) (2007), 'A History of Scots to 1700' ‹www.dsl.ac.uk› [accessed July 2008].

McArthur, C. (1981), 'Breaking the Signs: Scotch Myths as Cultural Struggle', *Cencrastus* 7: 21–5.

McArthur, C. (ed.) (1982), *Scotch Reels: Scotland in Cinema and Television*, London: British Film Institute Publishing.

McArthur, T. (1979), 'The Status of English in and furth of Scotland', in A. J. Aitken and T. McArthur (eds), *Languages of Scotland*, Edinburgh: Chambers, pp. 50–67.

McArthur, T. (1987), 'The English Languages?', *English Today* 11: 9–11.

McArthur, T. (1998), *The English Languages*, Cambridge: Cambridge University Press.

Macaulay, R. K. S. (1991), *Locating Dialect in Discourse: The Language of Honest Men and Bonnie Lassies in Ayr*, Oxford: Oxford University Press.

McClure, J. D. (1979), 'Scots: Its Range of Uses', in A. J. Aitken and T. McArthur (eds), *Languages of Scotland*, Edinburgh: Chambers, pp. 26–48.

McClure, J. D. (1981), 'Scottis, Inglis, Suddroun: Language Labels and Language Attitudes', in R. J. Lyall and F. Riddy (eds), *Proceedings of the Third International Conference on Scottish Language and Literature*, Stirling: University of Stirling, pp. 52–69. [Repr. in McClure, J. D. (1995), *Scots and its Literature*, Amsterdam/Philadelphia: John Benjamins, pp. 44–56.]

McClure, J. D. (1994), 'English in Scotland', in R. Birchfield (ed.), *The Cambridge History of the English Language, Vol. V: English in Britain and Overseas, Origin and Development*, Cambridge: Cambridge University Press, pp. 23–93.

McClure, J. D. (1997), *Why Scots Matters*, 2nd edn, Edinburgh: Saltire Society.

McCrone, D. (1992), *Understanding Scotland: The Sociology of a Stateless Nation*, London: Routledge.

McCrone, D. (1999), 'Opinion Polls in Scotland: July 1998–June 1999', *Scottish Affairs* 28: 32–43.

McCrone, D. (2001), *Understanding Scotland: The Sociology of a Nation*, 2nd edn, London: Routledge.

McCrone, D. (2002), 'National Identity in Scotland', ‹www.institute-of-governance.org/onlinepub/mccrone/bp__scottish__identity.html› [accessed July 2008].

McCrone, D., A. Morris and R. Kelly (1995), *Scotland – The Brand: The Making of Scottish Heritage*, Edinburgh: Edinburgh University Press.

McGinty, S. (2000), 'Bad news on home front', *The Scotsman* (29 Sept.), ‹www.scotsman.com› [accessed September 2000].

McGugan, I. (2003), *Inquiry into the Role of Educational and Cultural Policy in Supporting and Developing Gaelic, Scots and Minority Languages in Scotland*, Edinburgh: The Scottish Parliament Education, Culture and Sport Committee.

McGurk, J. (2008), 'Scottish newspapers "in crisis"', BBC News (15 May), ‹www.bbc.co.uk› [accessed May 2008].

Marshalsay, K. (1992), *The Waggle o' the Kilt*, Glasgow: Glasgow University Press.

Meech, P. and R. Kilborn (1992), 'Media and Identity in a Stateless Nation: The Case of Scotland', *Media, Culture and Society* 14 (2): 245–59.

The Metro (2006) ‹www.metro.co.uk› [accessed June 2006].

Miller, J. (1993), 'The Grammar of Scottish English', in J. Milroy and L. Milroy (eds), *The Grammar of English Dialects in the British Isles*, London: Longman, pp. 99–138.

Miller, J. (1998), 'Scots: A Sociolinguistic Perspective', in L. Niven and R. Jackson (eds), *The Scots Language: Its Place in Education*, Newton Stewart: Watergaw, pp. 45–56.

Miller, J. (2003), 'Syntax and Discourse in Modern Scots', in J. Corbett, J. D. McClure and J. Stuart-Smith (eds), *The Edinburgh Companion to Scots*, Edinburgh: Edinburgh University Press, pp. 72–109.

Miller J. and K. Brown (1982), 'Aspects of Scottish English Syntax', *English World-Wide* 3 (1): 3–17.

Moon, R. (1998), *Fixed Expressions and Idioms in English: A Corpus Based Approach*, Oxford: Clarendon Press.

Morning Extra (2008), 'Scottish newspapers "crisis"', BBC Radio Scotland (08:00hrs, 16 May), ‹www.bbc.co.uk› [accessed June 2008].

Munro, M. (2002), *Language and Cultural Identities in the Scots Comic Tradition*, Queen Margaret University College: Unpublished Ph.D. thesis.

Munro, M. (n.d.), 'Scots Language and Comic Performance', ‹www.scotslanguage.com› [accessed June 2008].

Murison, D. (1979), 'The Historical Background', in A. J. Aitken and T. McArthur (eds), *Languages of Scotland*, Edinburgh: Chambers, pp. 2–13.

National Newspaper Society (n.d.), ‹www.newspapersoc.org.uk› [accessed July 2008].

National Readership Survey (n.d.), *NRS*, ‹www.nrs.co.uk› [accessed July 2008].

Office for National Statistics (n.d.), *National Statistics Online*, ‹www.statistics.gov.uk› [accessed July 2008].

Oxford English Dictionary (1989), ed. J. A. Simpson and E. S. C. Weiner, 2nd edn; additions 1993–7, ed. John Simpson, Edmund Weiner, Michael Proffitt; and 3rd edn (in progress) Mar. 2000–, ed. John Simpson, OED Online ‹www.oed.com›.

Paterson, L., A. Brown, J. Curtice, K. Hinds, D. McCrone, A. Park, K. Sproston and P. Surridge (2001), *New Scotland, New Politics?*, Edinburgh: Polygon.

Petersoo, P. (2007), 'What Does "We" Mean? National Deixis in the Media', *Journal of Language and Politics* 6 (3): 419–37.

Pilrig, K. and K. McGlinchy (2005), *Nedworld: A Complete Guide to Ned Life and Living*, Edinburgh: Black and White Publishing.

Pittock, M. (2001), *Scottish Nationality*, Basingstoke: Palgrave.

Poussa, P. (1982). 'The Evolution of Early Standard English: The Creolization Hypothesis', *Studia Anglica Posnaniensa* 14: 69–85.

Press Gazette (no author) (2006), 'Scottish Sun Claims Victory Over Record', (2 June) ‹www.pressgazette.co.uk› [accessed June 2008].

Preston, P. (2006), 'Scottish papers fall off the rails', *Sunday Observer*, (22 Oct.), ‹www.observer.guardian.co.uk› [accessed July 2008].

Public Information Service (2003), *Makkin yer Voice Heard in the Scottish Pairliament*, Edinburgh: The Scottish Parliament Information Service.

Reah, D. (1998), *The Language of Newspapers*, London: Routledge.

Reid, H. (2006), *Deadline: The Story of the Scottish Press*, Edinburgh: St Andrew Press.

Robertson, J. (2002), *A Scots Parliament*, Edinburgh: Itchy-Coo/Black and White.

Robinson, C. (2008), *Say it in Scots: Scottish Wildlife*, Edinburgh: Black and White Publishing.

Robinson, C. (2008), *Say it in Scots: Wha's Like Us?*, Edinburgh: Black and White Publishing.

Robinson, C. and E. Finlayson (2008), *Say it in Scots: Scottish Weather*, Edinburgh: Black and White Publishing.

Romaine, S. (1982), 'The English Language in Scotland', in R. Bailey and M. Görlach (eds), *English as a World Language*, Ann Arbor: University of Michigan Press, pp. 56–83.

Rosie, M., J. MacInnes, P. Petersoo, S. Condor and J. Kennedy (2004), 'Nation Speaking unto Nation? Newspapers and National Identity in the Devolved UK', *The Sociological Review* 52 (4): 437–58.

Rosie, M., P. Petersoo, J. MacInnes, S. Condor and J. Kennedy (2006a), 'Mediating Which Nation? Citizenship and National Identities in the British Press', *Social Semiotics* 16 (2): 327–44.

Rosie, M., J. MacInnes, P. Petersoo, S. Condor and J. Kennedy (2006b), 'Mediating National Identities in the British Press', *Identity Briefings* 12, University of Edinburgh: Institute of Governance. ‹www.institute-of-governance.org/forum/Leverhulme/briefing_pdfs/IoG_Briefing_12.pdf› [accessed July 2008].

Rosie, M., J. MacInnes, P. Petersoo, S. Condor and J. Kennedy (2006c), 'Newspapers and National Identity in the Devolved UK', *Identity Briefings* 17, University of Edinburgh: Institute of Governance. ‹www.institute-of-governance.org/forum/Leverhulme/briefing_pdfs/IoG_Briefing_17.pdf› [accessed July 2008].

Saeed, A., N. Blain and D. Forbes (1999), 'New Ethnic and National Questions in Scotland: Post-British Identities among Glasgow Pakistani Teenagers', *Ethnic and Racial Studies* 22 (5): 821–44.

Schlesinger, P. (1991), 'Media, the Political Order and National Identity', *Media, Culture and Society* 13: 297–308.

Scobbie, J., N. Hewlett and A. Turk (1999), 'Standard English in Edinburgh and Glasgow: The Scottish Vowel Length Rule Revealed', in P. Foulkes and G. Docherty (eds), *Urban Voices: Accent Studies in the British Isles*, London: Arnold, pp. 230–45.

SCOTS (n.d.), 'Scottish Corpus of Texts and Speech Project', ‹www.scottishcorpus.ac.uk› [accessed July 2008].

Scots Language Centre (n.d.), 'Scots Language Centre', ‹www.scotslangua-ge.com› [accessed July 2008].

Scots Thesaurus (1980), ed. I. Macleod, P. Cairns and C. Macafee, Aberdeen: Aberdeen University Press.

Scott, M. (2003), 'Scottish Place-Names', in J. Corbett, J. D. McClure and J. Stuart-Smith (eds), *The Edinburgh Companion to Scots*, Edinburgh: Edinburgh University Press, pp. 17–30.

Scott, M. (2008), *Say it in Scots: Scottish Placenames*, Edinburgh: Black and White Publishing.

Scottish Government (n.d.), 'The Scottish Government', ‹www.scotland.gov.uk› [accessed June 2008].

Scottish Government (2007a), 'The National Conversation', ‹www.scotland.gov.uk/Topics/a-national-conversation› [accessed June 2008].

Scottish Government (2007b), 'A Strategy for Scotland's Languages' (Consultation Document), ‹www.scotland.gov.uk/Publications/2007/01/24130746/0› [accessed Nov. 2008].

Scottish Language Dictionaries (2008), ‹www.scotsdictionaries.org.uk› [accessed June 2008].

Scottish National Dictionary (SND) (1931–76), ed. W. Grant, W. and D. Murison, 10 vols, Aberdeen: Aberdeen University Press.

Scottish Parliament (n.d.), 'The Scottish Parliament', ‹www.scottish.parliament.uk/vli/language/scots/index.htm› [accessed July 2008].

Scottish Parliamentary Corporate Body (SPCB) (2004), 'SPCB Leid Policy', ‹www.scottish.parliament.uk› [accessed July 2008].

Sheppard, F. (2006), 'Scottish Sun leads in circulation war', *The Scotsman* (12 Aug.), ‹www.scotsman.com› [accessed August 2006].

Sinclair, J. (1991), *Corpus, Concordance, Collocation*, Oxford: Oxford University Press.

Smith, M. (1994), *Paper Lions: The Scottish Press and National Identity*, Edinburgh: Polygon.

Smith, J. J. S. (1996), *An Historical Study of English: Function, Form and Change*, London: Routledge.

Smout, T. C. (1994), 'Perspectives on Scottish Identity', *Scottish Affairs* 6: 101–13.

Strevens, P. (1980), *Teaching English as an International Language*, Oxford: Pergamon Press.

Stuart-Smith, J. (2003), 'The Phonology of Modern Urban Scots' in J. Corbett, J. D. McClure and J. Stuart-Smith (eds), *The Edinburgh Companion to Scots*, Edinburgh: Edinburgh University Press, pp. 110–37.

Stuart-Smith, J. (2004), 'The Phonology of Scottish English', in C. Upton (ed.), *Varieties of English: I: Phonology*, Berlin: Mouton de Gruyter, pp. 47–67.

The Sunday Herald (no author), (2006), 'Media Watch', (10 Sept.), ‹www.sundayherald.com› [accessed September 2006].

Tryhorn, C. (2008a), 'Scottish Sun rises again', *The Guardian* (8 Feb.), ‹www.guardian.co.uk› [accessed June 2008].

Tryhorn, C. (2008b), 'Scottish Sun pulls further ahead of Record', *The Guardian* (9 May), ‹www.guardian.co.uk› [accessed June 2008].

Tunstall, J. (1996), *Newspaper Power: The New National Press in Britain*, Oxford: Oxford University Press.

van Dijk, T. (1998), *Ideology: A Multidisciplinary Approach*, London: Sage Publications.

Vass, S. (2006a), 'Is The Sun setting on the Record . . . or is it just a false dawn?', *The Sunday Herald* (23 April), ‹www.sundayherald.com› [accessed April 2006].

Vass, S. (2006b), 'Eyeballing better ways to measure web traffic', *The Sunday Herald* (22 Sept.), ‹www.sundayherald.com› [accessed September 2006].

Vass, S. (2006c), 'News International considers full Scottish edition of Times', *The Sunday Herald* (22 Oct.), ‹www.sundayherald.com› [accessed October 2006].

Watson, M. (2003), *Being English in Scotland*, Edinburgh: Edinburgh University Press.

Wodak, R., R. Cillia, M. Reisigl and K. Liebhart (1999), trans. A. Hirsch and R. Mitten, *The Discursive Construction of National Identity*, Edinburgh: Edinburgh University Press.

Wood, R. E. (1979), 'Scotland: The Unfinished Quest for Linguistic Identity', *Word* 30: 186–202.

Wordsmith Tools (2003), Computer Software developed by Mike Scott, version 4.0, Oxford: Oxford University Press.

Wray, A. (2002), *Formulaic Language and the Lexicon*, Cambridge: Cambridge University Press.

Yorkshire Dialect (n.d.), 'Dictionary', ‹www.yorkshire-dialect.org› [accessed June 2008].

Index